THE FATE OF THE ANGLICAN CLERGY

THE FATE OF
THE ANGLICAN
CLERGY

A Sociological Study

Robert Towler
and
A. P. M. Coxon

First published 1979 by
THE MACMILLAN PRESS LTD
London and Basingstoke
Associated companies in Delhi
Dublin Hong Kong Johannesburg Lagos
Melbourne New York Singapore Tokyo

Typeset in Great Britain by
PREFACE LTD, Salisbury, Wilts

Printed by
UNWIN BROTHERS LIMITED
The Gresham Press, Woking

British Library Cataloguing in Publication Data

Towler, Robert
    The fate of the Anglican clergy
    1. Church of England – Clergy
    I. Title II. Coxon, Anthony Peter
    Macmillan
    301.5'8   BX 5175
    ISBN 0-333-25632-8

This book is dedicated with love and
respect to the memory of

NICOLAS GRAHAM CR

and with affection and gratitude to the

COMMUNITY OF THE RESURRECTION

to whom the authors, between them, owe
eleven happy years of student life

Contents

List of Figures   viii
Preface   ix

1 The Historical Background   1
2 The Clerical Profession   28
3 The Choice   56
4 Puritan and Antipuritan   89
5 Theological Colleges   116
6 The Training Process   144
7 The Career Structure of the Clergy   170
8 Becoming Marginal   187

Appendix I: Sources of Data   206
Appendix II: Statistical Tables and Additional Figures   208
Appendix III: Defining Characteristics of the Normal and Late
   Groups   224
Appendix IV: A Note on the More Recent Literature on
   Professions, with Special Reference to the Clergy   229

Notes   231
Bibliography   234
Index   245

List of Figures

1	Church of England ordinations, 1872–1975	30
2	Age of first thought of ordination: total sample	64
3	Age of first thoughts: normal and late groups	65
4	Age of application: total sample	69
5	Age of application: normal and late groups	70
6	Influences on decision to be ordained	72
7	Age distribution of ordinands, 1962	76
8	Ordinands' parental status	79
9	Recruitment and selection: school type	86
10	'Study of Values' (British version): profiles	95
11	Profiles on 12 variables	97
12	Importance attached to role components	111
13	Role-component scales for sub-groups	112
14	Importance of six role components	153
15	'How involved *ought* clergy to be in politics?' and 'How interested *are* you in politics?'	156
16	'How involved *ought* clergy to be in politics?' and 'How interested *are* you in politics?' – by college	157
A1	Study of values: comparative profiles for (1) British and American ordinands, and for (2) American college males	222
A2	Study of values: comparative profiles for Hostel of the Resurrection, Leeds, and Bishops' College, Cheshunt	223

Preface

This is a book of sociology. That is to say, it proceeds on the assumption that people in groups act in ways which are constrained by the structures and processes of groups; and it is those constraining structures and processes which are the object of study. Sociology is good sociology when it is based on empirical observations which are valid and appropriate to the problem under study, and when it infers social structures and processes from those empirical observations by a method which is also valid. The reader who is disinclined to recognise that society exercises an influence on people's lives, independently of their individual or shared conscious intentions, will find little of interest in the pages which follow, and we shall do nothing to persuade him to alter an initial prejudice. But, that said, we must add at once that we hope to address others besides sociologists, for we believe that a sociological understanding of the contemporary religious situation should contribute to every seriously interested person's grasp of the problems. Because we are both Christians, we care about the problems we discuss here. Indeed, our involvement with the ordained ministry of the Church of England is more intimate than that, for each of us began his student life intending to be ordained, and we were students together at an institution for ordinands from 1961 to 1964. Whether these facts have helped us to conduct better scientific studies, or have hindered us, must be for others to judge, but we have no desire to hide the facts.

This volume as it now appears was written by the author whose name comes first on the title page, and therefore I alone write this preface. The book's history is complex: Tony Coxon began his research on the social recruitment of the clergy in 1961; it was as a result of his influence that as an undergraduate I read sociology for my first degree, and subsequently chose the social-isation of ordinands as the subject of my research, research which he supervised. Our two doctoral theses formed the starting point for this book, but most of the material they contain has been discarded, and a great deal of fresh research has been done.

Although I have discussed its progress with Coxon at every stage and agreed its final form with him, the general argument, the additional research and the writing are all mine. It appears over both our names because it is his baby, whose upbringing he entrusted to me, and co-authorship seems the most accurate way of representing this relationship.

Formal acknowledgement must be made to the Social Science Research Council, a grant from which helped with the research reported in Chapter 7, but we are indebted to many people for their help, not least to the ordinands whom we pestered throughout the 1960s. Particular thanks are due to E. Grebenik, who, though he cares for none of these things, encouraged us both when he was Professor of Social Studies at Leeds; to B. R. Wilson, who acted cheerfully as mentor, examiner and adversary, and now is a friend; and to the Revd Hugh Bishop, without whose help this book might have been as badly written as are most books of sociology, but who cannot be blamed for the sociologese which remains.

University of Leeds,   R. C. T.
July 1978

1 The Historical Background

A study of clergymen today seems specialised almost to the point of being esoteric. It may interest the clergy themselves to consider the observations of others, but it may well be thought to be of no wider interest or significance. This in itself is an observation about the clergy at the present time, and it is in itself something remarkable, signifying the arrival of a wholly new era for religion and for religion's place in the life of a society. For, as far back in human history as we are able to see, the man or woman who was concerned primarily with magical or religious affairs was for that very reason an important person in society. The religious specialist, whether priest or necromancer or magician, was set apart from other people, and the history of religion consists in very large part in the history of such specialists. They had powers not vouchsafed to everyone, able to affect for good or for ill the fortunes of others. If today, therefore, an account of contemporary religious specialists seems marginal to the dominant interests of society at large, this in itself is a good reason for undertaking such a study. We may hope to discover what it is about the religious specialists of our own day which puts them on the periphery of society, and to see more clearly, thereby, the contemporary position of religion itself.

England affords a particularly interesting example, and we shall confine ourselves to this tiny example of religious specialism in the present work. The recruitment and training of clergy in the Church of England in the 1960s is a small topic indeed, but it requires only brief reflection to recognise that it has special interest. Why should recruitment and training be of interest, rather than a general study of working clergy? To know from what part of our society the clergy are drawn is vital, for only thus can we learn what sort of people they are, as compared with those whom they lead and serve. Only thus can we discover what kind of men the Church wants as its full-time officials, for selection takes place from among those who want to become clergymen, and unlike many other religions the Christian religion claims never to have recruited its specialists automatically from one group in society. Knowledge about the training given to clergy tells us what sort of specialists the Church aims to have: what skills they should possess, what knowledge they need, what attitudes and values should characterise them. What the clergy are supposed to be like will become clear through an examination of their recruitment and training, for requirements will be met only by finding the most suitable men and then by training them in a way appropriate to the requirements. Nor are these characteristics likely to prove merely formal, at variance with actual practice, for it is clergy who recruit, select and train new clergy, and so unrealistic ideals of what clergymen of the next generation should be like are tempered by the practical experience of men already themselves clergymen of long standing.

Why should the Church of England, among all the many Christian churches, be particularly instructive for an understanding of religious specialists in general? The reason is that, in several ways, the Church of England is well placed to be a representative case of religious organisations in the modern world. For longer than any other church, it has developed alongside, and in response to, a scientific industrial culture, which is the world's dominant cultural form and is still growing in influence. It is atypical only in being located in an advanced capitalist economy, which is a mode of economic organisation which many societies have gone beyond and many others will manage to avoid completely. And the Church of England is neither Catholic nor Protestant (it says it is both), but rather a national Establishment, formed as much by its conjuncture with secular influences as by the pressure of wholly religious factors. What we can'learn about the Roman Catholic Church and its clergy, on the other hand, tends to be specific to that Church and to be of only very limited value in teaching us anything about the ministry of the Methodist Church for example, and *vice versa*. The Church of England, as is its wont, stands in the middle.

And why should the decade of the 1960s have anything special to commend it ? Because, we maintain, it marked a clear turning point for the whole Christian Church, including the Church of England. The Second Vatican Council at last took the Reformation to the Church of Rome in a way the Council of Trent had failed to do (the parallels between Catholic history and the interpretation of Anglican history presented here are brought out well in Delumeau 1977); non-Western countries, instead of being the passive recipients of mission, moved into a position of leadership in Christendom; and the churches, unlike the sects which continued to flourish, began to realise that their decline was thenceforth a permanent fact of life. If by 'secularisation' we mean the displacement of the churches from a central to a peripheral role in the public life of a society, then we may say that the 1960s saw its acceptance in the West as a *fait accompli*. For a hundred years, at least, the Church had been regarded by those who opposed it as a threat, as a force to be reckoned with, but the 1960s saw the end of that era.

When, therefore, we turn from the global scene to the tiny clerical world of the Church of England, we see clear signs of the wider process. The number of men entering upon training declined sharply, and colleges began to close and to merge with one another. Young curates with families started to receive payments from Social Security, because their incomes had fallen below the officially defined poverty line. Religious and theological ideas underwent traumatic upheaval, symbolised by the publication of *Honest to God* and the rise of the Charismatic movement, which tended to polarise the clergy into radicals and conservatives, making irrelevant the traditional division between 'catholics' and 'evangelicals'. The most significant material changes to the Church of England were yet to come, as they still are, but in the course of the 1960s their inevitability became an unavoidable fact. Before then a person with sufficient insight might have foreseen changes; in the 1970s people began to watch an inexorable process in operation. The 1960s, then, were the last point at which it was possible to study the clergy of the Church of England as they had been, for solely economic factors guarantee the demise of the clergy as they have been known. A new pattern of ministry will emerge, financed in a new way, but its shape defies prediction.

It is no part of our intention here to foretell the future, though the range of possibilities which are open to the Church will find a place in our concluding remarks. Our primary aim is to throw some little extra light on the recent past, thereby completing a story. Clues to the next part of the story will be found in the one now ended, of course, but since the sequel has yet to be acted out we are all equally in the dark about it. In order that a study of the recruitment and training of Anglican clergy in the 1960s should make sense, however, it will be necessary to go back in time somewhat, and to sketch briefly and in broad outlines the history of the clergy of the Church of England, relying, as non-specialists, on such works as Chadwick's *The Victorian Church*. The phase of that history which is now rapidly drawing to a close began in the latter part of the eighteenth century, in the reign of George III, but it is necessary to go further back than that. Certain basic features of the clergy as a social group date from the Middle Ages, and to bring them properly into focus we need to start by looking at the mediaeval clergy, and then to consider the fate of the clergy in the sixteenth and seventeenth centuries, before we come to the beginnings of the modern period, in Hanoverian times.

MEDIAEVAL BEGINNINGS

Our concern is with the parochial clergy – that is, with the clergy who serve in parish churches and chapels. In the Middle Ages, however, the parochial clergy represented only one of four quite distinct groups which together comprised the clergy as a whole. Besides them there were the bishops, the monks and nuns in their abbeys and priories, and the friars. Often these different groups were opposed to each other, and the friars in particular stood out as the rebels and critics of the clergy as a whole. All were united, regardless of their differences, in their immunity from civil law, for they were answerable at law to their religious superiors through the ecclesiastical courts, instead of to the Crown. In many matters, such as sexual behaviour, others too were subject to ecclesiastical courts, but the clergy were answerable to religious authorities alone in everything. They were a section of the community set apart.

The primary concern of the clergy, in theory, was a purely religious one: they existed to instruct the laity in Christian doctrine and to administer the sacraments of the Church. In practice it was a very different matter, for in addition to their religious duties they performed most of the duties in connection with the administration of the country, the provision of education, medical and nursing care, and the laws concerning marriage and wills. In short, everything which required learning (rather than skill or power) was undertaken by the clergy, and by the clergy alone. At the top of the clerical pyramid, the bishops acted as ministers of the Crown to so large an extent that they were able to give only a minimal amount of time to the performance of their religious duties. In the ten years between 1376 and 1386, for example, 13 of the 25 bishops held high secular office under the Crown.

The parochial clergy were at the very bottom of this pyramid. They were poor, ignorant, and corrupt – the dregs of the clergy rather than the clerical norm. Very few of the priests who actually served the parishes were rectors or vicars charged with responsibility. Those to whom the formal responsibility belonged retained for themselves the incomes of the livings, and out of them they paid pittances to mass-priests, who could at least read, but who could understand Latin hardly any better than could their congregations. Yet it was these men who constituted the real parochial clergy; the impressive list of rectors or vicars boasted by many an English parish church – so far, at any rate, as the mediaeval period is concerned – is generally a legal fiction. The fine Norman names do not belong to men who ever served in those parishes, but to those who drew the incomes from them.

Taken together as the Second Estate, however, the clergy were the learned servants of the whole country. The learning and the service were subject to a complex division of labour, but their overall function is plain.

REFORMATION

In the Tudor period a secularising revolution took place which radically changed the position of the clergy and ushered in a new era of their history. With the dissolution of the monasteries and the reformation of the Church, the great wealth and power of the monasteries were removed at a stroke, and bishops ceased to rule the country as ministers of the Crown. Secularisation consisted in the passing of power from the hands of clergy to the hands of laymen, which is a story repeated more than once in English history. If the Church was stripped of its excessive power, however, it shed few of its less prestigious responsibilities. From the religious traumas of Tudor and Stuart times there emerged slowly an Anglican Church which still carried the burden of education, besides providing religious leadership. What had disappeared was the situation in which it was the clergy alone who were educated. While they retained sole responsibility for education, they shared the pursuit of learning with the sons of the rich who were destined for secular careers, and at the universities in the reign of James I poor students were the future clergymen and rich students were not.

As a result of all this the social standing of the clergy taken as a whole declined in the Tudor and Stuart periods. The scandalous poverty and ignorance of mass-priests was eliminated, it is true, but so was the power of the monasteries and the higher clergy. When the monasteries were dissolved, in 1539, much of their wealth was transferred to individual beneficiaries who enjoyed the favour of the King; but it also helped to found six new dioceses, to promote education, and to assist the navy. The monasteries had held many of the parochial benefices and, putting vicars or curates in charge of the churches, had received most of the tithes, but at the Dissolution this wealth passed to the Crown and to individuals, rather than to the Church, and thus did not materially assist the clergy. So in the period when the parochial clergy became the clerical norm their poverty was such as to preclude the gentry from joining their ranks or the daughter of a gentleman from marrying a parson. Gone were the 'criminous clerks', but gone too was the wealth of the Church, except for a handful of great bishoprics which went to sons of the nobility. From being a complex and diverse mediaeval Estate, the clergy changed into a much simpler entity, concerned with the religious affairs of the people, with education, and with the needs of the poor at the parish level. If priests were no longer hated and envied as belonging to a privileged estate, they were often despised and ill used. In the parish, parson was dominated by squire as being of a different order in society.

THE BEGINNING OF MODERNITY

It was in the years after the accession of George III, in 1760, that the fortunes of the Church of England and its clergy began to undergo a further change, as a result of which Gibbon was soon able to speak of the 'fat slumbers of the Church', and a new situation emerged which was portrayed by Jane Austen and other novelists of the nineteenth century. The reason for this change lay in the improvements in agriculture and the consequent substantial increases in land values, for the clergy, largely dependent as they were on glebe and tithe, benefited greatly from these new conditions. There was still a great gulf between the values of rich and poor livings, depending on their endowment, but, whereas in the reign of Queen Anne half the Church's 10,000 livings were worth less than £50 a year, a hundred years later only 4000 of them amounted to less than £150 a year. The improvement was not solely owing to increased values of existing endowments. Annates, or the first year's revenues of ecclesiastical benefices, the payment of which Henry VIII had transferred from the Papal curia to the English Crown, were surrendered by Queen Anne for the benefit of the Church, and the fund thus set up in 1704, called Queen Anne's Bounty, was used to assist the poorest livings.

The learning which since the Reformation had increasingly marked the English clergy was now, therefore, accompanied by a comfortable wealth, and so the Anglican clergy became renowned for scholarship, culture, and for the freedom from interference by anyone which they enjoyed. Only the slightest pressure was exerted by the bishops or by public opinion which might have compelled the clergy to exert themselves more than they wished. The result was that they became gentlemen, living on equal terms with the gentry as never before, and about half the livings in the gift of laymen were substantial enough to be given to their youngest sons or to sons-in-law.

We have given this sketch of the history of the clergy, as is general in historical accounts, from the perspective of power. A different story altogether would emerge if we made religious devotion and enthusiasm our yardstick for comment, instead of social power and prestige. From the perspective of power, however, the clergy were unfortunate, for in their newly found affluence they were soon to be overtaken by events. Their social status had risen in a predominantly rural England, in which settled villages rather than changing towns were the backbone of the country. No longer disfigured by poverty, the parsonage houses attracted men who had means of their own, out of which, together with their improved incomes, the parsonage houses themselves were extended, replaced or refurbished, and the churches beautified. This modern period in the history of the clergy, which is now ending, came in on a strongly rising tide of material comfort and power; but before long the tide began to recede, because the face of England started to change again. Villages declined and were eclipsed by rapidly expanding towns. With growing industrialisation the whole basis of the country's wealth began to shift from land to manufacture. The Church of England was ill prepared for the change and did not respond swiftly. Its churches were in the countryside long after the bulk of the population had moved to the cities. The incomes of its clergy were derived from the land, and they dwindled as commerce became the country's economic centre of gravity, and this was a change to which the Church responded even more slowly. The reign of Queen Victoria saw a gradual ebbing of the tide of clerical affluence from its Hanoverian high-water mark.

RISE AND FALL

The secularisation of the Victorian age and beyond bears a marked similarity to the process which took place at the close of the Middle Ages. In each period secular society changed substantially, and the new conditions no longer held the same influential opportunities for the Church and the clergy as had the old ones. The difference between the two is that in the Middle Ages the Church possessed wealth and privileges which were inalienable and immutable, thus giving it the power to withstand change, and making reformation possible only when forcibly undertaken by the Crown; in the modern period, by contrast, the Church's wealth has been superseded by the growing affluence of secular society, and its privileges have been gradually qualified and removed by Parliament. The periods are alike in that in the second, as in the first, the Church has lost a monopoly over some areas of public life and the clergy have lost a monopoly over certain jobs.

In 1800, if we take that date, rather arbitarily, to mark the beginning of the modern period of the Church, the clergy still had high incomes and enjoyed a high status in society. In a largely rural country dominated by the gentry, the clergy were among the gentry. They were ministers of a Church of England which was the Established Church in the strongest sense, for it was necessary to be a member of the Church to hold a high position in society: neither the universities nor Parliament were open to Jews, Roman Catholics, dissenters or atheists. When industry, commerce and democracy were introduced into this stable society, everything began to change. The increased wealth of the country depended on industry, which demanded that a large proportion of the population move away from the country into towns and cities. Industry depended on skills, which made it necessary to provide education not as an end in itself or as the proper training for a gentleman, but as the way of equipping competent workers. The greatly increased need for skilled labour made it necessary to recruit suitable workers from all sections of society and to train them appropriately, rendering social differences, though still noticeable and frequently noticed, less important in practice. And the wealth to be derived from industry and commerce became respectable wealth, making it possible for a gentleman to engage in activities which a generation before would not have been thought fit for him.

By 1900, then, a hundred years after the clergy had been at the zenith of their social standing, society had changed. The gentry, with whom they had been so closely identified through their land-based wealth, had waned in importance and been replaced by the newly dominant middle class. Social institutions, such as education, which previously had served to train and perpetuate the traditional elite class of gentlemen, had all been thrown open to provide the maximum number of men trained for skilled jobs. Civilised life had moved into the towns and cities, leaving the countryside a sleepy and impoverished backwater, and making gentility a less impressive virtue than affluence. But the change was far from complete. Many of the old values still exercised a strong influence, if not a crucial one, and successful businessmen aspired to the status of gentleman, which was still granted as of right to clergymen. Domestic service is one of the surest indicators of the existence of strong social differentiation, and domestic servants had by no means disappeared in 1900. Indeed, families of the new middle class employed servants, while the clergyman could afford fewer than he used to employ and fewer than his house and garden required. A rash of new public schools had been built in the nineteenth century to provide for the sons of businessmen the education proper for a gentleman and neces-sary for admission to the universities, but few clergymen could afford the fees at these new schools.

Now, as the twentieth century proceeds, the values of gentility are fast disappearing into the realm of nostalgia and eccentricity. The era to which the clergy of the Church of England were most fully adjusted has almost closed, and they have yet to find a place in the era succeeding it.

EDUCATIONAL CLERISY AND CLERICAL EDUCATION

The clergy's loss of social prestige marks the end of a period. In earlier periods, as we have indicated, they did not enjoy such high standing, and in this longer perspective they may be seen as returning to their normal condition from an atypical episode. Of greater interest in every way is the relationship of the clergy to education, and it is crucially important for our purposes, since the clergy's own educational history cannot be understood outside the context of their role in the education of others.

Until the Reformation, learning was effectively the perogative of the clergy. Every form of learning was clerical learning, and every theoretical discipline which has its origins in mediaeval culture was originally a clerical specialisation. The one exception to this general rule was the common lawyers, who became the first group of learned laymen in England, educated in the independent Inns of Court. In the fifteenth century these men were joined by others, who had received a university education but had not become clergymen; but, none the less, until the modern period all education continued to be under the control of the clergy. In 1800, therefore, local schools were all parish schools which, with the schoolmistresses, were under the direction of the parson; grammar schools were religious foundations, as were the colleges, such as Winchester and Eton, which were to become public schools, with the clergy firmly in control. Similarly the universities of Oxford and Cambridge were religious foundations, an integral part of the Church of England, where the fellows of most colleges were obliged to be clergymen. It was assumed that in a Christian country education must mean a Christian education, and the way in which this should be effected, it was further assumed, was by providing that the Established Church should be responsible for it. This principle was breached when, in the course of the nineteenth century, others besides members of the Church of England were admitted to degrees at Oxford and Cambridge, and it was still further breached when first primary and then secondary education was freed from any ecclesiastical control, so stripping the Anglican clergy of any priority in matters of learning, save that which they might earn for themselves by their own efforts. It removed their last important privilege.

While the long-term effects of introducing secular primary and secondary education were unquestionably more profound, it was the opening of Oxford and Cambridge universities to non-Anglicans which had the more immediate and more traumatic impact on the clergy. So long as these institutions remained exclusively Anglican, the notion of learning remained fused with the idea of Established English religion. A clergyman, by virtue of being a clergyman, was quite simply a man of learning. That professors and fellows were almost all clergymen served powerfully to underline the identity of scholarship and Anglican scholarship. The religious and the secular were not split apart as two distinct entities in education. The importance of the religious aspect of education was not questioned, and there existed no disagreement about the form which this religious aspect should take, since the Established Church imposed its own standards. It was the demand, eventually successful, of dissenters to equal treatment in the field of secular education which led to the separation of the religious element from it. This was a far cry from the cultivated harmony of science and religion which prevailed in the eighteenth century, but it was necessary if a variety of religious affiliations were to be given equal standing.

The struggle by dissenters from the Established Church to secure adequate provision for the education of their children was felt first at the primary level, and it was at this level that the implications of full concession were most far-reaching. It required the earnest religiousness of Gladstone in 1870 to effect it. That battle could be construed, however, as a political struggle, which indeed it was; but the issues at stake were recognised as being more than political when the struggle was carried into the universities. The change implied a notion of education and culture in which religion had no necessary part. More was involved, it seemed, than losing control of schools. That was bad enough, because it meant that the Church, traditional guardian of the Christian society, would no longer be able to guarantee that the young were taught in a manner and a milieu which would foster their moral and spiritual, as well as their intellectual, welfare. To compromise the principles of the university as a religious foundation, however, seemed to strike at the very roots of what it meant to be an educated, civilised and fully developed man. The Duke of Wellington, speaking in the House of Lords in 1834, went so far as to say that the admission of dissenters to Oxford and Cambridge might possibly endanger 'the existence of Christianity itself'. The fear was that, in a university which was no longer Anglican, scholarship, which was highly esteemed in England, would become wholly independent of religion, neither supporting Christianity by its researches nor being influenced and guided by it in any respect. Henceforth the education provided for the elite of society, moreover, would be one in which science and religion did not belong together, and religion thereby would be seen as something separate and apart, rather than being the matrix of all learning and the framework of culture.

It is ironical that the intimate link between the Church and the universities, which had played an essential part in the Elizabethan Settlement, should have been forged in the first place in order to control religion. As *The Oxford Dictionary of the Christian Church* puts it, in its article 'Elizabeth I', on her accession one of Elizabeth's

main difficulties was the religious question. Devoid of strong convictions, she sought to solve it according to political expediency. The country as a whole was still predominantly Catholic, though with a strong Calvinistic undercurrent. Elizabeth disliked the former because it denied her legitimacy, and the latter because it abolished episcopacy, which she held to be essential for the safety of kings. She therefore distrusted both Calvinists and Catholics and aimed at a compromise between the Lutheran political theory, with its emphasis on the prerogatives of the temporal ruler, and the episcopal organization of Catholicism, many of whose institutions, such as the celibacy of the clergy and the use of crucifixes and statues, she wished to retain.

The middle course was not easy to steer, and uniformity proved difficult to achieve, but under Archbishop Parker both compromise and uniformity were realised, and embodied in the Thirty-Nine Articles of Religion, passed in their present form in 1571, to which not just the clergy but all members of the universities of Oxford and Cambridge were required to subscribe. By exacting this requirement from the universities the State was able to check the troublesome puritan and Catholic thinkers who had threatened public order by subverting the young. Anglicanism, which had been brought into existence as an ecclesiastical compromise to tame lively religious ideas of an extreme persuasion, had become a religious tradition in its own right; and in the nineteenth century it clung tenaciously to a monopoly which originally had been thrust upon it. Anglican universities had been an important instrument in the making of a characteristic English culture, but that culture had now become deeply entrenched and the Church was unwilling to make any concessions to the dissent for the control of which it had in former generations been a tool. So deeply entrenched had the Church of England become that the fears expressed about the secularisation of the universities were, indeed, not groundless. There was no religious culture which could command respect outside the universities, for the two had been so closely identified as to become effectively identical.

The notion that a religious education could only be provided by uniting religious with scholarly profession was not simply a device employed by the Established Church to protect its vested interests. Roman Catholics maintained the same principle. They had no intention of taking advantage for themselves of the newly granted opportunity to enter Oxford and Cambridge and every effort was made to found instead a Catholic university, though with no more than fleeting success.

We see, then, that not only the Established Church but the whole Establishment strenuously resisted plans to open the universities to others than members of the Church of England. The reason was that the universities of Oxford and Cambridge played a key role in the whole complex of the dominant culture of the upper classes, and their secularisation threatened to do more than might have been done by any other single change to shake the cultural integrity of the Establishment.

The development of the Church of England after the Reformation had ensured that the clergy, being clergy of the national Church, had continued to receive their education within the national institutions. Those institutions had then been opened to laymen, and laymen educated within them went on to occupy positions in society which formerly had been filled by clergymen. But in 1800, at the beginning of the modern period of the history of the clergy, there was still no separation of clerical and lay education. The education of a clergyman was still exactly the same as the education of a gentleman; or, rather, of any other gentleman.

TOWARDS A SEPARATION

Even at the beginning of the nineteenth century not quite all clergymen ordained in the Church of England were graduates of Oxford or Cambridge, and it is with those exceptions that the story of ordination training in the modern period must begin, for they were destined to become the majority. Thomas Wilson, the Bishop of Sodor and Man who died in 1755, had himself trained the clergy to serve the Church in the Isle of Man, and the Bishop Wilson Theological College did not close until 1943. The remoteness of his diocese and the difficulty of obtaining suitable clergy made necessary a course of action so unusual as compared with the rest of the country. Clergy were necessary, however, and the expedient needed no particular justification. For similar reasons the Bishop of Chester, G. H. Law, founded St Bee's College in Cumberland in 1816, which continued to train clergy until 1896. Missionary colleges were also founded, such as that established in Islington by the Church Missionary Society in 1825. In all these instances there existed a pressing need which could not be met by graduates of Oxford and Cambridge and so special provision had to be made. The exceptions, however, did not call the norm into question, and, indeed, they were thought of as deliberately giving a more modest training, though one which was adequate in the circumstances. St David's College, founded in 1831 at Lampeter in Wales and granted a royal charter by 1833, provided a clear illustration of the point, for, within the limits of its slender resources, what was given there was plainly intended as an approximation to the education of an Oxford or a Cambridge college.

At about the same time as Lampeter was founded, a number of separate but related factors began to affect the whole situation of clerical training. In the first place, a new seriousness about what clergymen ought to be like was emerging. The self-confidence of the eighteenth century parson was being slowly undermined, here and there, as the influence of Wesleyan evangelicalism made itself felt in the Church of England, particularly in two ways. It did so directly, through the mediation of men such as Charles Simeon, a Fellow of King's College and vicar of Holy Trinity, Cambridge, from 1783 almost until his death in 1836, who managed to reconcile, through personal example, the enthusiasm associated with dissenters and the discipline of the Established Church. It also did so indirectly through the Oxford Movement, for in *The Christian Year*, published in 1827, John Keble made acceptable a degree of religious emotion which a generation earlier would have been highly suspect. Its acceptability was shown in his election, in 1834, to the chair of poetry at Oxford. John Henry Newman became vicar of the University Church at Oxford in 1828, when he still had strong evangelical sympathies, and when he lost those affiliations and began his association with Keble in 1830 the influence of the evangelical seriousness was transformed rather than abandoned. In both these ways, and in others less easily defined, a self-critical strain of thought entered clerical circles and challenged the complacent latitudinarianism of the past.

The struggle to open Oxford and Cambridge to dissenters had a further subsidiary effect, for it raised the wider issue of whether the universities did not in any case stand in urgent need of reform. Violent things were said and written, and though most of them were gross exaggerations it raised in people's minds the question of whether three years as an undergraduate was the most suitable, or the most seemly, way that could be devised for the education of a clergyman. Eminent public men could not help remembering how in their own undergraduate days they 'hurried unshaven or full of wine to their compulsory chapel'. This doubt about the suitability of the university as a nursery for clergymen conspired together with doubts about the carefree clerical style of a previous generation to make men ask serious questions about the training of the clergy.

AN EXCESS OF RICHES

In addition to this there was a problem stemming from another source, but also having implications for clerical education. It concerned the cathedrals. In 1831 Earl Grey's Reform Bill, which had passed the House of Commons, was rejected in the Lords by 41 votes, the bishops voting against it 21 to two, with six abstentions. Grey's Whig Cabinet was pledged to reform in Church and State, and popular feeling against the Church was high. The vote unleashed a storm of rage against the House of Lords, which was directed principally against the bishops. Riots took place throughout the autumn, and on Guy Fawkes day 1831 the effigies of local bishops replaced Guy Fawkes or the Pope on bonfires all

over the country. At a procession in Kent the words of the old song
were changed:

> Remember, remember
> That God is the sender
> Of every good gift unto man;
> But the devil, to spite us
> Sent fellows with mitres
> Who rob us of all that they can.

The election of 1834, however, returned a Tory House of Commons once more, and the short interlude during which Dr Arnold
of Rugby had written, 'The Church as it now is, no human power
can save' had passed for the time being. But, although the Church
was no longer in danger of imminent disestablishment, no one any
longer doubted that reform was necessary, and that it would have
to be substantial if popular feeling was to be assuaged.

The worst scandal, and therefore the situation most urgently in
need of reform, was the excessive wealth of some sections of the
Church. In the eyes of the public it was the Church as a whole
which was excessively wealthy, but within the Church the injustice was seen rather to lie in the fact that, for example, the
Archbishop of Canterbury received on average £19,000 a year,
while a curate received only £50 plus a house if his incumbent was
not resident, and in the conspicuous leisure and spectacular comfort afforded by a cathedral canonry. Measures were taken in 1835
to secure a measure of equality in the incomes of bishops, which
ranged from the £19,000 which the Archbishop of Canterbury
received to the £900 received by the Bishop of Llandaff. Attempts
were made to augment the lowest clerical incomes by a degree of
redistribution, and cathedral establishments were much revised.

The cathedrals were so conspicuously wealthy that concern
with them generated the problem of what they might be used for.
Durham was the prime target of criticism, and it quickly found a
solution. The 12 canons each received about £3000 a year; the
Dean was also Bishop of St David's, and three of the canonries
were held by the bishops of Bristol, Chester, and Exeter. This was
in 1831, and the days had not long passed since the eighth Earl of
Bridgewater had held a prebend at Durham for 49 years while he
lived in Paris. The solution they found was the establishment of a
college similar to that at Lampeter, which took a considerable

amount of capital and enabled the Bishop, van Mildert, to contribute Durham Castle as well as capital on his own account. The proposal was accepted quickly and Durham University was instituted in 1832 and given a royal charter. Being a Church foundation it was easily able to insist on excluding dissenters, and almost all the bishops expressed themselves willing to accept Durham degrees as qualification for ordination. One of the bishops who did not so agree gave as his reason the effect which the scheme might well have in encouraging the lower classes to aspire to the priesthood, while there were plenty of candidates available, who were more suitable as clergymen, from the classes above them. From the vantage point of the end of the century that reason was to sound almost sick in its conservatism, but it is something to which we shall return.

The case of Durham acted as a spur to the thought already being given to the problem of the cathedrals. No one knew precisely what they were for, though it was obvious that in practice they served to reward 'aristocratic blood, pastoral merit, political service, private influence and a certain quantity of learning', in Chadwick's phrase. It was plain that they ought to be of greater general service to the Church than a source of individual rewards. The search for a use for the cathedral close which would commend itself generally before long became linked with the growing awareness of the absence of any theological scholarship except that little which was embedded in the general scholarship of the university. Ancient practice, long abandoned, had surrounded the bishop with candidates for ordination, and the new idea was to make cathedrals places where ordination candidates might receive a fuller training in theology than could be offered by the universities alone. The idea appealed, and soon it commanded a wide acceptance. Small colleges were set up in the cathedral close of Chichester in 1839, and of Wells in 1840.

THEOLOGY AND THEOLOGICAL COLLEGES

The need for a better knowledge of theology among candidates for ordination deserves some attention, for belief that the need existed, and indeed was pressing, was to have wide implications for several decades and down to the present day. Where did this belief come from? For it was new. It derived, we should suggest, from the growing independence of secular scholarship. Individual specialisms and modern scholarly attitudes were beginning to emerge from the unity of eighteenth-century learning. The Whig dons at Cambridge who, at the time when the admission of dissenters was raised in the 1830s, pleaded for reform on a wider front provide evidence of this tendency. They were concerned less that the university should be thought to be so inedifying than that it should be so inefficient, and those who argued in this way were identified, by those who resisted their contentions, as astronomers, geologists, minerologists, ornithologists and entomologists, derisible in their specialisms. It had been of the essence of divinity that it informed the work of all scholarship, but these new disciplines developed under their own secular principles of scientific thought. It behoved divinity, therefore, to become increasingly theological, a discipline and a pursuit in its own right. The mood was not to produce its most tangible results until the last decades of the nineteenth century, by which time it had become the firmly held conviction of the majority; but it was abroad fifty years before that and, even at Oxford and Cambridge, was quietly having its effect.

As we have seen, two new theological colleges were founded in 1839 and 1840. The motives which lay behind their foundation were complex but we have suggested that important among them were the desire to provide a more serious training for ordination, the dissatisfaction with Oxford and Cambridge on that score, and the desire that ordination candidates might be taught more theology, to which end the cathedrals were to be converted into little centres of theological learning. The fear that the universities would become secular had not materialised. The Establishment conceded on another front, by granting a charter to University College, London, in 1836, as an avowedly secular institution which indeed offered no religious teaching at all. The respite offered to Oxford and Cambridge was only brief, however, and everyone knew that it could not last for long. Measures passed in 1854 and 1856 began the series of substantial changes by opening lower degrees to those of any religion or none, and the process continued until finally, in 1915, degrees in divinity were opened to any candidate at Cambridge, and, in 1920, to any at Oxford. Beginning in the 1870s, religious tests for dons were removed. The tide of university secularisation, together with a growing conviction that clergymen needed to be trained in theology, led to the founding of more theological colleges along the lines of Chichester and Wells. One was founded near Oxford in 1854, not beside the cathedral (which would have put it in Christ Church) but beside the bishop's palace (at Cuddesdon), reviving the most ancient custom. Lichfield (1857), Salisbury (1861), Exeter (1861), Gloucester (1868), Lincoln (1874) and Ely (1876) followed the cathedral pattern in rapid succession, and the Church of England found itself provided with a new system of ordination training.

The secularisation of the universities and the development of theology as a specialist discipline, as twin causes, had other effects beside the stimulation of these separate theological colleges. The first was the creation of specifically Anglican colleges, Keble at Oxford in 1870 and Selwyn at Cambridge in 1879, to provide what the universities as a whole could no longer provide. The second was the founding of an honours school of theology at Oxford in 1870 and of a theological tripos at Cambridge in the following year. As these developments proceeded, the first flush of fearfulness subsided and the recently secularised universities appeared less terrible than had been feared. As a consequence, theological colleges were opened within the universities themselves: St Stephen's House (1876) and Wycliffe Hall (1877) at Oxford, and Ridley Hall (1881) and the Clergy Training School (1881, called Westcott House from 1902) at Cambridge. The new system was now complete. Within the space of only a few years the old ideals of an integrated education in which divinity was the leaven, and of a scholarship in which divinity permeated the whole, had been abandoned. Roman Catholics followed more slowly, and were not to extend their tolerance of the secular university to present or future members of the priesthood for many years; but, whereas in 1867 it was declared by the Sacred Congregation for Propaganda that a Catholic in going to Oxford or Cambridge would 'commit the sin of exposing himself to a proximate occasion of mortal sin', the ban was lifted completely in 1895. Catholics had articulated, in typically precise words, the danger feared by the Established Church in the 1830s.

One effect of the changes which took place between the founding of Durham University in 1832 and the last theological colleges in 1881 was to have far-reaching implications. So long as the training of the clergy took place within the universities, ordinands were exposed to factional opinions within the Church, and were able to attach themselves to one party or another. If they were at

Oxford they could hardly avoid doing so. The lines of division, however, though they might be clearly drawn, did not correspond with lines within the university, and students could not avoid encountering contrary opinions in theology as in all else. But the theological colleges founded at Oxford and Cambridge in the 1870s and 1880s were clearly partisan, and this consequence of party spirit in ordination training spread rapidly. Before, it had been a matter of individual alignment and commitment, but with the appearance of party colleges it became a phenomenon which was positively inculcated. The change was remarked upon at once and has been a matter for adverse comment ever since. It was put succinctly by William Boyd Carpenter, Bishop of Ripon 1884–1911, when he said that theological colleges 'create, accentuate and perpetuate party differences within the Church' (Major 1925, p. 158). William Connor Magee, Bishop of Peterborough 1868–91 and Archbishop of York 1891, saw the danger coming only from one side:

> The theological colleges presided over, for the most part, by very High Churchmen, are rapidly turning out a number of young seminary priests; all moulded in the same pattern, set up with the same amount and kind of reading, and using the same party shibboleths and catch-words; often, of course, without understanding of their real meaning. (MacDonnell 1896, p. 60)

It was not a new accusation, for Bishop Samuel Wilberforce had been obliged to sacrifice his vice-principal of Cuddesdon College, H. P. Liddon, when the College was alleged to encourage popery. But, if the High Church party started the game, the Low Church party were not slow to join in, and were quicker off the mark in acquiring the patronage of livings for partisan trusts. A commission reviewing the colleges in 1942 came to a jaundiced conclusion: 'They have grown up in a haphazard fashion . . . they tend on the whole to encourage points of view representative of the "wings" rather than of the "centre" ' (*Interim Report* 1942, p. 13). Certainly the issue of churchmanship would never have assumed the proportions it did without the help of the theological colleges and their partisan stance.

THE CLERGY AND CLASS

Innovatory though the theological colleges were in Anglican ordination training, they changed the ministry very little. Their foundation was a response to secular changes, and represented the Church's response at the theological level to the emergence of secular learning.

We have already remarked on the irony of the Church's staunch defence of its privileged place in the educational Establishment in view of its origins as a ploy of the state to tame excessive religious zeal. The truly Establishment character of the Church of England first emerged in the eighteenth century, when, for the first time, clergy were numbered among the gentry. Having once achieved this position, the Church was extremely loath to lose it, and, indeed, treated as outrageous the idea that Anglican clergy might be drawn from the lower orders of society. It forgot that it had for centuries been otherwise, and completely forgot the novelty of the clergy's high status in English society. It was felt to be one of the great strengths of the Church of England, as compared with dissenting bodies, that its clergy were gentlemen. William Stubbs, the Regius Professor of Modern History at Oxford in the 1870s, and later Bishop of Chester and then of Oxford, expressed himself thus:

> There may come a time when, the doctrinal teaching of the Church remaining and retaining its hold on the classes of society that it now affects, it may still be so bad a speculation to bring up sons for the clerical office, that candidates must be sought in a lower grade; and that very large sphere and those many ways of usefulness which are now utilised by the clergy, as leaders of country society, and prominently interested in all social movements, must be given up; their sole means of influence being the sacerdotal, their spiritual or ministerial influence. I do not think it desirable that such a time should be hastened.   (Church Congress 1873, pp. 307–8)

Stubbs believed it was not just the greater influence of a gentleman which made it desirable that clergymen should belong to the gentry, but that there was intrinsic merit in this arrangement: 'Owing to the union of character of the clergyman with the social *status* of a gentleman, in fitting him for the latter [the

universities] have in a manner fitted him for the former.' (ibid.)
The same opinion was held by others, though the practicability
of the ideal was less certain in the 1870s than it had been twenty
years before. It was not universal, however, and Lord Malmesbury wrote to Disraeli in 1868 that 'the church cannot hold its
own with the new electors if it does not institute a class like the
bas clergé in Roman Catholic countries. They [i.e. the labourers]
have no sympathy with *gentleman* parsons.' (ibid.) The contrary
view, equally, was maintained. Bishop Samuel Wilberforce
reckoned it to be a fallacy that the poorer classes provide the best
clergy for the poor. Even those who wished to be on Malmesbury's side recognised the strong prejudice in favour of a gentleman parson, and Dean Howson of Chester told a Church
Congress that 'the title of B.A. without much knowledge of
divinity is more esteemed in the world than a good knowledge of
divinity without the title of B.A.' (ibid.)

Not everyone, however, ever believed it to be necessarily a
good thing that the clergy should be gentlemen. The evangelicals, despite Charles Simeon's efforts to civilise them, were prone
to revert to the enthusiasm of John Newton and others of the
eighteenth century, when St Edmund's Hall expelled six students for 'too much religion'. Nor were the Tractarians, despite a
strong Tory inclination, all of that mind, and Hurrell Froude
dubbed precisely the view spelt out years later by Professor
Stubbs the 'gentleman heresy'.

It was Stubbs who was proved right in the end, though, for it
was lack of a sufficient number of upper-middle-class ordination
candidates which drove the Church eventually to look to men 'in
a lower grade'. And, as Stubbs had anticipated, it was the declining incomes attached to livings which dried up the supply of
young gentlemen coming forward. Agriculture had been the
mainspring of the clergy's rise in status in the eighteenth century, and the same was now to be responsible for a reverse
process. There may have been idealists who were glad to see the
change coming, but it was thrust upon the Church by circumstances beyond its control. In 1837 the average income of an
incumbent was about £500, and by 1897 it had fallen to £246.
It is true that curates earned much more than they had at the
beginning of Queen Victoria's reign, and that more men were
incumbents than had been the case when fewer men held
several livings in plurality; but those same reforms had

stripped the Church of some of its richest preferments and therefore of their attractiveness for the sons of the nobility and the gentry. Already by 1863 a clerical writer was able to describe, with only slight exaggeration, the state of the Church of England in the following terms: 'This is a state of things that may well startle those who have been accustomed to look upon the clerical profession, with its glittering prizes, as the most attractive of all professions' (Phillips 1863, p. 4).

That the problem had become extremely grave by the end of the century is shown by the fact that in 1899 the archbishops set up a commission to investigate it, for the Church of England never considers what action it should take until action is well overdue. The Commission finally submitted its *Report on the Supply and Training of Candidates for Holy Orders* in 1908. By its terms of reference the Archbishops' Commission was charged to report on the 'advisability or the reverse, of seeking ordinands from different social grades'. It reported (*Report* 1908, p. 14) that it could not be contended:

> that poverty precludes from Ministerial service, or that God confines the vocation to the priesthood to one rank of the social order. At the same time it has to be recognised that in England for many generations past, owing to lack of educational opportunity for boys of poorer homes, the Ministry has, in fact, for good or ill, been thus confined, with the result that . . . a long established prejudice in favour of one particular class has been created . . . while on the other side, clergy drawn from the artisan and labouring classes are apt to be regarded both by their own people, and by other ranks, somewhat critically. . . . But it seems clear that the opening of a wider access to the Ministry . . . will place at [the Church's] disposal a far larger body of volunteers from which to make choice. . . . It will also reinforce the Ministry with men who, in intellectual capacity, zeal and self-denial in no way fall short . . . of the high standard at which the Church of England should aim.

Another, and much more profound, revolution had taken place in ideas about the clergy than that which resulted in the foundation of theological colleges. The advent of the colleges had been an adjustment on the Church's part to the secularisation of Eng lish education and a move to train more dedicated and worthy clergymen. Secularisation was not limited to education, however, crucial though that had been for the Church.

CHANGES IN THE MINISTRY

The massive movement of population from rural to urban areas, and the economic transformation which lay behind the migrations, had their own complex and far-reaching implications. The first effect of these changes was to diminish the Church's income. The second effect was to make the clerical profession, with its strong rural associations, relatively much less attractive than the newer professions which grew up with industry and commerce. And the third effect was to transform the work of a clergyman, who could no longer simply be a cultured and devout man. He had, instead, to organise and run a large city parish in which the children were in large schools, the sick in large hospitals, the workers in large factories. Clubs, guilds, Sunday schools and night schools, and many other things besides, were required. The building of new churches, by and large, had proceeded with the expansion of towns, but the increased need for clergy, if the rural churches were not to be left without pastors, was enormous. In the northern diocese of Ripon between 1836, when it was established, and 1872 the number of incumbents rose from 297 to 462, and the number of curates from 76 to 245. Indeed, in overall numbers the increase in clergy almost kept in step with the increase in population. In the second half of the nineteenth century there continued to be roughly one clergyman to every thousand in the population taken as a whole, though their distribution between town and country was absurdly unequal. The success was more apparent than real, therefore, when this factor is taken into account.

With these changes the whole conception of what it meant to be a clergyman had altered, and had become an altogether more religious one. Just as theology had been separated out as a distinctive academic discipline, and as the identity of clergyman had been 'prised apart from the idea of gentleman', so the notion of a clergyman emerged as one who was 'not as other men'. The clergy were no longer integrated in the social fabric of the country as they had been. They occupied a position which had become dislocated from secular society by secular changes, and they made a virtue of what was in any case a necessity by laying emphasis on the withdrawnness proper to the clergy,. and on their apartness.

The speed of these latest changes should not be exaggerated. Despite the establishment of theological colleges in the nineteenth century, the majority of men in the ministry at the time of the 1908 *Report*, 57·9 per cent of them, were graduates with no theological-college training. The bishops still exercised almost complete discretion in deciding whom they would ordain. All this was soon to end. The *Report* judged the theological colleges to be necessary, and a university training to be the most desirable preparation for it:

Universities, as such, do not provide a professional training for Holy Orders. They are places of Higher Education, not Higher Religious Education. They are a complement to Secondary education, not an alternative for Theological Training. A clear recognition of these two facts is of the utmost importance in estimating the place which our Universities should hold in the education of the Clergy. (*Report* 1908, p. 16))

The *Report* then made a formal recommendation that 'a University course should be regarded as a preliminary to, not an alternative for, a Professional Training', and, further, that 'a three-years course of Professional Training should be ultimately required, as a rule, of candidates for Holy Orders' (ibid., pp. 33–4). Finally, it recommended that 'a Central Candidates' Council should be created to supervise all matters concerned with the supply, recruiting and training of candidates for Holy Orders'. The recommended council was established in 1912, and in effecting this the bishops very severely restricted in practice, if not in theory, their discretion as to whom they should ordain.

A new view had finally been reached. Firstly, special ordination training was now regarded as necessary before men became clergymen – though reading for a university degree was still considered a desirable complement to secondary education. Secondly, the prerequisites for ordination were identified as intellectual capacity, religious zeal, and a spirit of self-denial. Together they added up to a ministry which was to be religious in a special way, and in a specialist way. This, decidedly, was a new conception of the ministry at the turn of the century.

Before the 1908 *Report* was published, two more theological colleges had been founded, each of which anticipated official acceptance of the new thinking. They were created under the auspices of Religious communities of men, by the Society of the Sacred Mission in 1891 and the Community of the Resurrection in 1902. The colleges, at Kelham in Nottinghamshire and at Mirfield in Yorkshire, were very different from each other in character, but both aimed to cut through the assumptions which were called into question by the *Report*. The Kelham college set out to provide a strictly non-graduate training, 'with no half-baked gentility'. It was a radical innovation, which prepared men only for overseas missions until after 1900, and which remained less than wholly respectable for a great deal longer; the first elevation of a clergyman trained there to an English diocesan see did not take place until 1973, the year after the college closed. The Community of the Resurrection's college held to the principle that it is desirable that a university education should form a complement to secondary education, and provided for candidates to prepare for university entrance, attend the University of Leeds, and then proceed to theological training at Mirfield. Places at both colleges were free and intended for those who otherwise could not have afforded the cost of training for ordination, and who, without training, would have been considered by the bishops to be unsuitable candidates. Both colleges were conceived as ways of combating the prevailing situation, which was described by Charles Gore, the founder of the Community of the Resurrection, as 'a Class ministry with a money qualification'.

To sum up, it is evident that the place of the ordained ministry of the Church of England in English society had radically changed by the beginning of the twentieth century from what it had been a century before, and with it had changed the training provided for clergy and the very conception of the ministry. As we have seen, the changes were the result, in part, of an upsurge of religious zeal dating back to the eighteenth century, and, in part, a response to gradual secularisation. We must be clear what we mean by 'secularisation' in this context. We do not mean that 'religiousness' declined. It would be hard to pin down the meaning of such a proposition, and evidence could be produced which would suggest that England was in some senses a 'more religious' country at the end of the nineteenth century than at the beginning. We mean that religious institutions, and the Church of England in particular, had become less central to the structure of English society. The clergy were crucial in this transformation, and it would be entirely accurate to say that the form taken by secularisation in many departments of public life was 'laicisation'. Various institutions which formerly had been dominated by the clergy, or in which the clergy had exercised a substantial influence, were now run almost wholly by laymen. This is not to say, we must repeat, that these laymen were 'less religious' than had been their clerical predecessors. In many cases the reverse may be true. But the Church, as an institution, had become greatly less significant a force in public life.

2   The Clerical Profession

INTO THE CONTEMPORARY WORLD

At first glance it is difficult to see why the Church of England was so alarmed about itself and its clergy in the first years of the twentieth century. Queen Victoria's reign had seen a massive programme of church-building. The population of England had grown enormously, but so had the number of clergy, from something like 14,000 in 1841 to more than 23,000 by 1911, making one clergyman to every 1800 people instead of the earlier proportion of one to every thousand. It was a regression, but not a landslide. Other signs were positively encouraging. Seven out of ten children were being baptised in 1913, compared with six out of ten 30 years before; the proportion of children being brought to the bishop to be confirmed had increased in the same period, and so had the proportion of the adult population making their Easter communion. All in all, the Church was holding its own in a most remarkable way.

The source of unease was the qualitative change we described at the end of the previous chapter rather than any numerical retreat. There had been no question of whether or not England was a Christian country when the Church had occupied a prominent position. Deprived of that privileged place, however, the Church was obliged to gain some other tangible hold over the population to be sure that it was still maintaining the place of religion in the life of the nation. In this task it was having no notable success. If it was not falling back, neither was it advancing in such a way as to inspire confidence.

From the years immediately prior to the First World War until the 1960s the Church of England maintained the same position. With small fluctuations, the proportion of the population being baptised, confirmed and making their Easter communions remained stable. In contrast with this, the period with which we shall be dealing saw substantial changes, for which no immediately obvious reasons suggest themselves.

Infant baptisms, as we have just mentioned, increased around the turn of the century. The rate rose from about 60 per cent of children being baptised in 1900 to slightly above 70 per cent in the 1920s, and then slowly dropped, again reaching the 60 per cent level. It continued to fall, however, and for the first time dropped below 60 per cent in 1958, falling below 50 per cent in 1958 and falling still further in 1970.

Figures for confirmations follow the same pattern. Between 2·5 and 3·5 per cent of boys between the ages of twelve and twenty were presented for confirmation between 1911 and 1961. In 1962 the figure fell below 2·5 per cent for the first time, and then continued to fall to 2·1 per cent in 1964, 1·9 per cent in 1966 and 1·7 per cent in 1968, until it was only 1·5 per cent in 1970. A similar pattern is revealed in the proportion of the population making their Easter communion; until 1934 the figure was 9 per cent, which fell to below 7 per cent in 1962, and, for the first time, to below 5 per cent in 1970.

These figures are all concerned with the broad features of church attendance and the use of Church sacraments which form the general context within which we must consider the clergy and their work, and the situation obtaining in the 1960s. The number of clergy themselves increased, as we have said, towards the end of the nineteenth century. If we take a broader view, completing the picture to the middle of the twentieth century, we find that the numbers rose to a maximum just after the turn of the century, after which they fell slowly to around the level of 1851. Indeed, disregarding clergymen over the age of 65, there were about 14,500 in 1851, 19,500 in 1901, and only 12,500 in 1951. It would appear that the modern period of the Anglican ministry (which, we have argued, began at the end of the eighteenth century) displayed a pattern of continued growth, in numbers and in vigour, for more than a hundred years. This period of growth was punctuated by the cry, 'the Church in danger' in the 1830s, but the response was one of renewed effort rather than one of retreat. The steady decline in the social status of the clergy and the encroachment of secularisation stimulated these efforts, which, on the whole, proved to be successful, until almost, it seems, a point was reached when the Church as an institution ran out of energy. The general position of the Church in society remained steady, but the number of men in the full-time service of the Church as clergymen gradually fell. Proportionately to a population which continued to grow, the number fell rapidly; and if we take into account the increasing average age of the clergy, it fell dramatically. The whole pattern is summarised by the following figures for the ecclesiastical provinces of Canterbury and York.

	1851	*1901*	*1951*
Population	17,000,000	31,000,000	41,000,000
Clergy under 65	15,000	19,500	13,000
Persons per clergyman under 65	1,000	1,600	3,300
Average age of all clergy	44	49	55

The numbers rose somewhat after 1951, but, as we have already noted, it was the 1960s which saw substantial changes. These are

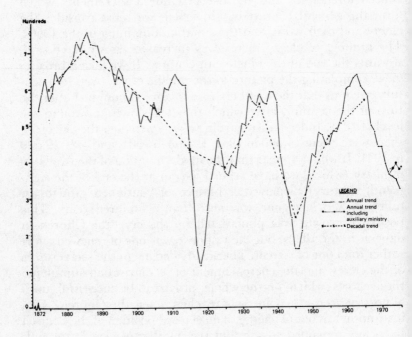

FIGURE 1   Church of England ordinations, 1872–1975

not yet reflected in the number of clergy, and, indeed, the pattern which has now emerged was unknown at the time when the research to be reported in the chapters which follow was being conducted. At that time the overall picture appeared still to be relatively stable. The way in which the numbers of men entering the Anglican ministry as deacons, illustrated in Figure 1, matches the other changes of the 1960s will be clear. At the beginning of the 1960s, however, it was obvious that the ministry was in a parlous state. What was not obvious was how close to a climacteric was not only the ministry, but the Church as a whole. But for the ministry the crisis of a numerical decline, so far from being the root of the problem, could be regarded as a symptom.

CLERICAL PRESTIGE

The problems experienced by the Church and its clergy have generally been interpreted by sociologists as a consequence of secularisation in the widest sense. As we have said already (p. 26 above), more is implied in this analysis than the removal of the Church and its representatives from positions of influence in society, for it goes on to propose that the culture and the thinking current in society have become 'less religious'. So, if contemporary society is not rooted in a religious culture, the clergy, as representatives of religious culture, are out of tune with the spirit of the age. As a social group they must be regarded as fundamentally irrelevant to society. B. R. Wilson, the foremost English exponent of this view, has written of the 'alienation' of the clergy, comparing today's clergy with 'the charcoal-burners or alchemists in an age in which the processes in which they were engaged had been rendered obsolete, technically or intellectually' (Wilson 1966, p. 76; cf. Gellner 1974). The explanation underlying this comparison may be accurate, but it is altogether too general to account for the specific changes of which there is evidence. For that reason we shall concern ourselves here with the ministry itself as a social group, considering the views of the clergy themselves who were about to enter upon their careers in the 1960s.

The loss of social prestige suffered by the clergy in the latter part of the nineteenth century continued into the twentieth century, and so did the secularisation (in the limited sense of the word) which had stripped the clergy of so many functions in society. We must consider each of these changes if we are to appreciate the situation confronting ordinands of the 1960s and make sense of their ideas.

Status and prestige are difficult concepts to deal with. In tracing briefly the status accorded to the clergy through a number of historical periods, we have had to be careful to see just who the clergy were in any particular era, but we have been able to enjoy the historian's luxury of treating the idea of status, or social standing, as being relatively unproblematical. Anyone who writes of an age which has passed has only a limited amount of evidence at his disposal. When we come to our own generation the quantity of evidence is so voluminous that the selectiveness forced upon us cannot fail to be obvious, and the presuppositions employed in making such a selection will be no less obvious. In assessing the status of the clergy we are addressing ourselves to one of the hardest tasks of all, for the evidence is unique in its contradictoriness. Herein lies a first clue to the true understanding of the contemporary clergy considered as a social group. As we shall see repeatedly, they are an aberrant group; they can be compared with other groups only at the cost of giving a distorted account of them. Nevertheless, the employment of this procedure is inevitable if we are to make use of sociological methods. Such a procedure would be impermissible from the start, but for one vital fact: namely, that the clergy refuse to regard themselves as a unique group in society. They insist on doing precisely what we hesitate to do: they compare themselves with other social groups, with which, strictly, they are not comparable. This is a methodological point which we need not labour.

On the one hand, to make a point we shall return to more forcibly below (pp. 182f.), the social status of the clergy is still very high; when given a list of thirty occupations and asked to put them in order of prestige, people in England still rank the clergyman well towards the top. He is reckoned fourth, in fact, after surgeon, general practitioner and solicitor; and the situation is not very different in the USA, where it has been found that the clergyman is ranked twelfth out of 90 (Richards 1962). On the other hand, the standing of the clergy is remarkably low if one takes any tangible evidence. Income and education are the most often employed criteria for measuring prestige, and neither of them would suggest that the clergyman ranks very high.[1] From having been the learned elite of society, the clergy's general educational standard has sunk greatly. By the 1870s and 1880s the proportion of deacons with university degrees had dropped to between 72 and 75 per cent (Chadwick 1972, p. 247), and by the 1960s and 1970s it was regularly dropping to below 40 per cent in some years. While more and more occupations were demanding a degree as qualification for entry into specialist training, the Church was finding that fewer and fewer of those admitted to its theological colleges had been to a university. The bench of bishops, too, has very largely lost its formerly high academic standing, for whereas in 1930 43 per cent held doctorates of divinity or other higher degrees, other than honorary ones, in 1973 only 7 per cent did. This does not mean that nearly half the bishops in 1930 were really scholars, for the universities of Oxford and Cambridge not uncommonly conferred doctorates on their members when they were consecrated bishops, but that practice itself testifies to the scholarly reputation of bishops in an earlier period.

Realistic comparisons of income are hard to make, because of the free facilities the clergy enjoy, chiefly the provision of a rent-free house. Under contemporary economic circumstances, however, the advantages which accrue from a tied cottage are extremely dubious, and this applies whether it is in the form of a rent-free council flat or an episcopal palace. The average income of a church living from all sources was very slightly over £1000 a year in 1962. All things considered, that level of remuneration did not accord with the high prestige accorded to clergymen.

The clergy are not alone in enjoying anomalously high status compared with their moderate pay. University lecturers and masters in grammar schools were also paid less in the 1960s than would have been expected from their high social standing, but in their case the contradiction was only between prestige and pay, not between prestige and education as well, as it was for the clergy, who in any case were reckoned more prestigious than either of them. The 1908 *Report*, referred to in the previous chapter, looked to 'poorer homes' to provide clergy who would be marked by a high standard of 'self-denial', thus anticipating continuing relative poverty; but in so far as it looked to those same homes for men of 'intellectual capacity' it trusted that by this means clerical prestige would be maintained, though in this its hopes have not been realised. Respect and dignity may be accorded to a group which is relatively poor, but such respect must be based on something. So far as the clergy are concerned it was formerly learning which provided the basis for this respect; what it is now is less easy to discern, and this brings us to the second set of changes which deserve consideration.

CLERICAL ROLE

If society is unclear about the reasons why the clergyman is rated high in social status it is just as unclear about what the clergyman is supposed to be doing. He is – simply, is – a clergy-man. The uncertainty and ambiguity as to the role of the clergy is shared by the clergyman himself, it seems, and some clergy feel that 'clerical status' is an impediment and encumbrance. A group of 50 French priests, writing to their bishop some years ago, argued that 'clerical status forces on priests a life-style and a kind of relationship with people which amounts to a major obstacle to the task of preaching Jesus Christ. Consequently it is necessary for us to rid ourselves of this clerical status before we can begin to work out anew how best we can fulfil the mission of the Church' (translated from a report in *La Croix*, 22 November 1968). There is a dead-weight of tradition which, for some at least, is frustrating as well as confusing. In England, as elsewhere, this problem is evidenced most clearly by the phenomenon of clergy leaving the parochial ministry (but see below, pp. 180). Sometimes they go into teaching posts or to jobs in the welfare services; sometimes they go to the increasing number of specialist posts within the diocesan structures and become youth chaplains, stewardship organisers, industrial or hospital or college chaplains, and so on. These are all posts which offer a more clearly defined context in which clergy may exercise their ministry. We are not maintaining that uncertainty of role is the basic problem of the contemporary parochial ministry, but only that it is the aspect of the problem most apparent to the clergy themselves – just as the shortage of men and of the money to pay them adequately is the aspect most apparent to Church administrators.

If we attempt to examine the role of the clergyman, it soon becomes obvious that it is a complex one, comprising many separate elements. The various strands which go to make it up have varied from time to time and from denomination to denomination, so that no single list of the components of his role would be universally applicable. In order to help us to see the sources of uncertainty in more detail we propose to consider a list devised for studying the problems of American clergy and to comment on each component in it in turn. Blizzard (1956, pp. 508–9) has proposed six aspects of the clergyman's role:

(1) teacher of the Christian faith;
(2) organiser of church societies and affairs;
(3) preacher of the Word of God;
(4) administrator of parish business;
(5) pastor of his people;
(6) priest, in his liturgical functions as administrator of the sacraments and leader of public worship.

This list would serve for a number of churches and will do well enough for the Church of England.

50 years ago all these tasks were performed by the Anglican clergyman, and by him alone. 50 years before that the clergy fulfilled various additional roles which we should now regard as secular and extra-ecclesiastical. Today, however, his monopoly over even his more domestic activities is subject to a process of erosion.

Teacher. The role of the clergyman as teacher is of ancient origin, and until recently it was based on his theological learning and on the level of his general education, in both of which respects he was distinguished from those to whom he ministered. The relative decline in the educational level of the clergy has already been noted, but we must also note that, even in the field of theology, so recently become a special discipline, the clergy no longer have a monopoly of skills. The proportion of those reading for degrees in theology who intend to proceed to ordination is declining; at the University of Leeds, for example, 57 per cent of those who passed through the Department of Theology between 1961 and 1965 were planning to teach in schools as specialists in religious education, while only 25 per cent were planning to enter the ministry of one of the denominations (Ling 1967). So long as the ordained ministry remains closed to women, this situation will of course be perpetuated, for that reason among others. While, therefore, on the one hand the level of educational attainment of the clergy declines, on the other there is an increasing number of lay people, men and women, who hold theological degrees. Many of these lay people are teachers, and this means that in the future more and more parishes will have among their laity people who are equipped to teach the Christian faith, far better equipped, in fact, than are their clergy, who have had less theological education and no formal training at all in teaching methods.

At the other end of the spectrum we find a similar process at work. Certain appointments in theology at universities were originally made possible by using the endowment incomes of cathedral canonries. This tie between the universities and the Church is now being rapidly dissolved, as the author of the Preface to *Crockford's Clerical Directory* noted in the 1973–4 issue:

> In England until quite recently the number of theological posts which did not carry with them some pastoral responsibility or some duties in respect of public worship were very few. A majority of the professors were residentiary canons of cathedrals, many of the lecturers were college chaplains, notably at Oxford and Cambridge. Durham had a similar pattern on a smaller scale, and at London, although there was not the same kind of cathedral connection, the greater part of the theological teaching was nevertheless done within the context of King's College and in relation to training for the ministry. The situation now is much changed. Certain professorships at Oxford and Durham and one at Cambridge are still annexed to canonries but we are informed that some of the holders of them find the cathedral responsibilities irksome. The majority of professorships in theology in England are now without any attachment to a worshipping community. As regards lectureships, these, outside Oxford and Cambridge, have generally been purely academic posts. Now at Oxford and Cambridge it is becoming less and less usual for lectureships in theology to be held by college chaplains. Of course this situation is mitigated by the personal attachments of individual lecturers and professors, but the fact remains that the leaders of theological teaching are increasingly people who have no formal and necessary connection with any part of the Christian Church. Theology and worship are divorced.

Nor is it only chairs at Oxford and Cambridge which are involved. Religious studies, which is what theology is developing into, is very predominantly a lay discipline, the scientific spirit of which is incompatible with the official task of conducting public worship.

Organiser. The second component of the clergyman's role which Blizzard distinguished is his role as organiser of the church activities, but a substantial amount of this work is now being handed over to the laity. Church societies, guilds, youth clubs and so on are increasingly organisations not only *for* the laity but also *of* the laity. This shift in emphasis is encouraged by Church policies, but it takes place in response to pressure from below as well. A survey of Catholic churches in Liverpool found that one of the most significant of the criticisms expressed by lay people took the form of rebellion 'at the extent to which the parish priest controls all parochial affairs' (Brothers 1963, p. 484).

Preacher. Preaching has had a chequered career as a clerical function. Since the office of lay reader, with licence to preach, was instituted in 1860, it has not been the exclusive responsibility of Anglican clergy. Laymen now preach much more frequently than in former days, and this is especially noticeable on formal occasions, such as university sermons. But in the routine life of parish churches it is the increasingly perfunctory character of preaching which is even more striking than the usurpation of the role by laymen. In the worship of evangelical churches, within the Church of England as well as in nonconformist denominations, the sermon retains its old pre-eminence, but elsewhere in the Anglican Church, as in the Roman Catholic Church, there is a tendency for the sermon to become something more in the nature of an impromptu chat. The practice advocated by the Second Vatican Council of preaching at every service seems to have spread, and the effect is the multiplication of sermons together with their devaluation. Anthony Trollope's wry comment in *Barchester Towers* applied to a day when 30 minutes was considered short for a sermon: 'There is, perhaps, no greater hardship at present inflicted on mankind in civilized and free countries, than the necessity of listening to sermons. No one but a preaching clergyman has, in these realms, the power of compelling an audience to sit silent, and be tormented.' Today the sermon seems no longer to be for the clergyman 'the pleasant morsel of his life', but to be an irksome duty. As the chaplain of a certain provincial university said recently after the learned diocesan bishop had preached, 'Of course we did not expect the bishop to spend twenty minutes preparing a sermon for the University Church, but he might have spared five.' In this aspect of his role, the contemporary clergyman, even if he attaches comparatively little importance to the preparation and delivery of his sermon, is like the vexed Dean and Chapter of Barchester in having ceded nothing of his right to preach every Sunday. The erosion of this clerical role, if our intuition is correct (for it is no more than intuition), lies in the declining enthusiasm of the clergy themselves.

Administrator. The administration of parish business is another part of the clergyman's work which he is only too glad to share with others. Responsibility for finance, for the care of the fabric, for the parish magazine and so on are the concern not only of the traditional churchwardens, but of such laymen as are fitted for these various jobs by their secular callings and can be pressed into service. Administration is a chore, and since the laity are ready to share responsibilities they may be pressed into sharing what are often irksome duties.

Pastor. The fifth component of the clerical role distinguished by Blizzard is that of pastor. By tradition it has been regarded as an important part of the duty of the clergy to care for members of the local church as their father in God and their pastor. Today, partly perhaps in reaction to a discredited paternalism, it is no longer so much the responsibility of the priest for his people which is stressed as the mutual responsibility of all the members of the church for one another. In the Church of England this is reflected in such ways as the institution of 'street wardens', whereby a local layman accepts responsibility for the pastoral care of a particular street or area, and in campaigns such as that conducted ecumenically in the 1960s under the slogan 'People Next Door'. So, at the same time as the clergy have been relieved of some of their obligations in the organisational and administrative fields, in order, presumably, to be able to spend more time in exercising their pastoral role, the obligation of lay people to discharge this same pastoral function is being stressed. The

result is that in all these ways the distinctiveness of the clergyman's role is being lessened.

Priest. The only component of the clerical role which it may be
thought necessarily remains distinctive, at least in churches with
a strong sacramental tradition, is the liturgical one. But even this
sixth component is no longer uniquely clerical in the sense in
which, until recently, it was. All modern liturgical thinking tends
towards stressing the fullest possible participation of the laity in
the liturgy, thus minimising the distinction between clergy and
laity still further, leaving the clergyman as the spokesman rather
than the supernaturally authorised leader, and substituting pres-
iding ministers where formerly there were sacred ministers.

The progressive erosion of the components which, taken
together, constituted a unique clerical role still leaves the clergyman as leader and co-ordinator of the parish. Now, a role of
leadership may be clear enough in an organisation geared to the
achievement of specific goals, but it is little more than honorific
in a voluntary organisation such as the local parish. In an
expanding organisation such as the early Church was, or as the
Mormons are today, expansion itself is the goal, and the clergy,
as full-time workers, spearhead the thrust. The Church of England completed its process of expansion, from a sociological
standpoint, many centuries ago, and was then left in a dominant
position in English society. Its clergy assumed myriad functions
of an entirely secular character, quite unrelated to expansion or
'mission'. When the 50 French Catholic priests proposed to their
bishop the necessity of abandoning entirely their clerical status
they were arguing that in order to start anew with a fresh *mission
de France* they would have to leave the past behind them, and
with it all the associations of a clergy who had completed their
task of conquest and had begun to rule.
   It follows from all this that the role of the priest in his parish,
and of the clergy as a group in society, is ambiguous and uncertain, because it developed gradually in order to meet the needs of
former ages and became fixed in a form appropriate to a society
which no longer exists. The parish does not need a paterfamilias,
because the parish as a natural community has vanished with
the development of cities, towns, and rural districts. The country
as a whole does not need a clergy who will minister to the people

in the ways their predecessors did, for it has secular Ministries of Education and Science, Health and Social Security, a Minister for the Arts, and so forth. The present Archbishop of Canterbury has advocated a Ministry for the Family within the Government. Only the final dénouement is to come: a Ministry of Religion.

We should maintain that these are processes of which the clergy themselves are aware. They may not express them in precisely these terms, but they are sensed clearly enough. And we believe that it needs no further argument to demonstrate that the dramatic decline in the number of clergy is a result of these processes.

What kind of group in society, then, are the clergy? With whom should one compare them when looking for illuminating companions?

THE CLERGY AS A PROFESSION

It is usual to treat the clergy as a profession, and to compare them with doctors, social workers and solicitors; they are regarded as working where possible in 'proper co-operation with the men and women of other professions' (Dunstan 1967). A Church of England report spoke not long ago of the distinctive role of the clergy explicitly in these terms:

> The clergy of the Church of England still take their place within the tradition of the learned professions of men whose responsibility is to serve people. There are responsibilities which are peculiar to the clergy and yet have to be spelled out more fully, but these as well as their more general responsibilities, can be discharged in a fashion which can be compared with the best practice of doctors and social workers.
>
> (CA no. 1703, p. 16)

Others doubt the accuracy of this approach, and this dissenting view links what we have said above with the question of whether or not the clergy constitute a profession:

> In some cases [the clergyman] earns about the same as an unskilled worker and this is perhaps how an unchurched society is coming to think of him – as someone who is not qualified as the twentieth century understands qualification. In an age

which is not particularly interested in faith it is difficult for people to understand what the clergyman is up to, and so they are apt to suggest that he isn't up to anything in particular. He is thrust on one side where serious issues are discussed – he isn't a social worker, he isn't a psychiatrist, he isn't a doctor, he isn't a probation officer, or a teacher or a welfare worker. He is granted a little elbow room in hospitals or prisons – after all it is well known that when people are unhappy, ill or dying they like a bit of religion, and the clergyman can at least talk about God without getting uncomfortable. But I believe there is a growing feeling in the community as a whole that the Church is played out and the clergy with it, and this is perhaps as obvious in the exaggerated respect – an almost superstitious awe – which is sometimes shown to the clergy and indicates how little religion is a part of people's ordinary, everyday lives. . . .

(Furlong 1966)

Perhaps Miss Furlong does not go quite far enough, for it may be that the Church and its clergy are sensed by some to be 'played out' even when it comes to what they understand by 'religion'. But her remarks anticipate our discussion, and it would not be right to dismiss quite so peremptorily the widely held and deeply respected conviction that the clergy constitute a profession, and that having said and accepted that, one thereby understands their nature and their problems.

The case for

Social scientists as a whole, though with notable exceptions, have shared the belief that a clergyman is a professional person. There are numerous reasons for this belief, which deserve to be stated, but one problem arises immediately: What does the sociologist mean when he speaks of a profession? We obviously must know the answer to this question before we can decide whether or not the ordained ministry measures up to the definition. Many different lists of defining characteristics have been proposed, no two of them exactly the same, but these

lists of traits contain a hidden similarity . . . that all of them derive from an ideal–typical conception whose closest concrete approximation is medicine and the priesthood. Ignoring variations in language, such lists report: high income, prestige and influence; high educational requirements; professional autonomy; licensure; commitment of members to the profession; codes of ethics; cohesion of the professional community; monopoly over a task; intensive adult socialization experience for recruits, and so on. (Goode 1969, p. 276. See also Parsons 1954, pp. 34 – 49; Caplow 1954; Greenwood 1957; Wilensky 1964; Etzioni 1969; Hickson and Thomas 1969; and Appendix IV below)

It will be simplest if we consider these characteristics under four headings: organisation, relationships with clients, the kind of authority exercised, and the relationship to the wider society typical of professions.

The essence of a professional organisation consists in the allocation of a scarce skill, making it available while maintaining its value. The skill need not necessarily involve technical intricacy, but it must be dependent on the judgement of the practitioner, which in turn must be informed by an understanding of the principles involved. A craft handed on from father to son, be it never so skilled and rare, is not professional; to be professional it must be grounded in a systematic body of theory. The builder knows from his own experience and from the experience handed down to him in his trade just what sort of lintel is needed for a certain window, but the structural engineer knows this without any experience, from a grasp of the theoretical principles involved. His knowledge, therefore, is not bounded by the limits of his experience or the experience of others, but only by the limits of human understanding. Professional skill consists in the ability to cope with the unfamiliar. All this means that there must be a body of theory; that the practitioners must be organised in such a way as to pass on the necessary knowledge; that they must preserve the necessary standards in their skills by vetting new practitioners and enforcing a code of professional conduct; and for these purposes they will naturally form themselves into an association which shares common interests and concerns. When we apply these criteria to the clergy it seems clear that they fulfil most of the conditions. They have their theoretical knowledge of theology and the religious tradition. In the convocations of Canterbury and York the Anglican clergy have one of the most ancient organisations in England. Canon law and ecclesiastical courts order their behaviour and discipline misconduct. Entry to the profession is controlled, for 'No man shall be accounted or taken to be a lawful Bishop, Priest or Deacon in the Church of England, or suffered to execute any of the said functions, except he be called, tried, examined, and admitted thereunto', as the Ordinal expresses it. The clergy live in a community of their own, with a directory of their members, and, if they do not all know each other, at least each knows a large number who between them know all the others; often they are the sons of clergy, marry the daughters of the clergy, and sire clergy. The organisation of the clergy is truly impressive.

A 'strictly professional relationship' is a phrase which has passed into the English language as part of general usage. One may know an architect or a dentist as a personal friend, but one may also pay a visit to him not as a friend at all, but solely in his professional capacity. In those circumstances, for the purposes of such a visit, the relationship becomes a professional one, governed by the appropriate rules, the essence of which is a contract. The advice he gives is not friendly but professional advice. The terms of the contract are such that, for his part, the skills he puts at your disposal carry the authority of his organisation, and would be corroborated by any number of his professional fellow practitioners; while for your part you trust his professional skill and you make due payment for it. There is a relationship between professional and client, not between Ann and Mary. It is depersonalised. Even if the client knows that the person whom he consults is an adulterous, inebriate, gambling bankrupt, he treats the professional *qua* professional with respect. The professional, for his part, gives his services without regard to his estimate of the client's personal worthiness, and, furthermore, such information as he learns about his client within the context of the professional relationship remains confidential to the relationship. The professional organisation exists, in part, to guarantee the contractual nature of professional relationships. It will defend the professional reputation of its members and secure due payment for their services; and if any one of them violates his side of the contract it will disqualify him. Now, the clergyman also has this type of relationship with his clients, even though it is often swamped by personal relationships. There remains, however, the contractual element at the root of the relationship, for the services which he renders are the same regardless of who the client may be. His obligation to render a professional service is, if anything, more strictly enforced than it is in other professions. The doctor or the solicitor is not obliged to accept a client, but a clergyman of the Church of England is not free to refuse his services to any parishioner without sufficient legal reason. You can compel the rector of your parish to officiate at your marriage, for example; he can delay the ceremony, and fix it at a time of his own choosing, but in the end he must render the service required of him, or suffer legal penalty. The 'seal of confession' is the phrase used to describe the solemn obligation of the priest to treat as confidential information which he receives when a penitent confesses his sins and seeks absolution through the sacrament of penance, and this too is an obligation which has legal standing. The clergyman may regard all his clients as friends, but beneath the friendship there remains a contractual relationship, the obligations of which he is powerless to abrogate, and these obligations must always, in the final analysis, take priority. In this respect the clergyman is bound by the contractual relationship characteristic of all professions, but he is bound more strictly. The doctor is not permitted to seduce a patient, but he may at least give medical treatment to his lover with impunity.

The authority of the professional, as we have seen from the contractual nature of the relationship, is not a personal authority but an authority of office. The authority of an Anglican clergyman is of this official, impersonal sort, as the words with which he is made a priest explicitly state: 'Take thou Authority to preach the Word of God, and to minister the Holy Sacraments in the Congregation, where thou shalt be lawfully appointed thereunto.' Nor is the nature of the authority ever ignored, for every act performed officially by the clergyman is accompanied, either explicitly or implicitly, by the qualifying formula, 'I . . . in the name of . . .'. So the form of absolution in the *Book of Common Prayer* runs, 'Our Lord Jesus Christ, who hath left power to his Church to absolve all sinners who truly repent and believe in him, of his great mercy forgive thee thine offences: And by his authority committed to me, I absolve thee from all thy sins, In the name of the Father, and of the Son, and of the Holy Ghost.' As if this were not enough to make plain the nature of clerical authority, the matter is spelt out still more explicitly in the twenty-sixth Article of Religion, which is entitled, 'Of the

Unworthiness of the Ministers, which hinders not the effect of the Sacrament'.

In the Church of England, because it is the Established Church, the clerical profession receives official recognition from the State. In return for the State's undertaking to guarantee the skills of the profession and oversee their exercise, the clergy are granted a monopoly over them. Thus, it is an offence to impersonate a clergyman of the Church of England, even if not done with intent to defraud. On the other hand, the royal authority which confirms the official, impersonal authority of the clergy, in the same Article of Religion takes care to specify measures which should be taken by the Church itself to vindicate the trust invested in it by the State: 'Nevertheless, it appertaineth to the discipline of the Church, that inquiry be made of evil Ministers, and that they be accused by those that have knowledge of their offences; and finally being found guilty, by just judgement be deposed.'

From this brief consideration of some of the typical characteristics of a profession it will be obvious why the clerical office has been traditionally regarded as a profession. The similarities are striking. But there remains one problem: what are the particular skills of the clergy the exercise of which is organised and institutionalised in so manifestly professional a manner? Our answer, stated baldly, is that the clergy have no particular skills at all; the similarities with the professions are all of form, and none of content. (An analogy might be found in the proposition that Communism, particularly in the USSR, is a religion; again the understandable similarities are of form, rather than of content, and the proposition hides much more than it makes manifest.) Thus stated, this answer is altogether too bald, however, so we shall approach the problem in another way.

The case against

Professional skill is composed of two elements. First, it is a service which is rendered to clients. It is less a matter of doing a job and more a matter of being consulted and of advice being sought. The professional sets out to help his client, to assist and to be of service to him. Hence there is an ideal of disinterested service built into the notion of a profession. This is because of the presence of the second element, which is the body of abstract knowledge upon which the professional draws in advising and serving his client. The profession is the guardian of this special theoretical knowledge, and it serves the community by putting it at the disposal of the inexpert layman. If the ordained ministry is to count as a profession it must be the guardian of its own proper corpus of knowledge, and it must employ this specialised knowledge in the service of laymen.

Now, there can be no doubt as to the ideal of service permeating the whole of the clergyman's role. His very title of minister implies it. Even the Catholic tendency to emphasise the primacy of the service of God does not eclipse the importance of the service offered to men, as witnessed by the Papal title of *servus servorum Dei*. The 'pastor' component of the clerical role consists in precisely this function of service. We have noted, however, that so far from dominating other aspects of the clerical role it is tending to diminish in importance in comparison with more purely administrative functions. In recent theological thinking what is stressed is the service to be rendered by the whole Christian community or by the local church as a whole, thus reducing the position of the clergyman to being that of symbol of the group, or its spokeman and organiser. The 'servant Church' is the fashionable mode in which the service ideal appears, and it does so at the expense of the particular role of the priest, who becomes the 'resource-man', the 'link-man', the 'ad-man' and the 'chairman'. This tendency casts considerable doubt on the notion that the clergy have any unique claim to express the ideal of service within the religious sphere.

Much the most serious objection, however, to the idea that the clergy constitute a profession arises when we ask what is their special professional knowledge. The common assumption is that theology forms the abstract theoretical knowledge of the clerical profession. But this cannot be so, for, in the first place, it has only recently become a necessary part of clerical training, and the ministry, if it is a profession at all, is certainly an ancient one. In the second place, a body of theory can count as professional knowledge only if it is the basis on which action is taken or advised. Were this point to be pressed it would have to be granted that the whole point of theology is only the derivation of a system of moral and ethical rules. In fact the clergyman does not give advice on the basis of his theological learning; rather he passes on his theological knowledge through his teaching and preaching. Apart from that it fulfils a function in the clergyman's life no different from that which it fulfils in the lives of his parishioners. In the third place, and this is a related point, theology cannot be the theoretical basis for specialised professional activity, because it is not specialised knowledge in the first place. Theology is only a theoretical statement of a religious view of the world. In large part it is no more than an explanation of how the religious view comes to be held, and it is the religious view, if anything, which constitutes the specialism. Theology is religious ' "knowledge about the world", raised to the level of theoretical thought' (Berger 1966, p. 113).

For all these reasons theology cannot be treated as the body of knowledge proper to the ministry as a profession. On this ground alone it seems as though it would be wholly misleading to treat the clergy as members of a profession. Social scientists have so regarded them out of unthinking deference to popular usage of the term. The clergy have so regarded themselves, and indeed in recent times have done so increasingly, because it gives them a niche in society.

THE ORDAINED MINISTRY AS AN OCCUPATION

The main point, however, at which we should wish to take issue with those who maintain that the ministry is a profession is a much more fundamental one. This point is the unquestioned assumption that the ministry is an occupation. Notwithstanding the fact that men derive an income from their status as clergymen, it is our view that so far from the ministry being that kind of occupation which we describe as a profession it is not an occupation at all. Would a hereditary peer who subsisted on his House of Lords allowance and Social Security benefits describe his occupation as 'Earl'? The comparison, we shall argue, is not facetious but illuminating. This will become clear if we look briefly at the historical development of the professions. The contemporary sociological character of the ministry as a social group may also emerge more clearly as a result, especially if the historical sketch in Chapter 1 is borne in mind.

In the eighteenth century Addison spoke of the 'three learned professions of divinity, law, and physic'. It was one of the earliest examples of the use of the word 'profession' to describe particular callings. The learned professions were those occupations which, in contrast to the contemporary trades and crafts, required learning as well as skill for their exercise. Addison mentioned three, but at an earlier stage in history, as we have already seen, both law and physic were practised by men within the ranks of the clergy. As Carr-Saunders and Wilson wrote in their book on the professions (1933, p. 290),

> The earliest phases of certain vocations, who have grown into professions, were passed within the Church. Education was so closely bound up with ecclesiastical functions that the priest and the teacher were distinguished with difficulty. Lawyers, physicians and civil servants were members of the ecclesiastical order who had assumed special functions.

In other words, certain vocations were open only to clerics. To be a clergyman in that period of history was not to have a particular occupation. It was to occupy a social position of an entirely different kind.

In the Middle Ages a person's social position was defined primarily in terms of what he was, not what he did. The prevailing mood of the society was static, changing but little from generation to generation. Even occupations which have a contemporary ring for us today had a different connotation then, when to be a mason or chandler meant one was the son and the grandson and probably the father too of a mason or a chandler. When a person changed his status in society it was, as it were, by fiat. A man might be created a knight, or he might take Holy Orders, or a woman might become a nun. Generally speaking, positions in mediaeval society were ascribed from birth, not deliberately and willingly chosen or achieved. Contemporary society is in the sharpest contrast with this pattern, although remnants of the older order remain, or have but recently disappeared. People still 'become wives' and find their whole lives changed in a moment. Until recently, many working-class men knew from earliest childhood what their occupation was to be, without any choice, and many more were forced into their father's occupation against their choice. By and large, however, our society today is oriented towards achievement and choice. The position a person occupies is defined by what he does, and who he is follows from it: not *vice versa*.

It would be well-nigh meaningless to ask what a mediaeval cleric did, but as times changed the range of vocations pursued by the clergy became progressively limited. After the national census had been instituted in England in the nineteenth century, however, the figures for the number of clergy were more than 10 per cent inaccurate, because a clerical schoolmaster, for example, was entered only as a schoolmaster for the national return. And in the heyday of the period of the gentleman parson, the question of what such a person *did* was patently absurd: his profession was divinity, but his occupation might have been the management of his stock or any other of the occupations of the squirearchy.

It would, therefore, be more accurate to say with Carr-Saunders and Wilson (1933, p. 294) that, from Addison down to the present day,

> Divinity found a place in the list only because it was at one time either the only profession or the basis on which other professions were built. It took its place with physic and law, as it were, by ancient right. Man had not observed that, since it had divested itself of duties relating to the ordinary business of life, its position on the list was anomalous.

The ministry presents itself to us, repeatedly, as an anomaly. There is nothing wrong with that. All we are trying to do at the moment is clear the ground of spurious assumptions. It will only lead to confusion if we proceed on the basis that the clergy represent a social group like this or that other one, when in truth they are a group *sui generis*.

PROFESSIONALISATION

It is sometimes argued that the anomaly presented by the clergy and from which many of their difficulties arise is only temporary, and is owing to the fact that the ministry has fallen behind the 'other professions' in its development. The Church Assembly report (no. 1703) quoted earlier takes this view in asserting that there 'are responsibilities which are peculiar to the clergy and yet have to be spelt out more fully'; the same view has been advanced by at least one social scientist (Schreuder 1965), and it is common in American writings about the ministry. We have only to reflect on the development of the professions to see that this analysis is wholly spurious. The first professions to emerge did so by struggling free from the juridical and intellectual discipline of the Church. The Inns of Court, as we have already remarked, were founded at the end of the thirteenth and the beginning of the fourteenth centuries, thus providing the country with the first group of learned laymen, the common lawyers, outside the Church. It was another 200 years before the next learned society, the Royal College of Physicians of London, was founded. The development of both these professions was made possible by their independence, and their body of theoretical knowledge was able to grow because it had been released from the broad theological presuppositions which previously it had had to subserve. In other words, it was precisely their separation from the Church, or from divinity as a profession, which made the evolution of the oldest professions possible. They were brought into being by separation from the parent body. The similarities they bore to the ministry were the direct result of their parentage and of the manner of their birth. They were learned as the clergy were learned, but in specialised areas; they were dedicated to the ideal of service as were the clergy, but in particular fields; they had organisations recognised by the Crown, codes of ethics, scales of fees, and so on, as did the clergy, but within their own proper domains. In time other professions came into existence, either by further fragmentation of law and physic, as with solicitors and surgeons, or by new processes of separation from the Church, as with natural science as it found fields of application. The form in which all of these successively emerging professions organised themselves was as close as possible to the ancient professions, but at a deeper level what was common to them all was a monopoly over some activity, guaranteed by the State.

The evolution of the professions is a continuing process but monopoly remains the defining characteristic of them all. Some new professions achieve the status and some have it thrust upon them. A 'Royal College of Hair Designers' would be of the former kind, while a 'Royal College of Tribologists' would be of the latter. But the evolution is more than mere proliferation, and the field of medicine provides a good illustration of the way in which change and development take place. The general medical practitioner who until recently was so familiar a figure and the very paradigm of the professional, despite the foundation in 1950 of a College of General Practitioners, is now all but extinct. The advance of medical science requires, among other things, that treatment should be given in hospitals and clinics where the appropriate equipment and techniques may most readily be made available. The complexity of modern medical science makes it inevitable that doctors be co-ordinated within a complex institution, thus displacing the solitary doctor in his own surgery, and making of him a mere agent of screening and referral. A large proportion of the contemporary general medical practitioner's work has little to do with medicine. To give what many of his patients come for requires compassion and common sense rather than scientific training, but the scientific training he has received is designed systemically to replace compassion with dispassionate diagnosis and common sense with scientific understanding. What has happened to medicine has happened to other professions: specialisation has proceeded to the point where the co-ordination upon which practice depends demands complex organisations, and professionals are perforce employees. Ironically, 'divinity, law and physic' are sociologically united again. They alone still offer the possibility of wholly independent practice when independence is totally out of the question for the overwhelming majority of professions. But it should be noticed that the doctor or the lawyer who chooses to remain independent thereby forgoes the chance of being in the vanguard of his profession. He forgoes specialisation, which is 'where it's at'. Nor can general medical practitioners, merely by forming a College of General Practitioners, make themselves into a specialism. They can become 'more professional', according to the contemporary meaning of the expression, only by becoming specialised. As they are at present they are not 'under-professionalised' but remain professional in a way understood by an earlier generation. The clergy, similarly, are not 'under-professionalised'; they are professional in a sense long, long extinct.

OCCUPATIONS AND THE ORDAINED MINISTRY

We have questioned the assumption that the ministry can usefully be regarded as an occupation and must now press the question, because both everyday speech and also much social science tends to give the misleading impression that our society is neatly divided into four status groups, and that every single person must belong to one of them. These groups are: child, worker, retired, and wife. Children, old-age pensioners and wives are permitted to work, of course, but they belong to a sort of penumbra surrounding the workforce proper. Some would deny that this applies to working wives, but the matter is very far from being clear and they are still a long way from being members of the workforce equal with their husbands, as women generally are far from being equal with men. The fourfold division of society is an elaboration of one which is more simple still, the twofold division into dependent and independent, for child and wife are but contrasting ways in which people may be dependants, and, although the retired worker is formally even more independent than he was as a worker, he may abruptly find himself, or more importantly he may feel himself, returned to the dependency of childhood. Although this impression of a population neatly divided into four main groups may be true in the broadest sense, it is none the less grossly misleading for three reasons. First, there are important exceptions. The most notable is that relatively small group of persons who have 'private means', though the group is far from small when one includes in it all those who have substantial 'private means' and who none the less count as members of the workforce, often as highly paid members of it. Secondly, it suggests that the category of 'worker' describes a relatively uniform status. Because they all confer the same status, occupations are classed together as so many peas in a pod, graduated only from the most highly to the most lowly paid, when in reality many of them are so different as not to be comparable. Thirdly, it throws a disproportionate weight onto the 'work' which defines the status of the worker. Since it is as a worker that the man defines himself, it is the job which dominates his conception of himself.

Even quite a short time ago there were people who, if asked what they did, would reply that they were 'gentlemen' or 'in service' or 'in the army'. The answer described the kind of life which they led rather than their occupation. The progressive division of labour and rapid specialisation of recent decades, on the one hand, and the ascendant ideology which regards all workers as essentially equivalent and of equal importance, on the other hand, have produced a situation in which people feel obliged to say what it is that they do, and therefore to feel that they themselves know what they do, instead of simply being content to be a member of some section of society. Or, to put it more precisely, their sense of belonging in society is overwhelmingly contingent on their occupational status. So the worth which a man attributes to himself comes to be dominated by his place in the finely graded structure of occupations, since the occupations are accorded varying prestige.

Occupations are evaluated according to a range of criteria, for each job demands a certain balance of skills, not all of which are equally highly prized. Intellectual, technical and personality skills are mixed in various proportions in all jobs, but in the prevailing climate of opinion which is so concerned with specialism and technique it is the claim to technical skill which is accorded the highest esteem. The more highly specialised and rare the skill, the more it is esteemed, as we observe with 'nuclear scientists' and 'heart surgeons'. The professions epitomise the jobs which require great technical skills based on great intellectual skill, or at least the intellectual skill on which the prestigious technical skill rests.

What we wish to point out is, in the first place, the highly specific character of occupations in our contemporary society which are increasingly defined by particular skills. Wherever possible the possession of a skill is formally recognised and certificated, rather than demonstrated on the job, and thus it becomes fixed. Once 'qualified' to do a specified job a person's skill cannot thereafter be called into question, and conversely a person is debarred from exercising any skills for which he is not formally 'qualified'. In the second place, we wish to emphasise the overwhelming importance attached to a person's occupation, and the concomitant disregard in which all other attributes which may characterise a person are held.

Now the clergyman, more than anyone else on the contemporary scene, is a jack of all trades. He occupies a unique position, but the uniqueness of his position has nothing to do with unique skills, or even with unique competence. There is nothing which he does that could not be done equally well by a lawyer or bricklayer in the congregation whom the bishop had ordained to the Auxiliary Pastoral Ministry. He does not have a job at all in any sense which is readily understandable today, and today, more than ever before, a person must have a job in order to fit into society. As a result the clergyman finds himself marginal to society. He is a strange creature who seems not to fit in anywhere. This applies to other people as well, such as the artist or the person of 'private means'; and generally they enclose themselves in a little world of their own, a community within the community which is marginal to society but within which the individual does not obtrude. The clergyman, however, is in a position which is marginal to society and at the same time highly visible. He is a public person who, alone in our society, wears a distinctive uniform at all times. When he discards the uniform, as many clergymen do today, he evades the problem posed by his marginality, but he does not solve it.

The immediate questions to which we shall turn in the following chapters concern the new generation of clergymen themselves. We shall look at how they come to be clergymen, at their backgrounds, the differences between them, the colleges in which they are trained, and the effect which training has on them; but behind all these questions lies the problem of their position in society. We shall address ourselves to it directly in a concluding chapter, albeit briefly, but one observation may not be out of place here.

The clergy show many signs of trying to escape from their uncomfortable marginality. Some quit the ministry for jobs in teaching or in the welfare services, while others go half way by involving themselves in voluntary organisations such as the Samaritans or by doing a little teaching on the side. Some try to find a specialism peculiar to the clergy in 'pastoral psychology' or 'clinical theology', or through management training courses. Some renounce their public status altogether and confine all their activities to the faithful remnant, retreating to within their local church and its congregation. Very few just stand and, as it were, allow the waves of marginality to break over them. And yet there would be much to be said for just that course of action, we are inclined to believe, and much is lost by the scarcity of men who are to be found taking it.

The Church and its ministry must change with the times, but the change need not necessarily be a process whereby they are moulded by the structures and ideology of secular society. There are those, particularly among the young, who suspect that the overweening emphasis on occupation and career is something which ought to be resisted, seeing it as an iron cage in which one does well not to be trapped. It may be so. The clergy could at least consider the possibility, and not rush headlong in the direction in which secular trends are pointing. The clergy as specially authorised representatives of the Church have, after all, a role which we have omitted to mention: the role of a prophet. It is not a role which readily admits of sociological analysis, except *post factum*, but it is no less important for that; on the contrary it may be more so. The prophet stands over against society, declaring the judgement of God; he is deeply involved in society and does not seek to escape from it; he is in the world but not of the world. The clergy of today have had a position marginal to society thrust upon them – and they must draw conclusions for themselves about the significance of this turn of events.

3   The Choice

Having argued in the last chapter that the clergy, so far from being a profession, are not even an occupation, we shall now do a complete *volte-face*. We shall proceed to consider the ministry as though it were a profession, comparable to medicine, law, teaching, nursing and so on. The reason is simple. The young man of 17 or 21 must decide how to spend his life, and the various possibilities which confront him must be compared so that he may set out on the appropriate training. The sixth-former who decided to apply for admission to a medical school rather than to a department of French must needs have compared the alternatives even if the choice was a foregone conclusion. The undergraduate student who decides between social work, the Civil Service and 'the Church' is similarly comparing possibilities. Inasmuch as the ministry is compared with a variety of professions which require postgraduate training, it is, by definition, comparable with them. The fact that in practice the ministry and the law are not comparable vocations says nothing at all about their comparability or otherwise from the perspective of a young man choosing how to spend his life.

THE CHOICE TO BE ORDAINED – IN THEORY

To choose the ordained ministry as a career seems to very few people something normal and unremarkable. Attitudes to such a choice always carry a burden of emotion. To some people it is a noble thing to do, while to others it is baffling, and to still others it is plainly wrong-headed, and the question 'Why do men choose the ministry?' has been found interesting for just this reason. All sorts of reasons have been advanced – spiritual, psychological and sociological. It is with the sociological accounts that we shall be concerned here, but not solely because we write as sociologists. We do not disregard what may be called the spiritual reasons; we treat them as all-pervasive but invisible,

56

for social science deals with the outwardly visible framework of events and not at all with their ultimate and transcendent significance. Where men have themselves given spiritual reasons for their actions we shall report them, as we might report their age or their political beliefs. But we are in search of general patterns which help to explain the present state of the ministry, rather than of explanations particular to individuals. Nor do we disregard psychological reasons; indeed, we have used certain psychological tests throughout our research and their value will be obvious in a later chapter. But, as we shall see, the occupational choice of the ministry seems not to be easily amenable to psychological explanations.

Theological and psychological approaches

The ministry is considered to be a 'vocation' as well as an occupation. The way in which the term is used tends to separate the ministry off from other occupations and to treat it as unique. An Anglican bishop not very long ago wrote, 'The Ministry is a gift and call from God. It is not a mere delegation of function or a convenient division of labour. It cannot be conferred by human appointment, nor can a man choose it by his own will. That cannot be said too often or too insistently' (Barry 1958, p. 7). The term 'vocation' is also used in this special sense of other occupations, especially of those which require a high degree of dedication and self-sacrifice; but only the ministry requires its new recruits to state solemnly that they believe themselves to be 'truly called' by God.

If Bishop Barry's words were literally true there would be nothing for us to explain: ordination would be the result of a call, not of a choice at all. Obviously, however, the real meaning of what he wrote is that a man must feel called by God for his decision to be a valid one in the eyes of the Church. It is all the more obvious from the parallel case of the bishop, who, though nominated by the Crown and elected by the dean and chapter of the diocese, is asked at his consecration, 'Are you persuaded that you be truly called . . . ?' This element of vocation is important sociologically as well as spiritually. Max Weber showed how powerful the sense of vocation could be when it was extended by the reformers to apply to any 'work in a calling [which for the individual] was a, or rather, the task set by God' (Weber 1930, p. 79), and what great sociological consequences this could have. A man's conviction that he is fulfilling the divine will can be overwhelmingly powerful, and its strength was increased rather than diminished by its extension in Protestant countries to worldly callings. As Weber went on to show, the forcefulness of the early Protestant sense of worldly vocation has been largely dissipated, and been replaced by a more cheerless, if no less urgent, sense of duty and obligation. But its application to the ministry enjoyed thereby a boost which has persisted. For a time the uniqueness of a calling to the ministry was eclipsed by the general secular sense of 'calling', but in the long run it has survived to be a distinctive mark of the Protestant ministry in a way which is not so distinctive of the Catholic priesthood or even of religious orders.

The concept of vocation has been used so generally to refer to the occupational choice of the ministry that theologians have been obliged to refine it and to draw out various elements which it contains. Richard Niebuhr, for example, has distinguished between (1) *the call to be a Christian*, (2) *the secret call* or 'inner persuasion or experience whereby a person feels himself directly summoned or invited by God to take up the work of the ministry', (3) *the providential call*, which 'comes through the equipment of a person with the talents necessary for the exercise of the office', and (4) the *ecclesiastical call* or 'summons or invitation extended to a man by some . . . institution of the church to engage in the work of the ministry' (Niebuhr 1956, p. 64). (In the Church of Scotland, for example, the call of a minister to serve a particular congregation is regarded more seriously than any initial 'secret call' he may have had to enter the ministry.) Niebuhr points out (ibid., p. 65) that conceptions of the ministry have differed as these four components of the call 'have been related to one another in varying orders of importance and modes of relationship'. Moreover, we can see that the differences in emphasis have tended to vary with the general structure and ideology of the church concerned. Thus, stress on the secret call at the expense of the ecclesiastical call has been typical of the small and informal group, together with emphasis on the special charisma, or spiritual gifts, of the minister. Larger and more formal churches, on the other hand, have seen the minister in more bureaucratic terms as the 'incumbent' of a 'living', and have tended to stress the ecclesiastical call while paying less attention to the secret call. This is to put the matter crudely, but the divergence is clear if we take two contrasting examples. The early Quakers, as Niebuhr points out (ibid.), 'not only maintained that the "inward call" or testimony of the Spirit [was] essential and necessary to a minister', but they denied the validity of the church call and seemed indifferent to the providential call. Roman Catholic canon law, on the other hand, though explicitly recognising what Fichter has called the 'objective' and 'subjective' aspects of vocation, states (Fichter 1961, p. 8) that 'any Catholic, who is not hindered by some legitimate impediment, may be admitted to religion, provided his motives are right and he is capable of discharging the obligations of the religious life'.

Concepts of the ministry held within the Church of England, though varied, are not extreme. As we shall see presently, Anglican ordinands who define themselves as 'evangelical' tend to see their vocations almost exclusively in terms of a secret call which is often referred to as 'inner conviction'. Thus, there were self-defined evangelicals who spoke of 'a sudden and direct and very clear call from God, 26 May 1960', or in terms such as these: 'I was called to the ministry by God. He used friends and relatives during six months to turn my thoughts to this work. The assurance word was delivered after a long weekend of prayer, by a convincing statement from my vicar.' On the other hand, 'catholic' ordinands, while not denying the importance of the secret call, tend to see it as of no more importance than the ecclesiastical and the providential call, and to feel that they are all combined in ways which cannot easily be separated.

Thus, the spiritual explanation of the decision to be ordained in terms of a call from God contains many different meanings. It is concerned with fundamental reasons, and in particular with the individual's understanding of what ought to be his reasons. It is concerned with the problem of why things happen, whereas we seek to understand only the patterns of how they happen. Theologians themselves recognise that talk about vocation often shifts from one level to another (Bennett 1959, p. 136), and recognise that the call to the ministry 'is not a matter of fact; it is a theological interpretation of a complex constellation of processes and experiences in the life of a person' (Wise 1958, p. 7).

The interest of psychologists in occupational choice has been greatly stimulated by attempts to develop effective techniques of vocational guidance. Their work in refining tests to identify the aptitudes which might fit children for particular occupations is of no relevance to the ministry, but their concern with 'interests' looks, at first sight, more promising. One line of research has tried to find broad patterns of interests, derived from early childhood experiences, which might predispose young people to choose one sort of job rather than another (Strong 1942; Roe 1953; Roe and Siegelman 1964), but attempts to validate the theory have failed, and it is easy to show that the complexity of interests in individual personalities can lead apparently identical persons in opposite directions (Super 1966). A more sophisticated approach has seen occupational choice as 'the process of implementing the self concept', and concomitantly has seen the task of the vocational counsellor as 'helping a person to formulate an adequate idea of himself, and to find a role appropriate to the kind of person he conceives himself to be and seeks to become' (Super 1963, p. 3). But this is a matter of helping young people to decide between manifold alternatives and, valid though it may be within that context, it can have little bearing on the explanation of occupational choice. Analytically oriented psychologists, as is their wont, have been much more bold in advancing explanations, which have ranged from the 'wish to relieve childhood anxieties by belief in the infallibility of God' (though it is not easy to see what this has to do with being ordained) to 'a strong curiosity about the human body, sublimated to a fascination with God and theology' (Menninger 1942, pp. 196–208) and to sublimated exhibitionism as 'a source of deep fulfilment' (Bowers 1963, p. 35). (We found Dr Bowers's book irresistibly funny and would recommend it to other irreverent persons as light reading.) But the accounts offered are all much too sweeping to be of value, except perhaps to the raw recruit to the psychiatric profession, for it results in such conclusions as 'Most clergy were lonely, set-apart children' (ibid., p. 97). The theological and the psychological approaches to occupational choice are inappropriate to our purposes. We are asking simpler and more superficial questions than either sets out to answer, and yet we believe that our questions have their own significance.

The sociological approach

A sociological account of occupational choice focuses upon the social patterns of choice, the institutional and cultural framework within which the decision takes place, and the social factors influencing the choice. Not only this, but it looks at the phenomenon of occupational choice from two points of view, for in a society such as our own, where choice exists, instead of occupational roles being ascribed at birth, the occupations themselves have to make a choice about whom they should recruit to their ranks. (Because of celibacy, the clergy were the first group in Western society to be faced with the problem. As was mentioned above, some occupations have only recently ceased to be self-recruiting, i.e. to recruit from among the children of their own number. We shall discuss self-recruitment to the Anglican clergy below.)

So occupational choice and occupational recruitment stand together as complementary processes. For the occupation there is a double problem: it must at the same time both be visible and attractive enough to be considered seriously by the potential recruit, and also be able to exclude those whom it considers unsuitable. Therefore, bearing in mind the perspectives of the recruiter and the recruited, the sociological problem is one of seeing which people are attracted and which are selected. We must gain some grasp of these facts before we can go on to consider training. The first problem, to put it another way, is to establish who are in training and how they got there.

THE CHOICE TO BE ORDAINED – IN PRACTICE

The most basic principle of a sociological approach to occupational choice derives from the work of Lazarsfeld, although, as he himself pointed out, it was acknowledged even before his forceful exposition (Lazarsfeld, 1931, p. 37). As stated more recently (Blau 1956, p. 532), the principle is this:

> Occupational choice is a developmental process that extends over many years. . . . There is no single time at which young people decide upon one out of many possible careers, but there are many cross-roads at which their lives take decisive turns which narrow the range of future alternatives and thus influence the ultimate choice of an occupation.

This approach has been embodied and extended in subsequent

work by Ginzberg (1951), Merton (1957b) and others to whom we shall make reference.

If the choice of an occupation is a process rather than a unique event we should expect it to proceed in stages; and in view of the structure of our educational system it would be reasonable to expect the stages to coincide with decisions which are built into education. With this in mind, and taking cognisance of psychological contributions to the theory of occupational choice, Ginzberg has suggested (1951, p. 192) that the process falls naturally into three separate phases: (a) fantasy choice, up to the age of 10 or sometimes 12, (b) tentative choice, from 10 or 12 up to 17, and (c) realistic choice, from 18 to 20 and allowing up to 24 for a firm decision to be reached. It seems obvious enough that these phases should apply to the choice of a profession, but not all occupations are chosen at the same age. Merton has said that this fact 'would contradict Ginzberg's notion of phase' (Kandell 1960, p. 29), but we should not go so far. It is no problem that most people leave school before they reach Ginzberg's period of 'realistic choice', for those who embark on training for a job are still in the process of reaching a definitive choice, while those who go straight into a job often change it subsequently for some other job and find what suits them by a process of trial and error. In either case the final choice is effectively made at about the same age.

First thoughts

It is a far from simple task to find out the ages at which people fantasised about doing a job, tentatively thought about it, and firmly decided on it. Even the phrases one uses in asking people have to be chosen with care, for if they have reached a decision they will have considerable emotional investment in it and may not take readily to the idea of childish fantasies. Using the more familiar phrase, we asked ordinands, 'At what age did you first think of being ordained?' and got the following sort of reply:

'18, though there were tentative thoughts from 15 onwards.'

'24 is the first serious thought, but romantic ideas from childhood; the latter not serious.'

'Seven years: this came in with being an engine-driver. First really seriously when I was 20.'

These early thoughts are brushed aside as mere nonsense even when they are mentioned, for ordinands in training appear to dismiss these first stirrings of the imagination, which might have been quite explicit at the time when they occurred and which probably will be recalled without embarrassment in later years and may even be recorded in memoirs. So we must assume that in answering this question ordinands in effect are reporting when they first 'seriously' thought about entering the ministry in the light of their present understanding.

In our 1962 survey (see Appendix I for details of the several investigations from which data are drawn; all were conducted by the authors, unless otherwise stated) we found that only 8 per cent of ordinands said they had first thought of ordination during Ginzberg's fantasy phase, while 49 per cent first thought of it during the phase of tentative thoughts, and 43 per cent in the realistic-choice phase; similar findings have been reported for other samples of Anglican ordinands (see Table 1; this and all other numbered tables will be found in Appendix II). To make sense of this information it will be necessary to separate out the group of older men in training, for the ages of the respondents in our 1962 survey ranged from 18 to 62. Older ordinands, or men said to have 'late vocations', represent a deviant group which has been recognised for many years as a distinct phenomenon. In the Roman Catholic Church they constituted a special problem for training – to such a degree that they were sent to separate colleges, for until recently the seminary system admitted possible candidates only at 11 or 18, and older men would have been like fish out of water in the higher division of an extended school system. Anglican theological colleges are different, admitting men who have already read for a degree and non-graduates of a similar age, and an older man does not obtrude so markedly. The distribution of ages at which men first thought of being ordained, given in Figure 2, is bewilderingly wide, with peaks at 16 and 20, and then falling off very slowly. If we define late vocations as those men who, excluding National Service, have worked in full-time employment for two years or more, and then redraw the distributions for the 'normal' and 'late' groups separately, two quite distinct patterns emerge, as will be seen in Figure 3.

That there were men with late vocations was well-enough known, but we are going to suggest that the two groups, normal and late, were different from each other in more ways and more

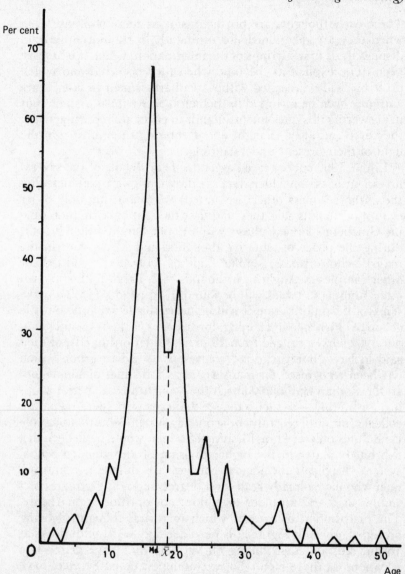

FIGURE 2   Age of first thoughts of ordination: total sample

Per cent

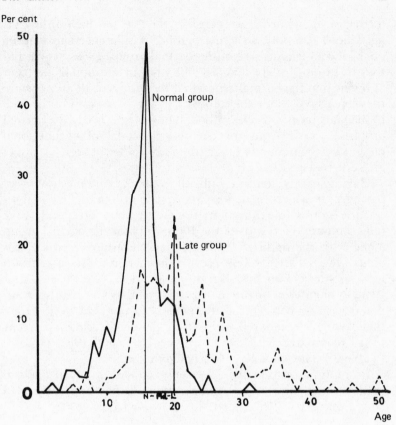

FIGURE 3   Age of first thoughts: normal and late groups

important ways than simply their age. We shall argue that they were characteristically different kinds of men from different social and educational backgrounds, and that their decisions to be ordained were made by different processes (see further Appendix III).

Of course, it could be that men who are older when they are in training actually thought of being ordained at the same age as did their younger fellow students, but were prevented from entering training by external circumstances. The distribution in Figure 3, however, shows that this was not so. It is plain that most of them were reporting the ages at which they first thought of changing their occupation, while the men in the normal group were making an original occupational choice. The impression is further strengthened if we consider the age at which ordinands left school. Not only is there a significant difference between the mean school-leaving age of the normal group, 18·43 years, and the late group, 16·68 years ($p < ·001$), but in addition 83 per cent of the men in the normal group first thought of ordination before they left school, while the same is true for 27 per cent of the men in the late group. It is clear, then, that we expect only the normal group to conform to the theoretical model of occupational choice, for the remaining late group are going through a distinct and different process.

Having learned that it is difficult to elicit accurate estimates of the ages at which men first considered ordination, we subsequently worded our questions somewhat differently, and, if we now compare the results of the 1966 study for the normal group alone with the findings for a comparable group, medical students, we shall see just how normal the men in the normal group were. A study of doctors in training found that 51 per cent first thought of entering medicine by the time they were 13 (as compared with 46 per cent of ordinands), 69 per cent by the time they were 15 (compared with our 72 per cent), and 86 per cent by 17 (compared with our 88 per cent) (Rogoff 1957, p. 111). (Table 2.) The similarity is strikingly close.

In an attempt to explain the range of ages at which medical students first think of becoming doctors, it has been suggested (ibid., pp. 111–12; cf. Hall 1948) that one cause lies in

> opportunities for hearing about the status and activities of physicians . . . the more frequent such contacts, the easier it is to identify with physicians, and to form the idea of becoming one. Having relatives (in the immediate or extended family) who are themselves doctors obviously facilitates both contacts and identification, and hence leads to earlier awakening of interest in a medical career.

A similar correlation holds for ordinands, among whom those with clerical relatives first consider ordination at a significantly earlier age than do those without (using the one-tailed difference of means test, $p < ·025$). Interestingly, however, this is true only for ordinands in the normal group.

When boys first think of ordination, is it ordination alone that they consider, or is ordination gradually selected from among a variety of early ideas? The idea of a 'secret' call would seem to imply the singularity of the ministry as a contemplated vocation, but in one of our small-scale studies we found that, among men in the normal group, 69 per cent had thought of some other job before deciding on the ministry.

It is interesting to note what other jobs they had considered: in descending order of frequency they were, schoolteaching, the armed forces or police, engineering, architecture, banking, medicine, and the Civil Service. This list shows considerable overlap with the jobs which had actually been done by older ordinands investigated in another small-scale study: the armed forces, the police, teaching and social services. The predominance in both lists of occupations oriented to either service or discipline calls for some comment. A simple view might indicate that one or two sets of values underlay these choices, prompting those who hold these values to find jobs which embody them. A sociological perspective tends to make us look at the influence in both directions, however, for not only do particular values make the choice of certain occupations more likely, but also, having chosen a certain occupation, there is a tendency for the appropriate values to be adopted (cf. Rosenberg 1957, pp. 17–19). We should expect there to be an interaction between the values a man holds and the values implicit in an occupation to which he feels drawn. What are we to say, though, about the apparently dissimilar values of service and discipline which characterise occupations associated with the ordained ministry in the minds of ordinands? Two points need to be made. First, service and discipline are by no means incompatible. It could be argued that both are concerned with order, aiming to serve, maintain or enforce an existing order rather than seeking to challenge or transcend it. Secondly, the ministry may indeed embody two discrepant ideals and therefore attract to its ranks men of rather different types. We shall discuss two different types of ordinand in the next chapter, but here it should be said that, if service seems to be more obviously related to the ideals of the ordained ministry, discipline and concern with authority have regularly been found associated with religious institutions, and this latter connection is one which will be seen at a number of points in our discussion.

The definite decision

So far we have considered only the early stages in the process of choosing to be ordained. There comes the moment for decision. It is not quite as simple as that, however, for 'an individual never reaches an ultimate decision at a single moment in time, but through a series of decisions made over a period of many years: the cumulative impact is the determining factor. It is important to ask why this is so: the actions following a considerable number of decisions are made at great cost and are more or less irrevocable' (Ginzberg 1951, p. 38). Only when a person enters into occupational practice may he be said to have decided finally, but the process whereby he reaches that point is largely irreversible and at each further step along the road it becomes progressively harder to turn back, both because of the specialist nature of training and also because of the high degree of commitment required.

The term 'definite decision' has been used to signify a choice which is firm but less than final. If the whole process comprises a chain of decisions, however, and especially if this is apparent to those taking them, the difficulty arises of identifying which decision is to count as the 'definite' one. The most satisfactory solution would be to take as definite that decision which seems to be so from within 'the actor's frame of reference', as the sociological jargon would express it. But that is no solution at all. We are dealing with a process over time and so with a frame of reference which is continually changing. This problem did not force itself upon us in considering 'first thoughts' of ordination, though assuredly it was there, but it cannot be ignored in the matter of a 'definite decision'. Thus, the study of medical students to which we referred earlier found that 'at each stage of medical school, most students feel that their decision was reached *in the course of that year*, or in the very recent past . . . as they progress through medical school, students continually update the time of final career decision' (Kandell 1960, pp. 203–4). ('Career decision' refers to the choice of a specialism rather than medicine generally, but the observation applies more widely. For an example of 'updating' see pp. 165f. below.) For these reasons there is as much to be said for choosing some arbitary point in the process of decision, so long as it is a point through which all must pass, as for using ordinands' own reports of when they reached their definite decisions to be ordained. The second strategy is no less arbitary than the first, for it involves an equally arbitary decision about when in the process to pose the question. We employed both strategies in various parts of our work.

All Anglican ordinands must at some point go before a selection board run by the Advisory Council for the Church's Ministry (ACCM), and for our 1962 survey we took applications to the Central Advisory Council for Training for the Ministry (CACTM), as it then was, as the point of definite decision.

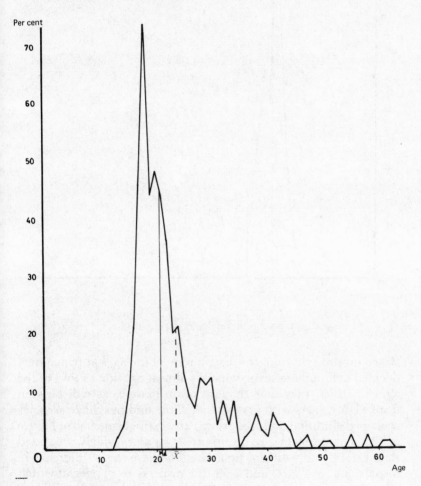

FIGURE 4   Age of application: total sample

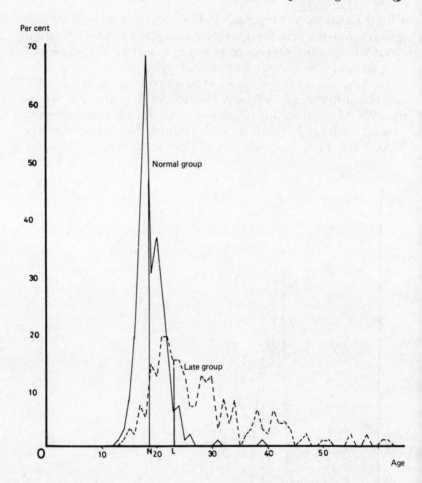

FIGURE 5   Age of application: normal and late groups

Based on this criterion, the distribution of the ages at which men decided definitely to be ordained is almost as wide as that of the ages at which they first thought of ordination, as will be seen from Figure 4. As with first thoughts, the findings make sense as soon as the normal and late groups are distinguished as in Figure 5. The means for the two groups are even more widely separated than before, and while for first thoughts there was a difference in dispersions ($\sigma = 3.95$ and 7.58) the dispersions of ages at which a definite decision was reached are still more different ($\sigma = 2.55$ and 9.77).

The comparison with the occupational decisions of medical students still holds (Table 3). Using ordinands' own definitions of when they definitely decided to be ordained, rather than their ages when applying to the CACTM, we find that 10 per cent of the normal group had decided by the age of 15 (it is 17·6 per cent for doctors), and 33 per cent by 17 (43·2 per cent for doctors). Clearly there are a proportion who decide early and stick to their early decision, and this phenomenon is common to ordinands and medical students, rather than a special feature of the vocation to the ordained ministry.

It seems plain that the decision to be ordained, though undoubtedly it carries spiritual significance, is a very ordinary process. Like the decision to enter any other occupation, it is almost wholly shaped by the structure of the educational system, and, indeed, if we remove the extraneous group of late vocations, we find that the timing of ordinands' decisions is indistinguishable from that of medical students, whose training is similar in its structure and duration.

We have seen something of how the decision to be ordained is made, and now we must look at the influences which bear on it, of which there are roughly four types. First, there are the influences of which an individual is aware as he looks back at his own decision; secondly, there are the direct effects of the Church's attempts to recruit men into its ministry; thirdly, there are the largely unseen influences which are known through their effects in the social and educational patterns to be seen in groups of men offering themselves for ordination; finally, there is the influence of the Church's own procedures for selecting some applicants and rejecting others.

'WHAT INFLUENCED ME WAS . . .'

An American Catholic study found that the relative order of encouragement major seminarians reported for their vocation was priest, mother, father, nun. For selected groups, the order was found to vary, coming out as mother, priest, nun, father for the poorer seminarians, and mother, nun, priest, father for those entering seminary when still young (Fichter 1961, pp. 22–3). Similar results have been found elsewhere. A Canadian survey found that a parish priest was most commonly reported to have been the main influence; and an American Protestant study cited by Moberg (1962) found the most influential people to be the pastor (34 per cent), mother (17·4 per cent) and father (11·2 per cent). We found the same to be true for Anglican ordinands in Britain (Table 4).

From our research the influence of the clergy appeared to have been much greater than any other source of encouragement and

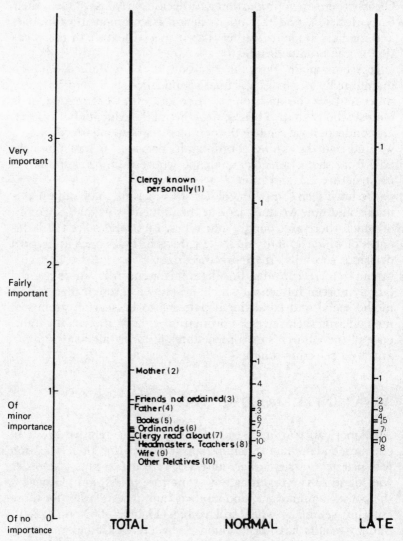

FIGURE 6   Influences on decision to be ordained

to stand in a league of its own. Figure 6 shows the order in which a number of influences were ranked and the unique position ascribed to 'clergy known personally'. In the course of interviews the following sorts of thing were said about these clergy who had been so significant:

'In him I saw what it would be like.'

'It was nothing he said directly. I've watched him work, and, when people have gone to him for help, it's then that I've felt most impelled to go into the Church.'

'When I knew him better, I watched him and saw his careful pastoral work.'

Something of the same kind comes across in remarks made by ordinands about books and films which portray the life and work of particular clergy. One said, for instance, 'First of all I saw a film about [Vincent de Paul] at an ordinands' gathering, and then I went into his life. At this time I hadn't decided, and this almost made up my mind – it gave me courage to admit I wanted to be ordained.'

We have seen that, in common with medical students, ordinands are likely to think at an earlier age about their future career if members of their immediate family belong to the profession, thus providing an accessible picture of what it will entail. It would seem that the same mechanism is at work here in the matter of influences on the decision, and it is a mechanism which is in no way peculiar to the ministry. De Wire (1959) compared a group of ordination candidates with a group of students who were planning to enter other occupations and found that they were alike in saying that both their parents and also practitioners of the occupation they were entering had influenced them in their choice. Thus, accountancy students, for example, may say that the most important people to have encouraged them to choose accountancy are accountants. De Wire argues, therefore, that the influence of clergy on ordinands is only a particular example of a more general phenomenon.

The influence of parents is different in kind, and what is looked for is encouragement rather than example. We found that about half the ordinands in our 1962 survey said that their parents had left the decision entirely to them, though mothers were generally more positive in their attitude than fathers. The married men all reported their wives as having given them strong encouragement (Table 5). In each case, however, ordinands said that support had grown. The hostile parents had become accepting, the neutral parents supportive, and the encouraging wives even more strongly so (Tables 6, 7 and 8). Of a mother it was said, 'Over the years her understanding has grown. At first it was "Just another job: a bit of a funny profession, but still. . ." Now she has a better religious sense and understands better. Mother has a little fund where she puts in a few shillings a week for my ordination present.' One ordinand said of his father, 'He has never opposed me or tried to influence me. He says, "If that's what you want to do, Okay." It'd be the same no matter what I wanted to do.'

We see the influence of parents only on the men who persist in their plan to be ordained, however, and it could be that continued opposition from parents would lead men to abandon their ideas of ordination. This seems unlikely, though, and support would appear to be the overwhelming response. Even a man's own doubts get supported by parental scepticism, as we see from the remarks of one ordinand made two years before he withdrew from training: 'I think she would prefer me not to be ordained. . . . I think she thinks that I ought to do something that is economically and socially "beneficient" to myself. . . she only came up with the 'not beneficient' line after my expression of doubts about my vocation. I don't think I came across it before.'

ADVERTISING FOR CLERGYMEN

Professions neither advertise their services nor advertise for recruits. It is assumed that the public will need professional services and will seek them, and it is assumed also that more people will want to enter a profession than it can admit, leaving the profession with the task of selecting the best applicants. It was with some amusement, therefore, that an observer noted that the Church of England, while maintaining stoutly that its clergy belong to one of the most ancient professions, mounted a poster campaign to attract applicants to its ministry (Wilson 1966, p. 79). This was in the early 1960s, when we were beginning our work, and we therefore investigated the effect of the campaign. Before it had begun and again after it had finished what were published as a matter of routine were leaflets giving simple information about entrance requirements, forms of selection, and so on, put out by the central Church agency; brochures distributed by individual colleges about their particular training; and booklets of a semi-devotional character about the work of the ministry, published by Anglo-Catholic or conservative evangelical tract associations.

When we asked a group of ordinands at a variety of colleges what they could remember of recruitment literature, 40 per cent said they could remember nothing. Indeed, most of that 40 per cent were not sure what was meant by 'recruitment literature' anyway, and when it was explained they pointed out that they thought its purpose had been simply to inform. Of those who did recall the literature in question, 60 per cent – representing only about one in three of all the ordinands questioned – remembered pamphlets issued by the central agency, which, at the time of the poster campaign, had adopted a tone of positive encouragement. The great majority of those who remembered other literature mentioned booklets sent out by conservative evangelical groups, which is the first piece of evidence of the evangelicals' greater efficiency in the Church of England.

As far as we could judge, the Church's attempts to boost the rate of recruitment met with little success and were a waste of time.

WHO BECOME ORDINANDS?

Who then, are the men that find their way to theological colleges and embark on training for the ordained ministry? Selection plays a part in determining who they are, but, since its contribution is the final influence, we shall leave it until last and consider first the general shape of the social group which ordinands as a whole constitute.

If we remove the late vocations, we find that in the 1960s ordinands were on average, aged $24\frac{1}{2}$, 73 per cent of them being between 22 and 26. This is what one would have expected, but the older men, as will be seen from Figure 7, were not that much older. Their average age was over 30, but their median age was

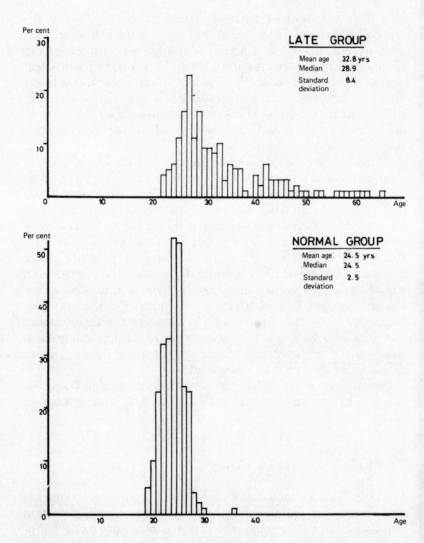

FIGURE 7   Age distribution of ordinands, 1962

less than 29 and the heaviest concentration of ages was in the twenties and very early thirties. The older ordinands are not so much older; they are men who proceed to ordination other than via the simple route of sixth-form, university, and theological college.

In the 1960s students who went to theological college straight from university did not, as a general rule, marry until they were ordained, or shortly before. Although the pattern was shared by other professions whose training was residential, in the case of the ministry it was a matter of definite policy; ordinands were required to obtain their bishop's permission before marrying, and the policy was strongly tinged with an ideal of self-denial demanded by the ministry, and, in the case of theological colleges run by religious communities, with faint overtones of monasticism. It is not surprising, therefore, that only 6 per cent of the men in the normal group were married at the time of the 1962 survey, although, according to the 1961 Census, 50 per cent of the general male population between the ages of 22 and 26 were married. The proportion remained steady throughout the 1960s, but changed subsequently. Russell (1976) reports that when our 1962 questionnaire (available in Coxon 1965) was used in 1973 by the Rev. Andrew Windross, when he was a student at Cuddesdon theological college, the proportion of married men in the normal group had risen to 25 per cent. This change was in line with general trends among graduate students, but represents a marked departure from the pattern of the 1960s and earlier.

In 1962, 44 per cent of the late group were married, but this too had changed by 1973, when 75 per cent were married, which is roughly the same as the proportion in the general population aged 25–34.

The change in the number of married ordinands over the period 1962 to 1973 is interesting in a number of ways. It is worth noting that there was a trend for the normal group to become more like the late group in this respect. The proportion of the late group who were married in 1962 was not much below the proportion for the general population of equivalent age (44 per cent compared with 75 per cent), while for the normal group it was a long way below (6 per cent compared with 50 per cent); in 1973, however, while the proportion of the late group who were married had increased to the point where it was almost the same as that for the general population (75 per cent compared with 79 per cent in the 1971 Census), the gross discrepancy for the normal group which had been found in 1962 was very substantially eroded by 1973, when the proportion who were married was 25 per cent, compared with 54 per cent in the equivalent age section of the general population. In the 1960s marital status was but one of the many respects in which the late group resembled the general population much more closely than did the normal group, as we shall see below. Ten years later, however, the distinctiveness of the two groups was much less marked. We consider this change to be a highly significant one and shall return to it.

The increase in the number of married men in training has another implication, too, which anticipates the argument of Chapter 5, where we discuss changing patterns in ordination training, and this deserves to be mentioned in passing. We commented above on the idealistic associations of remaining unmarried, and, while we should not for one moment wish to suggest that ordinands in the 1970s are less idealistic than were those of the 1960s, the unwillingness of a new generation to defer marriage does need to be noted. The implication, we should suggest, is that ordinands have a somewhat different attitude to their training, and that it is this changed attitude which is reflected in the lowering of the age of marriage. The period at theological college used to have the character of a 'total experience'; it was a time when men were wholly immersed in the atmosphere of a college and its various activities, and identified strongly, if not quite exclusively, with the college at which they were preparing for ordination. We suggest that now their sense of involvement is much more partial, and that this leaves them free to contemplate marriage and the compromised participation in college life which it entails. At this point, however, our concern is with the ordinands of the 1960s.

Not all the men who enter training for the ministry have a continuous history of religious practice. In our 1962 survey we found that 70 per cent of the men in the normal group said they had always been 'practising Christians', and this is a high figure when one bears in mind that according to the 1958 figures only 67 per cent of the population are baptised, only 50 per cent get married in church, 45 per cent are confirmed, 23 per cent receive communion at Easter and 19 per cent at Christmas, and only 14 per cent are on the electoral roll of their parishes (Paul 1964, pp. 17 and 20). A lower proportion of the late group, 55 per cent, said that they had been practising Christians up to the time when they decided to be ordained, showing again that they were less unlike the general population than were the normal group, and also suggesting a different pattern of occupational choice.

We have pointed out that the clergy enjoy high social status, but the men who enter the ministry come from a variety of social backgrounds. The Registrar-General's Office divides occupations into five categories: (I) professional; (II) intermediate and managers, (III) skilled manual workers; (IV) partly skilled; and (V) unskilled manual workers. Clergy count in class I, and high in it, since, as we have noted, when people are asked to rank a number of occupations according to their prestige the clergy generally come out as number four in the rank order (see p. 32). Taken as a single group, the ordinands in our 1962 survey came from backgrounds which, compared with the population, were over-representative of classes I and II and under-representative of classes III, IV and V. As will be seen from Figure 8, this pattern is rather dramatic if we take just the normal group of ordinands, and less so for the late group (see Table 9). In view of the fact that the occupation which ordinands are

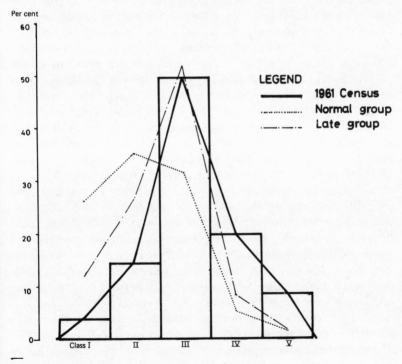

FIGURE 8   Ordinands' parental status

about to enter is in class I, this means that 73·6 per cent of the normal group were about to move into a class higher than that from which they had originated, and 88·7 per cent of the late group into a class higher than that of their last job. The rate of upward mobility is yet more spectacular if we base it on the clergyman's place as found in the ranking of occupations, making 84·4 per cent of the normal group and 94 per cent of the late group upwardly mobile.

A proportion of ordinands come from clerical homes, of course, and without them the rates of upward mobility would be absurdly high. The phenomenon of self-recruitment, or recruitment to the ministry of sons of the clergy, is interesting in its own right. The pattern is not unusual in the professions, and in various studies it has been shown that 51 per cent of law students have a lawyer in their families and 50 per cent of doctors a doctor (Thielens 1957, p. 134; Rogoff 1957, p. 112), although this is not self-recruitment in the strictest sense. We found that in 1962 8·6 per cent of ordinands in training were sons of clergy, 12·9 per cent of men in the normal group and 3·9 per cent of the late group. Even taking the 'normal' figure of 12·9 per cent, this is rather lower than might have been expected, although since the clergy make up only 0·107 per cent of the population it does mean that clergy sons have a 121 times greater than average chance of themselves becoming clergymen. The rate of self-recruitment was much higher in earlier generations. Drawing on studies in Scotland and England, Kelsall (1953) has shown that the proportion of clergy sons who chose to enter the ministry dropped systematically from 55 per cent in the period 1855–90 to 21 or 22 per cent in 1947–8, while the proportion choosing rather to go into teaching, medicine or the law rose from 20 per cent in 1855–90 to 79 per cent in 1926–35. But, whereas these figures are based on statistics on Cambridge and Scottish university graduates, our 1962 survey covered all theological colleges in England, and if we confine our consideration of the figures in the 1960s to the theological colleges associated with Cambridge we find that 25 per cent of Anglican ordinands were the sons of clergy. There is still a decline, but it is not quite so dramatic: 37 per cent of clergy sons at Cambridge in 1850–99 entered the ministry, 33 per cent in 1937–8, and in 1967 25 per cent of the ordinands were clergy sons. The proportion of ordinands who were clergy sons is not the same thing as the proportion of clergy sons who were ordinands, of course, but comparable figures are not available.

Ordinands at the Cambridge theological colleges, and presumably at the Oxford theological colleges as well, are an interesting sub-group. Not only does it contain a much higher proportion of clergy sons, but there is reason to suppose that with many of them an intention to be ordained was formed at a comparatively early age. Boys intending to enter the ministry are encouraged to read for a degree in theology, and we found that, of the Cambridge ordinands who were clergy sons, 62 per cent had first degrees in theology, while 38 per cent of the Cambridge ordinands with theology degrees were sons of clergy.

The educational backgrounds of ordinands are important, but it should be borne in mind how closely education and social background are linked. As Floud and Halsey have written (1961, p. 84),

> The English school system is heavily class-conditioned both historically and actually. In post-war years it has become the centre of fierce controversy as the outstanding support of the old, and an important source of new, class differences. It exercises a remarkable influence on occupational recruitment, setting firm limits to the freedom of individual choice and to possibilities of fluidity in the supply of labour. It is so organised as to demand that decisions which are critical for vocational choice are made at the age of 11 or 12, when they can reflect only the largely class-conditioned family environment of the child.

In the 1962 survey we found two distinct patterns for the normal and late groups of ordinands (Tables 10, 11 and 12). In the normal group, public-school ordinands left school at the same age as other public-school boys, while grammar-school boys are late leavers compared with other boys at grammar schools, and too few went to other kinds of school to warrant a mention. In the late group, on the other hand, public-school boys had been comparatively early school-leavers, grammar-school boys had left at the average school-leaving age, and the pattern for the rest was far too complex to be easily summarised. The normal group thus presented itself as homogeneous in terms of both types of school attended and also age of leaving school.

When we look at higher education we find that 54·9 per cent of all ordinands had a university degree or the equivalent, 79·3 per cent of the normal group and 27·2 per cent of the late group. The overall figure was more or less unchanged eleven years later, in 1973, when it stood at 52·2 per cent (but see p. 33 above).

The proportion of graduates entering the ministry has remained relatively stable in the recent past, but this must be viewed against the background of comparable groups. A recent study (Watts 1973) showed that in the period 1953–73, out of a total of 65 professional or quasi-professional organisations, 28 had raised their formal entry requirements to two GCE 'A' level and three GCE 'O' level passes, thus joining the five other professions which insisted on this level of qualification in 1953. The Church of England has fallen behind this pattern, but it has changed in another way. In an earlier chapter we remarked on the way in which the Church of England seemed to react to the secularisation of education by encouraging the study of theology. At the turn of the century, however, the form of learning thought proper for a clergyman was still that which derived from a general, liberal education, and the 1908 *Report* of the Archbishops' Commission assumed this. Of the graduate ordinands in the 1960s, however, 47·6 per cent were graduates in theology. They were responding to a mood very greatly changed since the turn of the century, well expressed by the then Archbishop of Canterbury in his introduction, entitled 'Theology as an Academic Study', to a booklet published by CACTM in 1962, under the title *Theological Training*:

> 'Shall I read Theology in my university course?' That question is often asked, and it is important that the advice given should be based upon some understanding of the character of a Theological course as an academic discipline. . . . Theology is a vocational as well as an academic subject, and competence in it is as necessary for the ordained minister as is medicine for the doctor, or law for the solicitor. By beginning his Theological study at the earlier stage [at university] a man can avoid superficiality, and it is important that . . . [clergy] should have studied the meaning of their faith with something of the *depth* that goes with an academic course.

The Foreword of the same booklet states, 'The University degree can, of course, be in any subject but those who are sufficiently clear about their vocation before going to a university should consider the advisability of reading Theology for their first degree, or at least part of their degree course.'

Another CACTM pamphlet published about the same time, *Ordination in the Church of England*, put the matter formally: 'Candidates are often encouraged to read for a degree in Theology at their university, unless there is a particular reason for their reading another subject.'

The principle seems to be that if the Church must have less, then at least it should have better. But the Archbishop's and CACTM's assumption that a theological degree is better than a degree in some other subject is a recent innovation. From the Archbishop's own words it would seem clear that the significance for him of a theological degree lies in part in the claim to professional status, comparable to medicine and the law, that it enables the clergyman to make.

SELECTION

The fourth factor involved in the recruitment of a group of ordination candidates is the choice by the Church itself of those candidates whom it wishes to accept from among the men who offer themselves for ordination.

The selection of suitable men is the responsibility of the bishops who will ordain them, but in practice the task is undertaken by the central agency of the Church, acting on behalf of the bishops. This has been the practice since 1945 and it was well established in the 1960s. The normal procedure is for about 20 candidates at a time to attend a residential selection conference with five selectors, one of whom, the chairman, is a senior clergyman, and another an administrator from the staff of ACCM, while the others are drawn from a panel of suitable clergy and lay men and women whose names are suggested by the bishops. Candidates must be at least 18 years old, and are individually interviewed by the various selectors in the course of a three-day mid-week conference which otherwise consists mainly of group discussions and corporate worship. After the candidates have left, reports are made by selectors and references are read. Just before the references are read, the fact that a candidate has attended a previous selection conference is divulged if this applies, but it is not known at the time of interview. On the basis of qualifications, interviews and references, one of four recommendations is made for each candidate: recommended for training; 'not yet recommended', usually signifying that the candidate should return to be considered again, after a period of time which may be specified; 'conditionally recommended', where the conditions attached usually concern the acquisition of certain academic qualifications; or 'not recommended'. The decision is communicated to a candidate by his bishop, for strictly speaking it is his decision and the task of the conference is confined to making a recommendation. Final acceptance is subject only to passing a medical examination.

What interests us here is the effect of the selection procedure on the composition of the group of men who go forward to ordination training. We need to know the influences it has, and the difference in make-up between the group of men who apply and the group of men who are recommended. The function of the conference is to select men first in terms of the 'rational' criteria which are laid down, such as educational attainment, and secondly on the basis of the candidate's 'suitability'. In so far as conferences select in terms of criteria which are formally laid down, their work is simply one of selection; but if their selection displays any consistent social pattern which is unrelated to formal requirements then it would be proper to describe this as bias, though we should not wish to imply conscious bias on the part of selectors.

The only information available is known as the Fayers–Heawood data, which are the figures for the period 1954–1960 collected by the then General Secretary of CACTM in the course of attending about a third of the selection conferences held during the period (Paul 1964, p. 275). What was recorded was whether candidates were recommended or not, cross-tabulated with the type of school attended and types of university, if any, at which the candidate had been an undergraduate student. We should expect the selectors to favour graduates, since this is the explicit recruitment policy of the Church of England, but any other pattern of preference would constitute a bias in selection.

What the data actually show is that, although preference is given to graduates over non-graduates, greater preference is given to graduates of Oxford and Cambridge over the graduates of other universities. So there appears to be a definite bias towards men from Oxford and Cambridge.

Secondly, the data show a bias in favour of candidates from public schools and against those from grammar schools. Furthermore, if we consider public, grammar and other schools, we find that there is much greater bias in favour of public schools as compared with grammar schools than there is for grammar schools as compared with other schools.

If we look at the trends over the period 1954–60 the evidence of prejudiced selection declines. At the beginning of the period there was a strong bias in favour of Oxford and Cambridge, but in the later years it lessened and ceased to be statistically significant. There was a consistent bias towards public-school candidates throughout the period, but at no point was it strong enough to be statistically significant, though it did approach significance in three separate years.

RECRUITMENT TRENDS AND RECRUITMENT POLICY

Education has been a recurrent theme in our discussion. This is not just because we are concerned with the education of the clergy, but also because of the importance of education to the history of the clergy as well as its importance to them individually at the present time. In the period we have considered, recruitment followed a pattern in which educational differences loomed large. But this is not all. The ordinands have careers ahead of them, and, although we shall devote a later chapter to the structure of clerical careers, it will come as no surprise at this point in the discussion to learn that Oxford and Cambridge men are over-represented on the bench of bishops. To illustrate the significance of education we shall briefly follow the influences of school type on the careers of clergy.

We have seen that the type of school a person attends is deeply embedded in the rigid structure of social class, and that it always finds an important place in a discriminating analysis. In Figure 9 we juxtapose such data as are available to show the process whereby an elite is formed, taking only the type of school attended as the criterion for comparisons. Starting with the population base and tracing the pattern through recruitment and selection to preferment to the episcopate, we see the inexorable consistency of the process. The most consistent preponderance is in the proportion of candidates who have been educated

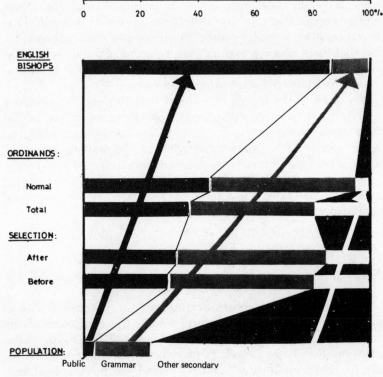

FIGURE 9   Recruitment and selection: school type

at public schools. Though only 3·5 per cent of the school-leaving population as a whole come from public schools, this proportional representation increases 25 times to the point where public-school men account for 87 per cent of the bench of bishops. Although the points of reference on Figure 9 are not drawn to scale as far as the passage of time is concerned, the gradient of the growth in public-school representation clearly indicates the most significant increases, which occur first at recruitment and then at preferment. The increase is far from insignificant during selection, and in the period between selection and the completion of training it is relatively less. The proportion of men from grammar schools also increases from 19·8 per cent in the population to 51·2 per cent in the normal group of men in training; but after that it shrinks again to a mere 13 per cent at the episcopal level, which is smaller than the proportion from which it started. So, although the ministry is over-recruited from those who have been to grammar schools, the higher ranks of the clergy are under-recruited from them. The group which suffers at every stage, and more at each successive point in the process, is that which was educated at neither a public school nor a grammar school. This 76·7 per cent of the school-leaving population are without representatives of their own kind among the bishops.

The exception to the trend just described lies in the greater proportion of men from other schools in our 1962 survey than in the Fayers–Heawood data for 1954–60. We have no positive evidence on which to base the proposition, but it seems likely to us that this discrepancy can be accounted for by the growth of the late group of ordinands between 1954 and 1962. There was no apparent reason why this trend should not have continued in the 1960s and 1970s, gradually altering the face of the ministry. It seemed possible that the Anglican clergy would shrink in numbers while at the same time they would come to have much more in common with the people whom they served. This was not to prove to be the actual course of events. In an earlier chapter we suggested that the 1960s represented the end of an era, and this is seen nowhere more clearly than here. In that decade the normal group fairly reflected ordinands as they had been. They were an elite group, drawn from a privileged social background and given a high standard of education. The late group, on the other hand, had some of the characteristics of an elite, but had the social and educational background of an average cross-section of the population. The trend from the 1960s to the 1970s has not been for the normal group to diminish in size compared with the late group, as looked very likely 10 or 15 years ago, but the discrepancy between the characters of the two groups has been very largely eroded. The groups themselves remain, but the non-elite character of the late group, which in the 1960s was still the exception, has come to be shared to a substantial degree by the normal group. In sum, the ministry has tended to become more representative of the population as a whole and less middle class, following the lead given by the late group in the 1960s, but not owing to the continued relative shrinkage of the normal group.

The new factor in the 1970s is the Auxiliary Pastoral Ministry.

With the advent of a group of clergy who serve the Church on a part-time basis, and who are trained without being withdrawn into conventional 'professional' education, there arises a real possibility that the whole pattern of recruitment to the Anglican ministry may change. When we look at the Church's policy on clerical recruitment over the previous hundred years from the vantage point of the 1960s, two things in particular are worthy of note. First, there is a growing concern with numbers. Understandable though this is, the statistical and organisational preoccupations seem to have supplanted, rather than complemented, concern with the quality of the ministry and the question of its proper role in the Church and society. Secondly, the question of social class no longer receives frank attention. In 1908 it clearly represented a problem which had to be tackled. In the 1960s, our evidence suggests, it still existed as a problem, though it may have assumed a less scandalous form, but it was no longer treated as a problem and indeed received no explicit attention. One is forced to conclude that class bias was accepted. It is difficult to put any other interpretation on the consistent pattern of recruitment, selection, and preferment described by Figure 9, occurring as it did, unchecked, 50 years after the resulting imbalance in the ministry had been recognised explicitly as an urgent and eradicable problem. With the approach of the 1980s, the situation is changing again.

If the Auxiliary Pastoral Ministry is recruited from a wide social range, and not predominantly from the professional classes, then the overall recruitment to the Anglican ministry could undergo a revolutionary change. Whether that would have any effect on the fate of the Church of England is, of course, another question.

4 Puritan and Antipuritan

At least one characteristic which distinguishes some ordinands from others has been mentioned in passing, and that is churchmanship. There are other distinguishing characteristics which have not figured in the discussion so far because we have been concerned with the process of occupational choice and recruitment, which involves the relationship of the clergy to the broad structures of the population to which they belong but within which they form a distinctive group. In other words, the focus of what we have said so far has been on those things which distinguish the clergy as a group, though before we shift the focus from the clergy in society to the clergy themselves we note again that we have already one major difference before we start. The normal and late groups are distinct because their members decide on ordination in different ways and they are recruited according to divergent patterns. But it does not follow necessarily that they will be distinguishable in religious terms, or even, say, in their political attitudes. Without forgetting it, then, we shall now put to one side the distinction between the normal group and the late group.

Most of the data on which we have drawn so far came from the 1962 survey, which covered a third of all the ordinands in training and included every college except one, the students at which refused, *en bloc*, to co-operate (exactly the same thing happened to Windross, though with a different college, when he repeated Coxon's 1962 survey in 1973). Now that we are narrowing down the focus and inquiring more closely into the attitudes and values of ordinands, and considering how they change over time, we shall draw on data from a much smaller group of men. We shall refer back repeatedly to the 1962 survey, but a study of the men who entered five colleges in 1966 will be at the centre of our investigation. The five colleges were chosen to be as representative as possible of the colleges as a whole, on the basis of what we knew from the 1962 survey, but data from them cannot be said to represent a random sample of ordinands and therefore cannot validly be supposed to apply to ordinands in general. There is no reason to think that these data are atypical of the general run of theological colleges and ordinands – indeed, everything possible was done to ensure that they should be typical, but there are none of the statistical guarantees on which we could rely when discussing the 1962 survey results.

Some readers may think it unfair of us to name the five colleges which we discuss in this and subsequent chapters, but we believe that it is entirely proper to do so. Of the five, St Chad's, Durham, is no longer a theological college in any case, and the same is true of other colleges mentioned by name at various points in our discussion; but throughout we have respected with the utmost strictness the confidentiality of individual students at the other four: Oak Hill College in north London; Queen's College, Birmingham; the College of the Resurrection, Mirfield; and Westcott House, Cambridge. What must be borne in mind is that our data refer to one year's intake well over ten years ago, and, although we believe them to be extremely instructive, they cannot be taken as a guide to the character of the four colleges today. In a period of fluidity and change in theological education every bit of evidence should be scrutinised, however, and we think that all theological colleges will benefit from an analysis of five groups of men entering five specific colleges, and not least those responsible for running the four colleges which remain open, though doubtless some features of their colleges from more than ten years ago will already seem strange and some characteristics of the groups of men studied will plainly appear as peculiarities of a single generation of students.

The 1962 survey provided evidence of the normal and late groups of ordinands. Everyone knew that there were men who had what were called late vocations and so the discovery of two groups was hardly news; what had not been appreciated before the findings of the 1962 survey were made public, however, was just how different the two groups are in very many respects. Age differences were shown to be of relative unimportance in comparison with differences in education, social class and self-recruitment to the ministry. It became clear as soon as we began the analysis in Chapter 2 that it would be gravely misleading to treat ordinands as a single group, and that the regularities which might exist would be masked unless we separated out the two groups.

Now that we are going on to look at the ordinands themselves
and the ways in which their attitudes and values change in the
course of training we shall need to be on our guard against the
same distinction's obscuring patterns which may be present,
because, for example, opposite trends which characterise the two
sub-groups might conceivably cancel each other out in the whole
group. We shall want to look at changes within each college as
well as across the colleges: we shall be on the watch for differences within groups of differing churchmanship, although they
will tend to be specific to colleges. Are there any other major
divisions? There have been many attempts to distinguish 'types
of vocation', some of which we mentioned in Chapter 2, but none
of them seemed to us very convincing. It was decided, therefore,
as a simple exploratory exercise, to employ certain standard tests
on the ordinands whom we proposed to follow through training.
We had no hypothetical types which we were trying to verify; we
wanted only to see in advance any distinctive sub-groups which
might require separate attention.

Three standard tests were used, and taken together they provided scores for each individual on 13 variables. The first six
variables are from the British version of the well known American 'Study of Values' test (Richardson 1965; Allport, Vernon
and Lindzey 1960). Though the test is commonly regarded as a
psychological one, it is concerned with assessing features of personality as they are manifested in peoples' values or evaluative
attitudes and so is of interest to the sociologist.[2] It will be necessary to say something more about the test but first let us look
briefly at the six variables. We have based the descriptions of the
six interests which follow on the manual to the test (Richardson
1965), and shall qualify these descriptions.

1. *Theoretical interest.* A high score on the theoretical variable
   signifies a dominant interest in the discovery of truth. The
   characteristically theoretical man assumes a cognitive
   attitude, seeking to observe, to understand and to reason.
2. *Economic interest.* A high score denotes someone who is
   interested primarily in practical things, and practical considerations take precedence over all others; concern with
   productivity, efficiency, and accumulation of tangible wealth
   follow naturally.
3. *Aesthetic interest.* This attitude, according to the Study of
   Values, is opposed to the theoretical, judging beauty and

harmony to be of greater value than truth or utility; the aesthetic person tends to be individualistic, finding interest in other people rather than in their well-being.

4. *Social interest.* A high score denotes someone who has an affective attitude towards other people, being concerned for them and their welfare; altruistic love is the characteristic, though not the only, form of concern.

5. *Political interest.* A high political score signifies a strong interest in power, leadership, dominance, influence or renown; the political man is more concerned with the power inherent in a situation than in its specific content.

6. *Religious interest.* The person who scores high seeks to comprehend the universe as a totality, and to relate himself to the whole. The religious attitude is one of striving after that unity that comes from a divine principle.

The variable which assesses a person's level of religious interest is of peculiar importance to us. The manual to the British version of the test, quoting from the American manual, which refers to the ideas of Spranger (1928), who originated this approach in psychology, has this to say of the religious scale:

> Spranger defines the religious man as one 'whose mental structure is permanently directed to the creation of the highest and absolutely satisfying value experience'. Some men of this type are 'immanent mystics', that is, they find their religious experience in the affirmation of life and in active participation therein. . . . The 'transcendental mystic', on the other hand, seeks to unite himself with a higher reality by withdrawing from life. (Richardson 1965, p.5)

The test would be a truly remarkable one if it did indeed measure accurately such a complex phenomenon. It has been suggested (Super 1949; Hunt 1968) that in fact it assesses something much more modest and circumscribed, and the findings we shall present will support that view. It seems that the person who enjoys fairly orthodox church activities and believes them to be important is more likely to obtain a high score on the religious variable than is the 'transcendental mystic' who eschews ecclesiastical institutions. We were not particularly hopeful that the test would help to distinguish types within the ordinand population, since earlier studies which have employed it 'find that it does not differentiate among types of ministers or seminarians' (Hunt 1968, p. 75).[3]

The next four variables are taken from the American 'Theological School Inventory', and adapted for use with British ordinands. The test was designed for use by counsellors in American theological colleges and most of its scales have to do with motivation. The results on those scales make little sense outside the context of counselling, and so we chose three variables which give a picture of the ordinand's conception of his own vocation (see above, pp. 58–9), expressed in religious terms, and one scale which is a personality variable. The four can be described, following the manual to the test, as follows (Dittes 1964).

7. *Natural vocation*. This variable is concerned with the respondent's assessment of his own suitability for the role of a clergyman. Nine items make up the scale, which reflects a vocational choice based largely on the respondent's careful thought and rational judgement of his own capabilities.
8. *Supernatural vocation*. This scale of 11 items focuses on the degree to which the respondent made his occupational choice as the result of what he defines as a non-rational response to a direct call from God. In the words of one item, he has 'answered a call more compelling than any rational personal assessment'.
9. *Concept of the call*. The 10 items on this variable are concerned with the same distinction as was used between a natural vocation and a supernatural vocation, but it assesses the degree to which the respondent believes that a supernatural type of call is proper to the occupational choice of the ministry. It asks not about the respondent's own experience of a 'call' to the ministry, but about his idea of what a 'call' should be.
10. *Flexibility*. The nine items on this variable are similar to those which measure 'intolerance of ambiguity', 'dogmatism' and 'rigidity' in other tests. This scale is concerned not with any aspects of motivation, but rather with a respondent's flexibility, particularly with regard to his beliefs and attitudes. Intuitively this is a useful measure, since it is some

indication of the respondent's idea of how he expects to react to the socialisation of theological education. The disadvantage is that it is not easy to measure flexibility, except as the inverse of rigidity, which is easier to assess. Although less readily interpretable, a rigidity or dogmatism variable would perhaps have been better in the Theological School Inventory than this scale.

The final three variables constitute the 'Eysenck Personality Inventory', which is a straightforward, wholly psychological test based on the theories of H. J. Eysenck.

11. *Neuroticism.* The neuroticism scale is unlike the other variables included so far in that the most 'normal' score is at the end of the scale opposite to neuroticism, since only very atypical people are entirely 'normal' in terms of this psychological model: they are abnormally normal. A high score indicates mental instability.
12. *Extroversion.* The variable measures what is meant by 'extroversion' in everyday speech, and is reckoned to be of psychological significance because it indicates, for the person who scores highly, that 'altogether his feelings are not kept under tight control, and he is not always a reliable person' (Eysenck and Eysenck 1964, p. 8).
13. *Lie.* The lie scale consists of eight questions. Its purpose is to rule out people from a whole study if it seems, from their score on this scale, that they are not being honest in their answers. Questions are of the kind, 'Are you completely free from prejudices of any kind?', such that the chances of someone answering yes truthfully to several of them are so low as to make the respondent look suspiciously like a liar. We had not intended to make use of this scale, but the results did not prove to be without interest and will be referred to below, although they were not used in the analysis.

It was not the intention of the study to examine psychological factors, but the Eysenck Personality Inventory was included in the hope that it might rule out purely psychological considerations from an analysis which was bound to verge on psychology, and this it did, bringing our findings into line with others which have sought to discover whether psychological factors discriminate between types of vocation to the ministry (Brown 1966).

The scores of the ordinands in our sample on variables 11 and 12, neuroticism and extroversion, approximate very closely indeed to scores for a sample of the general population. (Table 13).

The variables 7–10, from the Theological School Inventory, are designed especially for ordinands and of course there are no average scores with which to compare the results for the ordinands we were studying, apart from some American counterparts. The first six variables, on the other hand, contrast interestingly when we compare the scores from the ordinands with scores from a sample of British males. Figure 10 represents

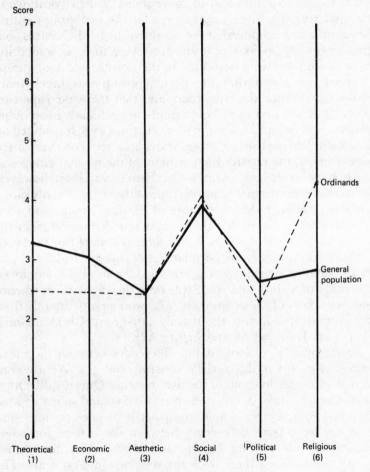

FIGURE 10   'Study of Values' (British version): profiles

the two sets of scores. Ordinands are very noticeably lower in
their scores on the first two variables, theoretical and economic
interests, and, not surprisingly, they more than compensate by
being higher on religious interest. (See Appendix II, Figure A1,
for a comparison with findings from another part of our
research.)

Before going any further we must ask whether there are distinctive patterns of scores for the normal and late groups. It is
true that the distinction has to do with processes of occupational
choice and of recruitment, but it could be supposed that if the
groups were of different educational backgrounds the differences
might extend to values and to conceptions of their vocations to
the ministry. When the mean scores for the two groups within
the sample are examined there do prove to be differences, but
they follow no obvious pattern. However, there is something
more to be taken into account. As the normal and late groups
emerged, we found that the normal group was much more
homogeneous than the late group, and that the wide dispersion
which characterised the whole sample of ordinands in so many
respects was reduced when the normal group were considered on
their own, leaving the late group widely scattered on every attribute. Indeed, the relative homogeneity of the normal group was
one of its most striking features. On these 12 variables, however,
the scores of the normal group on nine of them are actually more,
not less, scattered than are those of the late group, and so it
appears most unlikely that the normal–late distinction gives the
key to two patterns of scores. Nor is there reason to fear that such
a distinction is hidden by peculiarities of this particular sample,
for the small-scale studies at Leeds and Cheshunt also employed
the Study of Values and there was only the slightest divergence
between scores of Leeds students, who were predominantly from
the normal group, and the mainly late-group Cheshunt men
(Appendix II, Table 14 and Figure A2).

So we proceed to look at the differences between the mean
scores on each variable for the separate colleges. We are concerned with only four out of the five, because Queen's, Birmingham, had an intake of only four men in 1966 and so is included
only in figures for the whole group. It is at once obvious that
there are very large differences between the colleges on some
variables while not on others, and that by far the widest
divergence between them is on the religious-interest scale. The

mean score for the whole sample is 42.9, but the mean at Oak Hill
is 50·9, and at St Chad's only 33·3 (Table 15). In fact, what most
clearly distinguishes the variables is the degree of difference in
the mean scores of the various colleges, which is over 10 on 5 of
the 12 variables. Moreover, it appears that the divergence between Oak Hill and St. Chad's recurs on all the other variables for
which there is a large difference of college mean scores. The
mean scores of Westcott approximate quite closely to those of St
Chad's, but taken together the two colleges stand out as contrasted with Oak Hill. In Figure 11 we represent the mean scores
for the two colleges on all the 12 variables. When the mean
scores for the normal and late groups are inserted, a pattern
which was at first far from obvious becomes clear, for the means
for the two groups fall between the extremes of Oak Hill and St
Chad's, the means for the normal group being consistently close
to St Chad's and the means for the late group consistently nearer
to Oak Hill.

The pattern of mean scores for the religious-interest scale,
where the differences are most marked, is repeated even where
the dispersion is very much less. The pattern ranks the colleges

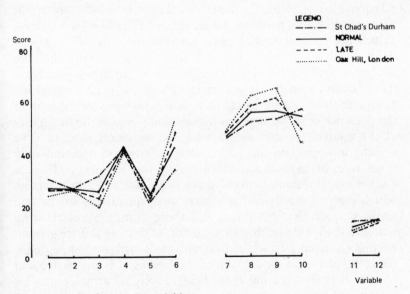

FIGURE 11   Profiles on 12 variables

in the following order: Oak Hill, Mirfield, Westcott and St Chad's. Allowing for Westcott and St Chad's to swap places, for their means run very close to each other, the pattern holds for religious interest, natural vocation (though the dispersion of means is small), supernatural vocation, and concept of the call; and in reverse order for aesthetic interest, flexibility, and theoretical interest (where again the dispersion is relatively smaller).

What is the factor which ranks these colleges so regularly? It might be the normal–late distinction, though that seems unlikely, for, while St Chad's contained only normal-group men, there were a number of the late group at Westcott, and Oak Hill, conversely, had a large proportion from the normal group. In any case, divergences between the colleges are much stronger than those between the normal and late groups. At first glance it seems that it might be churchmanship, for St Chad's is catholic and Oak Hill evangelical. But Mirfield, too, is catholic, more obviously so than Westcott. These are the only two obvious possibilities, and neither seems likely. We shall leave these questions for a moment, and investigate further the scores of all respondents on the variables rather than concentrating exclusively on the college groups.

By looking at the various mean scores we have ignored the relationships between the variables. There is a difficulty about using correlations between the six scales of the Study of Values, as has been mentioned already, because they are not independent. In this instance, however, they comprise only half the variables, and so, bearing the difficulty in mind, we perform a factor analysis on the intercorrelations of the twelve variables. Factor analysis is a statistical technique which enables us to infer the presence of some factor or factors, unknown at the beginning of the analysis, which account for the variation in data. The results, however, do not tell us what the factors are, but only their role in explaining, statistically, the variation. It is a dangerous technique because there is no guarantee that factors which exist as statistical facts have any equivalents in the real world outside the technique, and there is no way of showing either that they do or that they do not. It may help if we give an example of what a factor analysis might do with some imaginary data. Suppose that for a group of children aged between five and 15 you had data giving their height, weight, arm length, leg length and measurements round the hips and round the chest.

The first factor to emerge from the analysis might be one to which every single one of the variables contributed. The second might be concerned with height and length of arms and legs, and the third with weight and girth. If such results were to come out of a factor analysis, one would suppose that the first factor was age, the second fatness and the third skinniness. There might be others which had no obvious meaning, and, indeed, which truly had no meaning at all.

The factor analysis on the scores of the ordinands on these twelve variables produces a first factor which accounts for 25 per cent of the variance in the data, followed by five factors each of which explains about 10 per cent of the variance (Table 16).[4] The first factor is of immediate interest because it brings together five of the variables which we noticed from Figure 11 as having widely and regularly dispersed mean scores among the colleges. So it would seem that the regularity obtains for individual scores as well as for college mean scores. We must now ask what this factor is.

The data which comprise the scores on these 12 variables were collected over a period of time. The panel study took three years to complete and the data used here were collected between the spring of 1966 and the summer of 1967, in three stages: variables 7–10 in an initial interview, variables 1–6 at the time of a second interview, and variables 11 and 12 at the time of a third interview. The first round of interviews in the 1966 study were conducted before the ordinands entered training, in their homes and in a variety of unlikely settings, and subsequent rounds of interviews were all conducted in the colleges. The overwhelming intuitive impression gained from interviewing a large number of ordinands in succession was a certain broad variation among their religious attitudes. To put it crudely, for originally it was no more than a crude impression, some of the ordinands seemed to be noticeably more religious than others, or at least to be religious in a markedly more serious and devout way. This greater religious seriousness was conveyed both in the course of the interviews themselves and also in the informal conversations which preceded and followed them, and it came across most strikingly not only as a tendency to be especially interested in religious matters but also as a tendency to talk about other things within a religious frame of reference and as if they had some religious bearing. For these ordinands religion seemed to be the major interest in life, and topics of conversation which had no religious relevance were quite noticeably avoided. What made this religious seriousness in some ordinands more notable still was the attitude of studied indifference to religious affairs which was affected by others. It was not just an absence of obvious piety and enthusiasm which made this contrasting type of ordinand stand out, but a positive distaste for piety and religious enthusiasm.

In describing ordinands as 'religious' and 'irreligious' we are applying a very specific meaning to the word 'religious'. In the more general sense, two men who enter upon training for the ministry undoubtedly manifest an equal commitment, and must be regarded as being equally religious. The narrower meaning of the word refers to what may be thought of as a sectarian form of religiousness (cf. Wilson 1959). It entails a complete involvement in the religious institution to the exclusion of all else, as opposed to a qualified, or partial, involvement; it entails a sense of supernatural summons, and a feeling that one has been singled out by God, rather than a natural sense of human service which may admit of a religious interpretation; and it entails a feeling of being apart from 'the world', at home in the holy religious institution in a way not possible in wholly secular institutions.

We shall call the religious type of ordinand a *puritan*, and the irreligious type an *antipuritan* (cf. Towler 1969).

We shall briefly characterise the puritan and the antipuritan, bearing in mind that what we are reconstructing is a pair of contrasting impressions which were gained before the 1966 study had advanced far, and well before the factor analysis, or even the Study of Values test, had been employed. We can best characterise the two types of ordinand by considering the three ways in which they seemed dissimilar. In the first place, as we have said, the puritan tends to live in a wholly religious world. The church provides activities which fill most of his time and his spare time is devoted to pursuits which are consonant with this dominant religious interest. Probably he subscribes to religious magazines, plays football for a church team and perhaps sings in a group which draws its members from several churches. He may go to a religious youth camp for his holidays, or else visit places of religious interest abroad. The antipuritan, on the other hand, treats church activities as something of a chore. They occupy only a small proportion of his time and energy, and are regarded as a necessary duty which must be fulfilled. But, in the second place, he is very committed to some apparently secular interests. He is interested in politics, and is quite keen on music and the arts. In the late 1960s the cult of *The Lord of the Rings* was at its height, and one or two antipuritans said emphatically that they found more inspiration in Tolkien than in the Bible. In fact the arts seemed to figure quite large in the life of the antipuritan, while the puritan by comparison appeared to be philistine. His books were low-brow if they were not religious, his pictures and ornaments all had religious connotations, and his records were of Cliff Richard or church music rather than of Bob Dylan or Beethoven. In matters of taste the general impression made was that the puritan's taste was bad, if he had any taste at all, for a busy church life can leave little time for anything else. This characteristic absence of good taste extended to such things as dress and was particularly apparent at Oak Hill, where puritans predominated, all with clean short hair, inexpensive shoes, mass-produced clothes which were well cared for, and modest cars, well polished and free of litter. St Chad's and Westcott had an altogether more studentish air in every way. The contrasting styles are more readily understood at colleges which have their own traditions and which make an impact on students quite quickly, but the same styles were readily discernible before ever the men arrived at the colleges. In the third place, there are differences between the puritans and the antipuritans in their attitudes to religious worship. The puritan really enjoys services and prayer meetings and his own private devotions. They are a source of satisfaction and even of pleasure, and sometimes of immense emotional relief. In fact religion is something which in his own experience truly 'works' and he feels the better for it. The antipuritan, on the other hand, is almost completely detached. Worship and prayer are matters of observance and obligation, and if on occasions there is an emotional component it is made light of in company, for only in private and in confidence will it be discussed seriously.

The 12 variables in the tests suggest ways in which the pictures of the puritan and antipuritan might be completed. The first factor, which is the only one in which we are interested, ties together low aesthetic interest and high religious interest with a strong sense of a direct call from God, a belief that every ordinand should feel himself so called, and a low degree of flexibility. The particular sense of vocation is a special application of the puritan's strongly affective and experiential attitude to worship and religious affairs in general; and *mutatis mutandis* for the antipuritan. The role of flexibility is seen in the way in which the puritan is highly committed to religion within the narrow confines of the ecclesiastical world, while the more flexible antipuritan seeks to find inspiration and meaning in the full range of secular culture and institutions, with the church as no more than a background, or perhaps a foundation.[5] But the very generality of the flexibility scale means that its involvement in this syndrome of two types of vocation merits rather careful attention.

In the small-scale studies at Leeds and Cheshunt we employed the Melvin–Eysenck test, which assesses on one scale a respondent's conservatism or radicalism, and on another his 'tough-' or 'tender-mindedness'. We found that, whereas the ordinands whom we studied were distinctly unlike the general population in that, the more radical their score on one set of items, the the more highly they scored as tender-minded on the other set, in general experience the two scales are virtually unrelated (Eysenck 1954, p. 135). This in itself is interesting, but it was found, further, that the ordinands had low scores on certain items in the test contributing to tough-mindedness which were drawn from the F (fascistic) scale used by Adorno and others to measure authoritarianism. Two other 'tough-minded' items were concerned with anti-semitism, which is another of Adorno's measures of authoritarianism, but there was unanimous agreement among the ordinands that 'Jews are as valuable citizens as any other group', and, as we have said, a low score on other items indicative of authoritarianism. These findings are at variance, at least superficially, with the results repeatedly obtained by Adorno and others as reported in *The Authoritarian Personality*, according to which religiousness is associated with the various manifestations of authoritarianism.

Studies of authoritarianism using the tests and scales we have mentioned have found that, for a whole series of indicators of religiousness (including declared religious affiliation, frequency of church attendance, and psychological importance of religion) religious people consistently score as being more prejudiced and ethnocentric than non-religious people. The dispersion is great, however, and the mean score for any one denomination generally approximates to a central, neutral point. It has been found amongst religious people that those who adopt a critical attitude to the Church and who oppose institutional religion, or at least are critical of it, or who emphasise the moral or rational aspects of religion, score very noticeably lower as authoritarian than do those people whose religiousness is conformist or submissive. 'The fact of acceptance or rejection of religion is not as important as the *way* in which it is accepted or rejected' (Sanford 1950, p. 208).

This conclusion from the studies on authoritarianism is verified by the interview experience of Adorno and his colleagues, who emphasise three points, drawing on that part of their work: first, that the very rarity of religious people who score low on authoritarianism is significant; secondly, that there is a general tendency for religious people to adopt all the features of a 'conservative' ideology, which is associated with ethnocentrism, and religion is one of those features; and, thirdly, and this is important for the present discussion, 'only fully conscious, very articulate, unconventional Christians are likely to be free from ethnocentrism' (Adorno *et al.* 1950, p. 742). Almost all the ordinands in our small-scale study, it seems, were either the rare religious people who score low, or else 'fully conscious' Christians.

There is one other clue in Adorno's work, for he mentions (ibid., p. 739) that the term 'hypocritical' is often used to refer to religious people by those who score low as authoritarians, and sometimes by those who score high. The implication is that the use of this term suggests a critical stance towards the Church. Now it so happens that one item in the Melvin–Eysenck test is the proposition, 'Most religious people are hypocrites'. In the group we studied 14 per cent of the ordinands agreed with this statement, and if Adorno has identified correctly the characteristics of Christians who score low on authoritarianism we should expect this same 14 per cent to have scored very low on the items from the F scale; and this proves to be so. Most score zero out of a possible four on the items drawn from the F scale, and with one exception the others score only one. In our first use of the Melvin–Eysenck test the ordinands were asked to express the degree of their agreement or disagreement, and when the responses were checked it was found that, the lower the person's score on those F-scale items, the more emphatically did he express agreement that 'most religious people are hypocrites'. Anti-'conservatism' is perhaps reflected in the political allegiance of these 14 per cent for, with the one exception just noted, they were all something other than conservatives – either 'not in sympathy with any party' or socialists or liberals.

It will be obvious that this 14 per cent from the small-scale studies at Leeds and Cheshunt were fairly extreme in their non-conformity and unconventionality, but what applies to them might *a fortiori* apply to those who scored high on the flexibility scale. At least it gives an insight into the quality of the religiousness of these manifestly religious people. On the other hand, we should notice that, despite the differences in religiousness between ordinands, they differ, as a whole group, from what we know of the general run of people, and of religious people as a whole. In the first place, radicalism among ordinands, unlike others, tends to be strongly associated with tender-minded attitudes. That is, the more unconventional and critical of the *status quo* an ordinand is, the more he will hold to humanitarian ideals of kindness, compassion, and so on; and, similarly, the ordinand who is conformist and conservative will tend to be tough-minded and to approve of sternly disciplinarian attitudes to crime and so on. Secondly, the high religious commitment of these ordinands generally is not accompanied by fascistic authoritarianism and almost never by anti-semitism. Among our group of ordinands at Leeds and Cheshunt 56.7 per cent were pure non-authoritarians, i.e. they scored positively on not a single item indicating authoritarianism, and 23.7 per cent were low authoritarians, leaving 6.2 per cent to score moderately and 9.3 per cent to score highly on authoritarianism and a mere 4.1 per cent to be pure authoritarians. These ordinands as a group were, in this respect at least, dramatically unlike those to whom they would eventually minister, for well-nigh incontrovertible evidence exists to show that religious people generally are more authoritarian than non-religious people in their attitudes. The conflict between clergy and laity on political and social issues is an equally well known and amply documented modern phenomenon (Glock and Ringer 1956; Campbell and Pettigrew 1959; Hadden

1969). We can see that this conflict existed in embryo among this group of ordinands while they were still some time away from ordination. Having said that, however, we must remember that these remarks concern the interpretation of high scores on the flexibility scale only, and that high scores on that scale were strongly associated with high and low scores on various other scales; this leads us to suppose that something other than straightforward authoritarian conservatism, or its converse, is involved.

As we saw above, there was considerable variation in the scores of the ordinands on the religious-interest scale, and we have singled out those with high scores as more religious in this narrow sense, calling them puritans. In other words, the religious-interest scale measures a particular sort of religiousness. That it can be mistaken for religiousness *tout court* by those who constructed the test, whom we assume to have had no special religious axe to grind, tends to suggest that this narrow meaning we have attached to the word 'religious' is a not insignificant part of common usage, and perhaps that what we are calling 'puritanism' can be taken by some as being the same thing as religiousness.

Before we consider the other characteristics it will be useful to consider the colleges again, for in our 1966 study it was there that we first observed clearly the variation which we have subsequently identified as being the result of the presence of two groups, the puritans and the antipuritans. Among the group in the 1966 study, which effectively numbered 76, 25 of the men may be described as puritans and 22 as antipuritans.[6] At St Chad's there were eight antipuritans out of the 14 students, and no puritans; at Oak Hill there were 19 puritans among the 22 students, and one antipuritan; at Queen's, Birmingham, there were three puritans out of four men, and no antipuritan; of the 15 men at Mirfield there were two puritans and one antipuritan; and at Westcott there were 12 antipuritans out of 21 students, and one puritan. So, although there is the concentration of puritans at Oak Hill, and of antipuritans at Chad's and Westcott, which we expected to find, only slightly over half of the men at the latter two colleges are of the anticipated type. The relationship between type of vocation and college is obviously not a simple one.

CHURCHMANSHIP AND OTHER DIFFERENCES

The notion of parties distinguished by different types of church-manship within the Church of England is not difficult to under-stand *per se*, because every comparable organisation is divided into parties; but the particular alignments in the Church of Eng-land are hard to grasp because they are so deeply embedded in the Church's long, and sometimes obscure, history. A High Church party already existed in Elizabethan times, exemplified by men such as Bancroft and Hooker, which stood for resistance to the incursions of puritanism into the Anglican establishment, and it continued into the seventeenth century with figures such as Andrewes and Laud. In the eighteenth century the term 'Low Church' came into use, contrasted with these High Church sym-pathies, which were suspect after the succession of William and Mary; but originally the term 'Low Church' was used to describe views which were latitudinarian or liberal. In the nineteenth century both expressions came back into use with more specific connotations. 'High Church' was the label attached to those who emphasised the continuity of the Church of England with the pre-Reformation Church and who, valuing the traditions of Western Catholicism, were in sympathy with the writers of the *Tracts for the Times*, and joined themselves to the Oxford Movement. 'Low Church' came to be applied specifi-cally to those men influenced strongly by evangelicalism who were also critical of liberalism. So the term 'Low Church' was no longer used, as it had once been, to describe those who had liberal tendencies; those who espoused such ideas came to be referred to as the 'Broad Church' party, of whom Dr Arnold of Rugby, Bishop Hampden and Archbishop Whateley were not-able members. Still later, the term 'Broad Church' gave way to 'modernist' as the description of those who held even more radi-cal views affecting both the Catholic Church and the various Protestant Churches, including the Church of England.

We shall refer here to three groups: catholics, modernists and evangelicals. We recognise that these labels imply generalisa-tions which, like all generalisations, are no more than approxi-mations. Many complexities and variations of belief are gathered under each of these umbrellas. But none the less the labels are a useful shorthand description of different types of churchman-ship. 'Modernist' is the most unsatisfactory of the three labels, since it was so specific to one historical period, but we shall employ it while bearing this in mind, not least because our analysis will tend to undermine the tripartite division from which we start.

In the 1960s there were many clergymen and ordinands who felt less than comfortable with these labels, but there can be little doubt that they were worn. The modernists were out of sympathy with both the catholic and evangelical parties, seeing certain other considerations as more important than the things which divided those two groups. Others were out of sympathy with the two major parties without wishing to think of themselves as modernists; they were in some ways the latitudinarians of the 1960s, and sometimes they called themselves 'Central Churchmen', but we classed them with the modernists because they shared the objections to the 'two-party system'. A great many Anglicans, however, and most ordinands, were ready to describe themselves as catholics or evangelicals, even if with strong reservations. Catholics who were definite and extreme in their identification designated themselves as Anglo-catholics, leaving their more cautious brethren to refer to themselves as Prayer Book catholics, meaning that their sympathies would not permit them to stray far outside the usages permitted by the *Book of Common Prayer* interpreted in a catholic sense. Anglo-catholics, by contrast, made free use of the Roman Missal and looked to Rome for guidance. The evangelicals were sub-divided into conservative and liberal evangelicals. The former group were strongly committed to belief in the supreme authority of scripture and in the importance of a Christian's having a personal experience of conversion. The latter group placed rather less emphasis on these beliefs but shared with the conservative evangelicals a dislike of strong Church authority, preferring individual commitment, and thus feeling themselves generally at one with other non-extreme Protestants and opposed to the spirit of the Church of Rome.

In the 1966 study, 40 per cent of the ordinands described themselves as catholics, 25 per cent as modernists, and 35 per cent as evangelicals. (The proportions are broadly similar to those of 47 : 23 : 30, found in the 1962 survey, because the colleges chosen for the 1966 study were selected deliberately to reproduce the churchmanship proportions found in the 1962 survey.) We have seen that the colleges are very broadly associated with the churchmanship parties, although some recruit men much more exclusively from one party than do others. So it is not surprising that at St Chad's most of the students when they entered the college referred to themselves as catholics, leaving one in ten to call themselves modernists. All the men entering Oak Hill were evangelicals. Almost all of the 15 Mirfield men were catholics, except for 2 modernists. Westcott House was evenly divided between catholics and modernists. In view of the association which we have seen between the colleges and the two types of vocation, we should expect to find churchmanship and vocation type to be related. Of the 30 men who said they were catholics, half were of neither the puritan nor the antipuritan type, but 11 were puritans and 4 were antipuritans. Of the 13 modernists, 10 were antipuritans, 1 was a puritan, and 2 were neither. There were 25 evangelicals, of whom 20 were puritans, 1 was an anti-puritan, and 4 were neither. (Table 17.) So almost all the puritans are evangelical, and the antipuritans are either catholic or modernist; conversely, evangelicals are puritans, modernists are antipuritans, and catholics are a mixture.

One of the important differences between the churchmanship parties concerns their ideas about church worship, and associated with these different patterns of worship are contrasting ideas of the role of the clergyman. For the evangelical, preaching is the central activity of the clergyman in church and it tends to dominate his whole conception of his work. The catholic emphasis on the sacraments, on the other hand, leads to an emphasis on the clergyman's role as priest, while the modernist, with his characteristic lack of interest (comparatively speaking), in what goes on inside church, sees the clergyman primarily as teacher and pastor. We have already mentioned these several components of the clergyman's role and shall return to look at them in some detail in Chapter 6, but it is of interest to note here that among the puritan and antipuritan types of ordinand a clear pattern emerged in this matter. Of the 16 who said that the clergyman was first and foremost the preacher of the Word of God, 15 were puritans, and only 1 an antipuritan; of the 10 who saw his role chiefly as the celebrant of the sacraments, 9 were antipuritans and 1 was a puritan; while, of the 7 for whom the clergyman is principally a teacher of the Christian faith, and the 14 for whom he is the pastor of his flock, there is an almost equal division between puritans and antipuritans.

Now, it may be thought that we are being repetitive in dealing first with churchmanship and then with the priority ascribed to the various components of the clergy role, since the two are so closely tied to each other, but we have a specific point in mind. When the 1962 survey was repeated in 1973 by Windross, he found that ordinands were extremely reluctant to accept churchmanship labels, and that there was only a low consensus within the colleges as to churchmanship. On the other hand, students in 1973 were ready enough to embrace one rather than another model of the clergyman's role, and there was high consensus within colleges as to which model was the most satisfactory one. Thus, at St Stephens House, Oxford, perhaps the most unambiguously catholic of the colleges, 28 per cent of the students in 1973 did not classify themselves as catholics at all, but all of them rated celebrating the Holy Communion as among the clergyman's principal functions.

So in a sense we are more interested in the ways in which ordinands perceive the clerical role than in the churchmanship labels they choose, for in the long run the former are of demonstrably greater significance, since they give some indication, even if only very approximately, of what the men think that their future work should be about.

The clearest way of representing the differing ideas which ordinands have about the clergyman's role is by drawing their assessment of a variety of different role components on a scale, ranging from 'completely unimportant' at one end to 'extremely important' at the other. At various stages of our work we have used different lists of components of the clerical role. In the 1962 survey a list was used which closely followed one employed by the Columbia University Seminar on Professions. It has the added interest, of which we shall not take advantage here, of having been used with very similar results on Jewish rabbis (Sklare 1955). In the 1966 study we used a list based on the work of Blizzard (1956). The two lists are as follows.

1962 survey
(a) Administrator of church affairs
(b) Celebrant or officiant at sacraments and services
(c) Leader of the local community
(d) Preacher of the Word

1966 study
(1) Teacher of the Christian faith
(2) Organiser of church activities
(3) Preacher of the word of God
(4) Administrator of church affairs

(e) Official of the Established Church

(f) Pastor and father of his parishioners

(g) Counsellor, adviser and confessor

(5) Priest and celebrant of the sacraments

(6) Pastor and shepherd of his flock

Not only are these two lists rather different, but in addition we used different methods of assessing the importance which ordinands attributed to the items. In the 1962 survey questionnaire the men were asked to put a number 1 beside the item which they considered most important, a 2 beside the next in importance, and so on to produce a ranking. In the 1966 study, which used interviews, the ordinands were shown a card with the list on it and asked to say which of them was the most important single one. The question met with a resistance which is not surprising, since all these components are supposed to represent essential aspects of a clergyman's work, but they were asked then to say for each component whether they regarded it as important, very important, or of comparatively little importance.

Figure 12 shows the scales of importance attached to the several components of the clerical role in the 1962 and 1966 projects according to the respective lists. The different methods produce strikingly similar results, and two things stand out. First, ordinands distinguish sharply between those aspects of a clergy man's work which have a clear religious significance, and put them into a different category from the merely functional aspects of the work. This is a finding which others have reached, but it contrasts with the results of studies which have attempted to gauge the proportions of his time which in practice the clergyman spends on these various activities (Blizzard 1956 p. 508). But, in the second place, we see that this splitting of the role components into two categories is not the result of one component's being paramount, regardless of churchmanship (see pp. 151–4 below). No ordinand will put priest or preacher first unless he is respectively a catholic or an evangelical, while some of each party will ascribe greatest importance to a component of the role unrelated to churchmanship allegiance. The comparison between party groups is made in Figure 13, where the catholic, modernist, and evangelical scales are represented separately.

DEGREE OF IMPORTANCE:

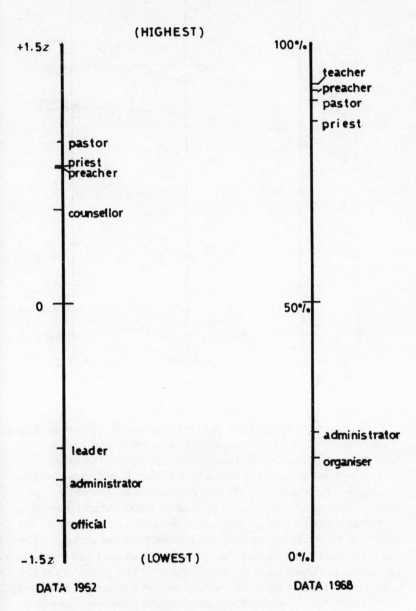

FIGURE 12   Importance attached to role components

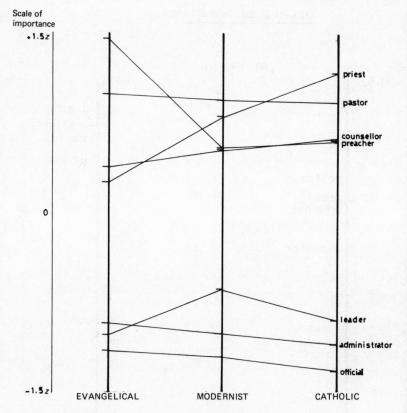

FIGURE 13   Role-component scales for sub-groups

It is only the evangelicals who have so great a consensus in
their ranking of one role component as being of first importance
that they achieve a dramatically high score on the scale. But
when the total group of ordinands is broken down into churchmanship sub-groups the dichotomy between 'normative' and
merely 'functional' aspects of the role is barely affected at all.

At the bottom end of the scale there is one feature worth
noting in view of what we have said about puritans and antipuritans, and that concerns the clergyman's role as leader of the local
community. Although it is consigned to a low position on the
scales of each churchmanship sub-group, it is regarded as rather
more important by the modernists, who number many antipuri-

tans among their ranks, than it is by the catholics, who have some antipuritans among them, and by the evangelicals, who have none. This would make sense if we were right to ascribe to puritanism as a religious attitude a degree of rejection of secular society, for this would naturally express itself in a concomitant rejection of the role of the clergyman as secular spokesman.

We shall look more closely at some of these differences between ordinands when we come to discuss the changes which take place during training, but one further difference deserves to be noted in this context, for it has a direct bearing on the distinction between puritans and antipuritans. This is the divergence of attitudes displayed by ordinands to questions of sexual morality. They were asked whether they thought that sexual relations outside marriage were always wrong, and although this is a wholly inadequate way of assessing a man's moral values it is indicative of two things: the extent to which absolute rules are thought to be operative, and, more important for the present purpose, the degree of conformity and conventionality which an ordinand displays. There are remarkable differences among the answers received from the men, who, at the time when the question was first asked, were waiting to enter theological college. Of the 21 men about to go to Oak Hill, 20, or 95 per cent, said that sexual relations outside marriage were always wrong; only 66 per cent of the men going to Mirfield thought so; 32 per cent of those going to Westcott; and 27 per cent of those going to St Chad's. When we look at the figures for puritans and antipuritans we find that 20 out of the 25 puritans thought sex outside marriage always wrong, while only 5 out of the 22 antipuritans thought it so.

One other finding relates to the degrees of conformity among the ordinands. As we explained above, the lie scale of the Eysenck Personality Inventory was not used in the analysis, since it was utilised only as a check on the reliability of respondents in filling in questionnaires honestly. The answers which must be given to the various questions which make up this scale if the respondent is to score positively are these:

(1) As a child, did you always do as you were told immediately and without grumbling? YES
(2) Do you sometimes laugh at a dirty joke? NO

(3) Are you completely free from prejudices of any kind? YES
(4) Do you sometimes boast a little? NO
(5) Do you *always* answer a personal letter as soon as you can after you have read it? YES
(6) Do you sometimes put off until tomorrow what you ought to do today? NO
(7) Have you sometimes told lies in your life? NO
(8) Would you rather win than lose a game? NO

Clearly, there are all sorts of reasons why a person may actually be answering honestly in answering one of these questions in such a way as would count towards the lie score, but when a number of questions are answered in this way the evidence cannot be ignored. The mean score for a large sample of respondents is reported as being 1·383 (Eysenck and Eysenck 1963, p. 14), and for the ordinands in the 1966 study it was 1·146. But the scores for the ordinands seemed to show some signs of following a pattern and the means were not the same at all the colleges: they were about 0·5 at St Chad's, about 1·0 at Westcott and Mirfield, and about 2·0 at Oak Hill. There is nothing in the least suspicious about a score of 2·0, but the difference in mean scores between colleges is noteworthy. In their discussion of the scale, the Eysencks point out that some people score highly because they give answers which they conceive as being right rather than wrong in the moral, or desirable, sense, rather than in the sense of being true or false. Disregarding scores at particular colleges, there proves to be a definite association between scores on the lie scale and answers to the question about sexual morality (Table 18).

To sum up our conclusions thus far, we believe that we have shown in Chapter 3 that the normal and late groups among ordinands follow distinct processes of occupational choice and are recruited according to patterns which contrast sharply. Now, in this chapter we believe that we have presented sufficient evidence to make it a reasonable supposition that there are two other readily recognisable groups among ordinands. One is the group of puritans, who are more conventionally religious, conformist, relatively disinterested in a world beyond the Church, and broadly, though not exclusively, evangelical. The other is the group of antipuritans, who are irreligious in the special sense defined above, who are non-conformist, and highly involved in secular culture outside the Church. If it is asked whether these two pairs of groups, normal and late, puritan and antipuritan, can be correlated with one another, the answer is that they cannot (Table 19). The dichotomies are separate and distinct, and both must now be borne in mind.

5   Theological Colleges

So far we have looked at men as they approach training for the ministry. We have considered what sort of backgrounds they come from, what routes they follow, and what sorts of men they are. Once a man actually enters upon his training his intention of being ordained quite suddenly ceases to be an aspiration; it becomes an imminent fact. He enters his theological college as a layman and he will leave it as a clergyman. Thus far in his life, a clergyman has been someone to whom he has related as a special sort of person, who occupies a role about which he has a variety of ideas. At the end of a period in limbo he himself will occupy that role, and it will be him whom people will approach as a special sort of person. People will have new and unfamiliar expectations of him in his new capacity, and his world will be a very different one after he is ordained, at least it will appear so to him because he will be looking at it, and having to act in it, from a new position. In the course of his time at theological college he will have the only opportunity offered to him to learn the role of the clergyman – not just in its academic aspects, but as a particular way of life with its own attitudes, values, opinions, and self-image. It is a period of transition or, in sociological language, of socialisation to a new role.

How much a man changes in the course of his time at theological college, and in what ways he changes, is what we shall examine in the next chapter, but the college is the only milieu in which socialisation to the new role can take place before ordination. If the change is not effected at college, it will come in the experience of clerical practice, when the man is expected to act out a role which he is still only learning. This process of socialisation is an important one with far-reaching implications. Robert Merton has written (1957b, p. 287),

Ratified by more than two generations of use in psychology and sociology, the technical term socialization designates the processes by which people selectively acquire the values and

116

attitudes, the interests, skills and knowledge – in short, the culture – current in the group of which they are, or seek to become, a member.

The socialisation with which we are concerned is professional socialisation, i.e. socialisation into membership of a profession, and it is much more specific than most other forms of socialisation, both in the content of the particular culture which is appropriated and also in the length of time over which the appropriation takes place. Of course it is in any case an on-going process, for it never ends abruptly when a man is ordained, and, indeed, it would be a mistake to imagine that the process is ever completed in the sense of producing a 'fully socialised' person (cf. Wrong 1961).

In discussing occupational choice we compared clergy with doctors, and the comparison is again instructive, because the roles for which medical students and ordinands are preparing are crucially different, and this has consequences for the characters of the two processes of socialisation. The doctor's role is more cognitive than affective, and therefore much of the emphasis in training falls on the acquisition of information, of technical skills, and of theoretical principles, leaving social skills and appropriate role relationships to be learned as an incidental part of training. Ordinands, by contrast, are being socialised into a role which is more affective than cognitive, and sociologically this has the paradoxical consequence that the experience of training in a theological college is more intense and complex than it is in a medical school. The culture which must accompany clerical skills is difficult to spell out, as, indeed, are those very skills; their acquisition depends on more subtle processes than are afforded by the lecture room and the laboratory. So, if at a theological college the social interaction, the involvement, and the commitment are more intense than they are in a medical school, that is not because the training is a religious one, but because the culture which is being learned is altogether more diffuse. Since the skills being acquired are not objective, instrumental and cognitive, but subjective, intuitive and affective, the attitude engendered by training cannot be one of cool detachment: it must be an attitude of committed involvement.

In another way medical and clerical training are alike as two forms of professional preparation, for the particularity of any professional role, especially when it is compared with the roles learned in childhood (referred to by sociologists as 'primary socialisation'), entails also a trained incapacity to perform other roles, and even the incapacity to perceive normal social situations except in the blinkered manner which has been inculcated as the professional one. Doctors and clergy alike may experience difficulty in responding to death, for example, except with the professionally prescribed offer of comfort and support peculiar to medicine and the Church. This trained incapacity can have serious consequences for those who drop out of training, the more so as training proceeds, and still more if a man with several years of professional experience quits his profession. The number of alternative occupations which are open to the drop-out diminishes as the role to which he has been socialised becomes more specialised, with the result that drop-outs from medicine or the ministry, medical training or ordination training, find themselves doing jobs with dramatically lower status than medicine or the ministry. The 'spoilt priest' of Roman Catholic folklore, the most extreme case of the general phenomenon, not only found himself a religious and social leper, but also discovered with a rude shock that he had spent long years in being trained for nothing except priest-craft (Fichter 1961, pp. 185–204).

In drawing this comparison between medicine and the ministry we are portraying one particular model of ministry, however, and we shall suggest that it is not the only one.

TWO MODELS OF ORDINATION TRAINING

The traditional training of the Catholic priest marks one end of a continuum along which the various forms of training can be ranged; the other end is marked by the training received by Anglican clergy prior to the founding of the theological colleges in the nineteenth century. No example of either extreme remains in our own day, but the two models are still useful, because they draw attention to significant aspects of more 'mixed' kinds of training, which make sense when seen as elements of a form of training which has now passed away, or as elements of a form which is only just emerging.

We may call the two models 'open' and 'closed'. The typical

seminary in the Catholic Church before the Second Vatican Council was an almost wholly closed institution. Boys generally entered the minor seminary at the age of 11 and received their ordinary schooling in a deeply religious environment, shielded from secular influences by an institution run by priests and dominated by the notion of priesthood. As a boy moved up through the institution from lower forms to higher ones, from minor seminary to major seminary, from ordinary lessons to philosophy, and from philosophy to divinity, his daily life gradually, and by almost imperceptible steps, changed so as to approximate more closely to that of a priest; and always the boys a year ahead were one year closer to ordination. He entered as a very young schoolboy, and left the seminary as a fully qualified priest. The very term used to describe his training at the seminary – namely, his 'formation' – signifies that it was designed to embrace every aspect of the person and to mould a whole person of a very particular kind. The book learning acquired in the course of 'priestly formation' was but one part of the process, and the most general assumption underlying this closed model of training was that retreat and seclusion from the world were necessary in order to produce a clergyman. The candidate was withdrawn from the world as an ordinary person – indeed, as an unformed child – and returned to it a new person. The same principle underlies this kind of training wherever it occurs. The person leaves the world as a layman, a common man, and after a period of seclusion returns to the world as something quite different and special: a priest. What goes on within the walls of the seminary is less important than that there should be walls, for the seclusion itself is what is important if the man's previous acquaintances are to accept him as a new kind of person, changed from him they knew, and if the man himself is to emerge with a securely established, new self-image. What lies beneath this model of training, of course, and what gives it point, is a conception of the ministry as something set apart, sacred, and radically different from the laity. It is this difference which marks off the clergy that makes it necessary for ordinands to withdraw from the world in order, thereafter, to return recognised and recognising themselves as changed into members of a race apart.

The open model of training for the ministry knows no withdrawal from the world. The training may be long and arduous, but it is not in the least secluded. A contemporary example roughly corresponding to this model is the training of ministers for the Church of Scotland, which, typically, is a course of intensive training in all branches of theology, conducted under the auspices of a university. The open model imposes no rules of residence beyond the normal requirements of the university, and such association between fellow ordinands as takes place does so only as an incidental consequence of studying together for the same examinations. A common culture does arise to a certain extent, of course, but it is the by-product of the common course of studies, and it is these academic studies which define the purpose of training. The similarity to medical training of training for the ministry according to this open model will be immediately apparent, and disparities we noted earlier arise because most clerical training, in England at least, is strongly tinged with elements of the closed model.

The purpose of training for the ministry which conforms to the second, open model is the acquisition of defined knowledge, skills and information, all of which are tested and then certificated at the end of the course. The man does not emerge from his training as a different person, but as the same person equipped for specialist tasks, and this is because the conception of ministry which underlies this model of training is of service to a congregation by one who is the exact equal of the layman, not his better in any sense. Nor is he sacred or set apart, but, rather, he is called by the congregation, and in the presbyterian tradition he is literally called (see above, p. 58), to render the service and ministry for which he has been trained, to the congregation which has called him, and that congregation is not under his jurisdiction, but is self-governing.

These two models of training would be of little interest here but for two things. First, training for the Anglican ministry has at present gone almost full circle, from the open model at the beginning of the nineteenth century, through an increasingly important element of the closed model, beginning with the founding of the theological colleges and culminating in the full development of the catholic colleges in the first half of the twentieth century, and now back to the open model again. Now the emphasis increasingly is on academic theology, colleges have moved into deliberately close proximity with centres of secular learning, and their secluded character is being systematically changed. So, the distinction between the two models of training is important, because it tells us, both negatively and positively, the direction of current trends. Secondly, and following on from the lesson to be learned about training, the distinction is important because it indicates a basic shift which is taking place in the Church of England's conception of ministry, and alerts us to a piece of evidence which is vital in discerning the future of the Anglican ministry.

It is not possible to say unequivocally whether a change in the conception of ministry is leading to a change in training, or whether a shift in training is engendering a new idea of ministry. We should argue that both processes are at work at the same time. On the one hand, ministry is increasingly conceived in more democratic and egalitarian terms and less in terms of sacerdotal elitism, as we observed in an earlier chapter, and obviously this has had implications for the way in which clergy are trained. The same shift has occurred in the Roman Catholic Church. The decrees of the Second Vatican Council made direct changes in the training of priests (*Decree on Priestly Formation*, October 1965), but in encouraging the Pope and the bishops to consult rather than to rule sovereignly and in princely style, and in exhorting the laity to an active apostolate, the decrees promoted a sense of democratic participation which was inimical to the old style of priesthood. On the other hand the strong trend towards the inclusion, in courses of training for the ministry, of more theology, which conforms to the patterns and standards of secular scholarship, has itself served to undermine the 'sacralising' character of training, and thus to encourage a move away from sacerdotal conceptions of ministry, in favour of more professional conceptions.

We should maintain that the influence of a changing model of training on conceptions of the ministry is an important one, and one the importance of which has not been sufficiently recognised.

Of all the factors which have changed the character of Anglican theological colleges in the recent past and which continue to exert an influence, the most striking is this insistent cry for ordinands to read for degrees in theology, and for theological colleges to improve the academic standards of their teaching of theology. We have already noted the official ratification of this policy by the Archbishop of Canterbury, and commented on its origin, plain for all to see, in the desire to have clergy who are accorded a professional standing comparable with medicine (see above, pp. 40 and 82). The effects of this policy have been felt in a variety of ways by the colleges, of which the most obvious has been the pressure for colleges to be associated with university departments of theology. When the number of ordinands dropped sharply in the late 1960s and early 1970s, some theological colleges were closed and others were reorganised, and the most important single factor which decided the fate of a college was its proximity to the facilities afforded by a university. Thus, the colleges most at risk of being shut were those, such as Ely and Lichfield, which had been founded in cathedral cities in which there was no university; others escaped only by being merged, as were Salisbury and Wells, and Ripon Hall and Cuddesdon. The result has been that greater emphasis is laid on academic pursuits, which bring students under influences which originate outside the colleges, and less on the internal life of the colleges themselves and their exclusively religious culture. On the whole, the colleges have moved a substantial way along the open–closed continuum and now approximate much more closely to the open model than they did even ten years ago.

Some further implications of the changes in ordination training will become clearer if we examine the open and closed models from a purely sociological point of view.

GOFFMAN AND ETZIONI

A monastery is a typical example of the kind of institution which Erving Goffman, in his now celebrated book *Asylums* (1961), calls a 'total institution'. By this he means any establishment which encompasses the entire lives of its inmates, and of course this is every bit as characteristic of the closed type of ordination training as it is of a monastery. Whereas for most people in our society the activities of working, recreation, and sleeping go on in different places, in the company of different people, and under different sets of social rules, the central feature of the total institutions Goffman describes can be defined as 'a breakdown of the kinds of barriers ordinarily separating these three spheres of life' (ibid., p. 313). Other distinguishing features of total institutions are the following (ibid., pp. 313 – 14).

1. All aspects of life are conducted in the same place and under the same authority.

2. Each phase of a member's daily activity will be carried out in the immediate company of others, all of whom are treated alike and are required to do the same thing together.
3. All phases of the day's activity are tightly scheduled ... the whole system of activities being imposed from above through a system of explicit formal rulings and a body of officials.
4. The content of the various activities are brought together as parts of a single overall rational plan purportedly designed to fulfil the official aims of the institution.

A theological college which is fully residential, has strict rules which severely limit the access of visitors and the opportunities for ordinands to go outside, and in which the teaching, catering, worship and recreation are organised by the college approximates quite closely to Goffman's characterisation of a total institution. The principle of seclusion on which it is based positively encourages the various 'total' elements, since they act as a barrier against the outside world.

The theological college run by the Society of the Sacred Mission at Kelham in Nottinghamshire, which closed in 1972, had much of this character. It was in the country, in its own ample grounds, and ordinands were associate members of the religious order, with the result that they were subject to all the discipline of the religious vows as well as being *in statu pupillari*. A brief review of the life of Kelham will provide a picture of the closed type of training. All students were required to follow a Rule, which included the following.

1. Attendance daily at matins, mass, sext, evensong and compline.
2. Corporate meditation or mental prayer, daily for a period of 30 minutes.
3. Private confession was not obligatory, but it was strongly encouraged and most students followed the practice.
4. Lectures were compulsory, as were set periods of private study.
5. Manual work on three afternoons a week was compulsory and entailed such jobs as gardening, scrubbing and sweeping.
6. Obligatory tasks each weekday morning before the beginning of academic work. These were referred to as 'departments' and included 'Domestic' (domestic chores), 'Grub' (refectory

duties), 'Chapel', and 'Spuds' (potato preparation). 'Grub' was the most time-consuming of the tasks, which rotated fortnightly.

Kelham students had the holidays normal in higher education, but in term time the whole of the ordinand's day except for a weekly 'holiday afternoon' was spent within the grounds of the institution. Since rooms were shared by three students, and since meditation was corporate, even sleeping and private prayer, which elsewhere might have afforded some privacy, were communal activities. The college had a complex structure of diverse roles and some authority was delegated to student officers, but all authority derived from the Society and was mediated through the college principal, called the Warden. Below the Warden were lecturers, who supervised academic activities, and chaplains, charged with the spiritual well-being of the ordinands. Among the students themselves there was a senior student, with responsibility over the whole student body; there were also class seniors, responsible for classroom order and the like, and room seniors, responsible for each room of three students.

Except for the weekly holiday afternoons, Kelham students spent the whole of their time in the immediate company of others, though the other people involved were not always the same. The Rule they all followed had a certain degree of flexibility, but it assumed that all activities were communal and that no individual student had legitimate personal or private needs which were not met by its provisions. The whole daily routine was tightly scheduled for everyone, and each activity was heralded by the ringing of bells all over the building. Activities followed immediately one after another, except for gaps of about ten minutes after matins, after morning work, after lunch, between afternoon work and tea, and between dinner and compline, but even these short gaps could be superseded by 'departments', by compulsory showers, by talks with chaplains, and so forth. The rational plan which governed daily activities and their overall structure was explained formally and informally in terms of the 'maintenance of a disciplined devotional life'. Talks to students at the beginning of a new year, always a valuable source of sociological data in theological colleges, emphasised that rules and restrictions existed to 'deepen spirituality'.

One important feature of the total institution, according to

Goffman (1961, p. 317), is a series of mortification processes:

> Upon entrance [the recruit] is immediately stripped of his
> wonted supports, and his self is systematically, if often unin-
> tentionally, mortified . . . he begins . . . some radical shifts in
> his moral career, a career laying out progressive changes that
> occur in the beliefs he has concerning himself and significant
> others.

The process is typically an entirely open one, and is clearly seen
in the stripping and bathing which mark admission to prisons
and mental hospitals, but it may assume rather more subtle
forms: 'in religious institutions we may find sociologically
sophisticated theories about the soul's need for purification and
penance through disciplining of the flesh' (ibid., p. 318). At
Kelham there were indeed mortification processes. The new student, who was called a 'probationer', wore civilian clothes, while
other students wore a modified monastic habit; at one time the
probationer was required to wear short trousers, but even ordinary clothing served to mark the newcomer as an outsider. The
process of 'clothing' was ritually prescribed, and in his second
term the recruit was given a cassock, blue scapular and black
belt; he became an 'aspirant' for the remainder of his first year,
at the end of which he became an associate member of the Society of the Sacred Mission and exchanged his belt for a black
girdle with two knots in it. These ceremonies took place solemnly
in chapel, in the presence of the whole community, and a prom-
ise of obedience was read by the recruit, and instruction was
given in the Rule and in the 'Spirit of the Religious Life' by a
professed member of the Society.

Kelham represented a form of the closed model of training
which was unusually pure in the Church of England, but the
model itself was widespread, and most aspects of the life at
Kelham, like the Rule, domestic duties, and regulations about
periods of work, had their watered-down equivalents in many of
the other colleges which provided fully residential training for
unmarried men. Other characteristics shared by many colleges
are common to almost every residential establishment, from an
army barracks to a nurses' home, and four of these deserve brief
mention. The first is a peculiar institutional slang. Perhaps the
most common piece of theological college argot is the word

'topos' to refer to lavatories, but in one or more of the colleges other terms enjoyed wide currency in the 1960s, such as 'Moab' (wash-place), 'spike' and 'spikey' (High Church, addicted to ceremonial excess), 'prot' and 'protty' (Low Church), 'tat' and 'tatty' (ecclesiastical paraphernalia, *objets réligieuses*, fondness of same), 'crud' and 'gungey' (second-rate, inferior, spoiled). And of course each institution has its own individual folklore and its quota of culture heroes. A second common feature, connected with the first, is an annual Christmas concert, which serves to articulate, to celebrate and to reinforce the peculiar culture, and which provides an occasion when staff may be ritually polluted by students. Grievances and complaints can be aired with complete impunity in this ceremonial context, and the event acts both as a safety valve and also as a way of reasserting the collective solidarity of the institution. A third is the house magazine. A fourth feature, which merits particular note, is the stress laid on sexual segregation and the general obsession with sex, with sexual taboos and with the violation of taboos. The mandatory celibacy at Kelham was no more than an obvious manifestation of this common phenomenon, which appeared in heterosexual and homosexual forms in many colleges. Sexual deprivation is one of the most widespread forms of deprivation with which an institution denies individuals expression of their individual identities, thus asserting the priority of the institution over the individual.

Training for the ministry according to the closed model takes place, then, in a college which conforms quite closely to what Erving Goffman describes as a total institution. What we have argued is that this kind of training takes place in isolation from the wider society, and in a wholly different environment, because the ministry is conceived as being something set apart, exercised by men with a very special identity which marks them off from the general run of humanity. At the other extreme, the open model of training does not require residence at all. It focuses on specified knowledge and skills, and, no matter what they are, whether scholarly learning or the skill of open-air preaching or the manual acts of the mass, their acquisition cannot possibly necessitate the students' spending together their hours of sleep and leisure.

This distinction between two models of training is perfectly obvious, and yet its implications are not always grasped as readily as is its existence. Thus, we find churchmen advocating more emphasis on academic theology as an integral part of training for the ministry, and arguing that men should be entirely free to marry and live outside a college while they are training, since, if anything, it enhances their capacities for serious and sustained study, while the same churchmen want to continue talking of the importance, in training, of developing a 'deep spiritual life' and therefore of setting aside a generous amount of time for private prayer and attending religious services daily. They fail to recognise that they are wanting to have their cake and eat it, for the demands of the traditional regime of religious devotion which is thought to lead to a deepened spiritual life are simply incompatible with the proper demands which should be expected from a wife and young children, which make serious study quite difficult enough in any case. At the most general level there is a contradiction between, on the one hand, arguing that clergy are no different from the laity except in their liturgical function and their professional theological skills, and, on the other hand, insisting on a routine of devotion for ordinands which would be totally impracticable for any but the most exceptionally placed layman; and yet current trends in ordination training are leading to precisely this contradiction.

Another implication of the two models of training for the shape of the ministry is brought out by Amitai Etzioni's theory of complex organisations (1961a). Etzioni's work was concerned with forms of compliance, i.e. the bases of good order, in an organisation, and this is relevant for our purposes since it will be obvious that there is an intimate connection between the authority under which an ordinand receives his training and the authority he will regard as legitimate as an active clergyman, and also between the sense of involvement a man has with his training and the sense of involvement he will have subsequently with the Church. Etzioni suggests that we may usefully distinguish three major forms of authority, or power, which an institution can exercise over its members, and also three major forms which the members' sense of involvement can assume. When they are combined in the following way,

Power	*Involvement*		
	Alienative	Calculative	Moral
Coercive	X		
Remunerative		X	
Normative			X

the combinations marked X are described by Etzioni as being 'congruent'. Thus, coercive power encourages a negative or alienated sense of involvement with an organisation such as a prison, and the alienative involvement in its turn evokes the exercise of coercive power as the only kind appropriate, and so the power and the involvement are congruous with one another. A similar congruity exists between remunerative power, which relies on material reward, and the kind of involvement Etzioni calls calculative, which seeks to maximise material gratification; and between purely normative power and a sense of moral involvement in an organisation. If coercive power and remunerative power rest on the threat of physical and material sanctions, respectively, normative power relies for its strength on the threatened use of symbolic, non-material sanctions. It is so called because it rests upon certain norms assumed to be accepted by a consensus of everyone concerned. The schoolboy who is made a prefect has had his conduct symbolically rewarded, for the reward has no material significance of any consequence, and he is as strongly sanctioned if he is subsequently reduced to the ranks; the headmaster or housemaster who allocates and manipulates these symbolic rewards and sanctions is exercising normative power over his charges. By moral involvement is meant that kind of association and commitment which is given freely and for its own sake rather than from any ulterior motive, as one might be involved in one's marriage, unless it were entered into for money, or in a political party, unless one joined in the hope of gaining material benefits from membership.

Clearly, both coercive power and alienative involvement are largely irrelevant to contemporary Western churches and forms of training for the ordained ministry, though they are not in principle antipathetic to religious organisations. We should argue, however, that both of the other two combinations are relevant to the ministry and shed some light on characteristics of clerical training. The closed model of training obviously involves very extensive compliance by ordinands in its running, and its very existence depends on their conforming to a set pattern in almost all aspects of their daily life. Ideally, this wide-ranging compliance is effected by the exercise of purely normative power and by a wholly moral involvement in the process on the part of students. The open model of training, by contrast, requires much more limited and partial compliance on the part of ordinands, extending only to a part of their lives and leaving unregulated the greater proportion of their time. Since the purpose of training, i.e. the satisfactory acquisition of specified capabilities, is so objective, the sense of involvement in the process leading to the final result tends to be predominantly calculative; detachment from training is possible because the goal of training is defined in so detached a way. Concomitantly, the authority responsible for training exercises a power over ordinands which is tinged with only a minimum of normative ideals, for it provides services which the men themselves need in order to complete their training and qualify successfully. The power wielded by the educators may not be remunerative in the literal sense, but it is without emotional overtones and matched to the business-like attitude of its clients.

IMPLICATIONS OF THE TWO MODELS

Now, if these two very different forms of compliance mark the two models of clergy training, we think it impossible that they should not predispose ordinands to adopt markedly different attitudes, when they become clergymen, towards both those under their authority and also those to whom they are responsible. The combination of normative power and moral involvement seems likely to engender a natural respect for authority and generally to be consonant with the Catholic tradition of Church order; while the other combination, of remunerative power and calculative involvement, may be more consistent with the individualism of the Protestant tradition, cultivating an independence which asks for, and gives, obedience only on an *ad hoc* or contractual basis.

The evidence discussed in the last chapter tended to point away from the division between Catholic and Protestant (or catholic and evangelical) traditions, and in a later chapter we shall argue that the distinction between radical and conservative tendencies is of greater importance, and so it may seem inconsistent for us to appeal here to a distinction we call into question elsewhere. The issue is complex, and in order to clarify it we must repeat that the two models of ordination training are not described here because they are important as a pair of models,

but because of the current tendency for the open model to dis-
place the closed; the purpose of delineating each has been to
throw light on this trend. The trend itself, we maintain, is modern and conservative (not to be confused with 'Conservative', or
what another terminology would describe as 'liberal bourgeois'),
and derives its impetus from Protestantism, though it is not
limited to that tradition. It is modern, despite the fact that in
another sense it represents a return to the Anglican pattern of
150 years ago, because the emphasis on the acquisition of a
specialist knowledge and skill, rather than on the transition to a
particular social status, is in keeping with the modernising tendency to appeal to achieved qualities and to denigrate those
which are ascribed. It is conservative because in embracing a
specialist role for the religious professional, and laying stress on
a particular knowledge which is uniquely his own, it disqualifies
the clergyman from his more universalistic role as the man
charged with the tasks of representing the whole community and
passing a religious judgement on every aspect of society and its
culture. It is a tendency, therefore, which has the effect of locking
the ordained minister within the confines of a religious world
with clearly drawn boundaries, and thereby rendering him politically impotent. It derives its impetus from the Protestant tradition because it continues the Reformation struggle to assert the
equality of all men, different in their callings, but with identical
opportunities for salvation and damnation.

FROM THE MODELS TO EMPIRICAL REALITIES

None of the colleges which are studied in depth approximated to
either of the extreme models we have just discussed. All were
residential colleges with some kind of rule, and all allowed a very
substantial amount of freedom to individual students. They were
very far from being identical, however, and, if we describe the
manner in which normative power was exercised, this will bring
out one respect in which Oak Hill again differed from other
colleges; this is a point to which we shall return at the end of the
next chapter.

In most theological colleges in the 1960s, the exercise of normative power was obvious both as exercised from above by the
principals and their staffs, and also in the form of social power

exercised informally within the student body, mostly by the more senior students over their juniors, but also among peers. Conformity to the rules and requirements of the college needed to be explicitly enforced very little. When it did require enforcement, the first sanction applied to a deviant was the disapprobation of his peers; if this failed he incurred the disapproval of more senior students and others outside his immediate circle of friends. In both instances the normative sanctions were of a purely personal kind, consisting, for example, of 'taking the micky' out of the person concerned, for students at few theological colleges would pass judgements based on some form of religious condemnation on their fellow students, for such invoking of religious principles to back up moral judgements was itself strongly disapproved behaviour. It lay open the one making the judgement to the charge of being 'pious' or 'holier than thou' – a heinous crime, since it usurped the form of power reserved to the staff of the college, whose part it was to invoke any further sanctions against a deviant student. 'Friendly advice' was the first treatment to be administered, by the principal or one of his staff, and if that failed to be effective the religiously legitimated authority of the college was formally invoked in censuring the man's conduct.

In practice, a principal only occasionally needed to make his disapproval explicit, but behind this disapproval always lay more than merely normative powers, the use of which was implicitly threatened whenever the purely normative religious authority was invoked. For example, a principal had it in his power to curtail a man's training by recommending that his grant be stopped and removing him from the college, but this was an ultimate weapon and of only immediate application. In the longer term, before the ordinand could leave the college to be ordained, he would need a letter of commendation from the principal to the bishop who was to ordain him, and the threat of the withholding of this acted as a further deterrent. Furthermore, the ordinand was in effect almost wholly dependent on his principal's goodwill in finding a 'title' – the technical ecclesiastical term for the first appointment a curate receives; and, in the still longer term, since Anglican theological colleges tend to be used as clerical labour exchanges, he might well expect to seek a second job, and later a parish of his own, through the good offices of his ex-principal. Thus the principal's 'remunerative' power, his powers to affect an ordinand's future for good or for ill, were so far-reaching, and known to be so by principal and student alike, that the purely normative power exercised by the principal was effective and quite awesome. It was extremely difficult, moreover, for a student to appeal against the judgement of his principal, the ultimate basis of which was his personal judgement on normative criteria.

On a day-to-day basis, order was maintained by the principal's censuring a student when necessary, and in so doing possibly suggesting difficulties which the future might bring. Beyond this the only immediately available power he had was expulsion or the threat of expulsion, but it may be doubted whether this constitutes more effective power than a severe censure in an institution the very existence of which is based on the assumed legitimacy of religious authority. Furthermore, expulsion from a voluntary, normatively based institution is fundamentally disruptive, and indeed often damaging, to the institution itself. In practice, those who leave of their own accord, as well as those who are forcibly ejected, commonly find themselves abused and criticised after their departure, as the organisation re-establishes the strong fabric of its normative structure. The vehemence of the condemnation which often ensues is incomprehensible if one seeks to understand it as as a response of individuals, instead of as the reflex response of a corporate body motivated by the instinct of corporate self-preservation. George Tyrrell clearly understood this when he reflected on the reaction to his leaving the Society of Jesus:

> Corporations and crowds are non-moral agencies, and, judged by the standards of individual ethics, seem to commit atrocious crimes, which, in fact, are no more crimes than the ravages of sea and storm, or of brute passion, or of other natural forces. Every society vomits its deluge of slander upon the seceder whose secession is constructively an act of reprobation. The convert from Anglicanism to Rome or from Rome to Anglicanism; the ex-Jesuit or the ex-Freemason have all to pass through the same baptism of the cloud of suspicion and the Red Sea of slander.   (Petre 1912, vol. II, p. 279)

So, the exercise of normative power in the form of a religious judgement is the severest sanction available to the principal of a theological college. Its seriousness and its possible long-term implications are such that sensitive principals will often temper it with fatherly advice or with good-humoured chaffing, according to personal disposition, rather than administer it neat.

We have said that at most colleges students criticised each other only in ways which did not imply religious condemnation, and that judgements based on religious principles were considered to be in the poorest possible taste and beyond the pale of approved student behaviour. Oak Hill was an exception to this general statement, for this college was characterised by a religious seriousness and an earnest moral tone which itself would have been unacceptable in most colleges, but which allowed Oak Hill students to comment on each other's conduct and religious behaviour without jest and without any embarrassment. A degree of evangelical zeal not only permitted but positively encouraged a sense of mutual responsibility, and in this atmosphere normative pressures were exerted from all sides. Nor did the principal and his staff escape condemnation. Although we did not observe that such condemnation was publicly expressed, it was the only college at which students were heard to pass serious judgements on what were considered to be the principal's culpable faults. It is interesting that the main charge laid against the principal was that of Erastianism, for it throws light on the ethos of the college. Many of the students, and in particular the brighter and more vocal ones, had little concern for the college or for becoming clergymen as such, conceiving themselves as preparing for the activities of evangelism and ministry, to which the status of clergyman was purely incidental; for them, the college existed solely to facilitate this training, and had no intrinsic virtue or reason for existing. Similarly, the Church of England was seen as an institution the justification of which rested entirely on its capacity to 'bring men and women to Christ', and the history and traditions of which were in themselves at best valueless, and at worst a hindrance to the work of the gospel. A principal who expressed a certain respect for the Church of England as such, and who sought to create a sense of pride in membership of his college, was therefore highly suspect, for such concerns could not fail to distract men from the single-minded purposes of their lives, their college, and their Church.

Oak Hill was very like other colleges in outward appearances, but unlike them in the instrumental attitude to it, and to its training which characterised many of its students. A typically strong sense of personal calling to the work of the ministry meant that the authority of the college could have only a limited impact on a student, and that the religious judgement of an individual fellow student could be a potent force. One can imagine that at other evangelical colleges the ethos of mutual criticism among students might, for various reasons, have been more widespread and much more ferocious than at Oak Hill, where it was comparatively mild, but, in displaying this trait at all, Oak Hill was unlike the other colleges we studied at all closely. In view of what we saw of it in the last chapter, its peculiarity in this respect is not surprising, for it stands in a long tradition of puritan enthusiasm.

An institution such as a theological college must necessarily be somewhat precarious in the puritan atmosphere of exclusive concern with salvation, but it is rendered equally precarious elsewhere by an equivalent concern with other extrinsic goals, such as the acquisition of skills in academic theology. We have distinguished closed and open models of training, and it could be argued that a theological college as a distinct institution has a place only within ordination training which tends towards the closed model. The open model, and training which approximates to it, has no need of a separate institution. We suggest that the present trend in training is likely to put the future existence of the colleges in jeopardy, and all the more so as they are compared with effective open schemes of training such as are being devised for the Auxiliary Pastoral Ministry.

THE CAREER OF A COLLEGE

The general shape of ordination training is also subject to pressures of a further kind, for the colleges are institutions which tend to develop purposes of their own which do not always continue to serve the aims for which they were established. When this happens to individual colleges it has its own effect on ordination training as a whole. We shall consider briefly the development of one college, run by the Community of the Resurrection at Mirfield in Yorkshire, by way of illustration. It must be emphasised in the strongest terms that there is nothing unique

about this college's development, and one might as easily have
used another as an example. It was chosen only because it is a
college with which we were familiar.

As was seen in the first chapter, the colleges founded in the
middle of the nineteenth century met what was seen as a need of
the time. By the turn of the century a new need, no less pressing,
was felt, and it was to meet this new need that the College of the
Resurrection was founded, in 1902. Early numbers of the *Quarterly Review* of the Community of the Resurrection, itself founded
only in 1892, made plain how the need was seen and how the
Community proposed to meet it. Charles Gore, the founder and
first superior of the Community, expressed the problem thus (see
above, p. 26; the quotations which follow are from numbers of
the Community's *Quarterly Review* published between 1903 and
1908):

> What I want English churchmen to realise is this – we in the
> Church of England have been for many years sinning a great
> and grievous sin, really stifling . . . the leading of the Holy
> Spirit of God, because . . . we have been making no effort to
> enable men, into whom God was putting the desire of the
> ministry, to realise that desire without great expense which
> was beyond their means.

The problem was to be solved, or a solution was to be attempted,
by the founding of the college, and the policy was quite clear:

> We do not accept and train [students] for whom parents or
> friends can afford the cost of education at University, or at a
> Theological College where payment is required. All are men
> to whom the free training offered by our scheme is essential.

The aim was simple.

The importance of a university course was strongly emphasised, and from the outset it formed an integral part of the training. The Community set itself the task of giving, free of charge, a
training for ordination which should be the peer of the best
available already, and for this it was thought that three years'
reading for a degree was essential. It was an ambitious aim, for
only just over a third of those ordained in 1902–6 had been to

both a university and a theological college:

> We are convinced that the Church requires not only more
> priests, but better priests; we do not advocate what is com-
> monly called the 'seminary system', for we desire our men to
> think for themselves, and we value highly signs of strong indi-
> viduality and independence of thought and character.

The course extended over five years, and at the beginning students were given only a month's holiday each year. In the first
year the men lived in the newly built college at Mirfield and
studied there for the first year of an arts degree at Leeds. (The
College of the Resurrection was made an affiliated college of the
University of Leeds in May 1904, the year in which the university received its charter.) Their second and third years were
spent 12 miles away, in Leeds itself, where they lived in a hostel
while they completed their studies for a degree. Thus, in October
1904 the Hostel of the Resurrection was inaugurated as a university hall of residence which was also an integral part of the
college. Having graduated, the men returned to Mirfield to
spend their two remaining years 'under the direction of the
Superior in a wide and thorough grounding in theology in all its
branches, based on a devout and intelligent study of the Bible'.
The training, which was undertaken by members of the Community and tutors appointed to assist them, also included 'practical work, skilled teaching, mission work, etc.', and so each
student was attached to a parish mission and also addressed a
Men's Bible Class in the area.

The scheme of training got off the ground quickly and in
1904–5 only 18 men could be admitted from among the 100 who
applied. By 1906 there were 46 students; four did not have the
necessary qualifications to begin their degree studies and so were
at Mirfield preparing for university entrance, a further 14 were
at Mirfield reading for the first year of their degree, and 28 were
in Leeds completing their degrees, of whom 6 graduated the
following year. The Community was obviously pleased with the
progress that had been made, and with the number of men
admitted who would otherwise have been debarred from ordination, and from time to time it published breakdowns of the occupations of the fathers of men admitted. In 1907 it was: priests 2,
clerks 4, artisans 5, tradesmen 3, music teachers 2, railway servants 2, relieving officer 1, butler 1.

At first the students studying in Leeds had only temporary accommodation, but work soon began on a permanent building which was to become the Hostel of the Resurrection, and the first part of it was opened on 21 April 1910 by Lady Cavendish in the presence of the vice-chancellors of the universities of Leeds and Manchester. Although the new building gave increased accommodation, the pressure for places was outstripping the college's capacity and in that year only 40 men could be selected from among 400 applicants, and only 11 of the 40 men selected could actually be admitted. This, it was felt, testified to the amount of previously untapped potential, which had been doubted by many writers of memoranda to the Archbishops' Commission, and vindicated the foundation of the college.

With some adjustments, like the adoption of normal vacations in the place of the original month's annual holiday, the whole scheme of the College of the Ressurection had come into successful operation by 1913. The Great War disrupted the college with everything else, but its work was resumed in 1918 and became thoroughly established in the inter-war period. An extra wing was built onto the Leeds hostel and opened in 1928, completing the design, after which the whole period of three years which students took to read for a degree was spent in Leeds.

The college flourished for a few years after the end of the Second World War, and the hostel with it, for many men returned to resume their training after a period of war service, but, with the passing of the 1944 Education Act, the fundamental *raison d'être* of the College of the Resurrection had disappeared. That Act and the related legislation provided the means of free or maintained access to higher education for precisely those men whom the college had been founded to support, and so ordinands, who hitherto would have depended on the Community's scheme of training, became free to read for a degree wherever they chose. The demand for places dropped steeply, and consequently the whole scheme was adjusted in a variety of ways. At the hostel, which was most obviously affected, a number of suitable men who were not ordinands were admitted to residence; not uncommonly, the ones selected were those who had religious sympathies and were thought possible candidates for ordination, though the Community of the Resurrection's characteristic method of encouraging such ideas was always ostentatiously to discourage them.

As the old need was met by State provisions, however, a new

need appeared, and attempting to satisfy it seemed to offer the possibility of filling places at the hostel which otherwise would have gone to non-ordinands. Early in the 1950s the hostel admitted its first students as 'qualifying candidates' (QCs). These were men, usually from working-class homes, who could not qualify for university entrance, and they came to the Hostel to study for GCE examinations, under the guidance of members of the Community and of lay tutors, as an alternative to studying at 'night school'. The intention was that such candidates, once qualified, should proceed as undergraduates, and the scheme was made possible by the funds available now that undergraduates were supported by local education authorities.

The numbers of men from Leeds wishing to go on to the college at Mirfield inevitably dropped, and consequently the college too changed its character as it accepted a higher and higher proportion of graduates from other universities, especially from Oxford and Cambridge, and the original conception of the college and the hostel as a single institution was greatly attenuated. By the time of our studies in the 1960s, the two were sister institutions, though under the authority of a single committee of the Community, and Leeds men who went on to Mirfield were no longer the norm.

With the benefit of hindsight it is possible to see that in the late 1940s the College of the Resurrection, or, more accurately, the Community which ran it, faced a clear choice. The purpose for which the college had been founded disappeared with the 1944 Act. It might either have transformed itself into an ordinary theological college, with its own special ethos and the high prestige it had earned, and disposed of the buildings in Leeds for which it had no further use; or else it might have sought some new need to replace the special purpose it had once served, which it might have found either in the needs of potential ordination candidates abroad, or in the special requirements of the men who were to join the QC scheme. The choice was not seen, however, and the Community fell between not two but three stools, continuing with the college at Mirfield, and with the hostel at Leeds, and extending its work with ordination training in the West Indies and southern Africa. Having become established over a period of forty years, the college appeared to be a necessary institution, and what had been created as a means to achieve a very specific end became an end in itself. The new and meritorious needs at home and abroad, moreover, were ill served by the college's continued existence. In southern Africa, for example, where the Community was doing uniquely valuable work, the importance of which bore comparison with the task discerned by Gore and others in England at the beginning of the century, personnel were not available because they were staffing the college at Mirfield. Because of the persistence of this institution the Community of the Resurrection found itself doing exactly the opposite of what it had set out to do: it had founded the college to fight injustice and privilege and waste, and the continued existence of that college, with a high proportion of men from Oxford and Cambridge and privileged homes, acquiesced in injustice and promoted waste by taking resources which might otherwise have been employed in enabling the dis-privileged to realise their potential.

The problem of ordination training overseas is beyond the scope of this discussion, but at home the QC scheme flourished for a while, and some QCs distinguished themselves in their subsequent university examinations and the scheme was thus vindicated, for there had been those who had suspected that only the incorrigibly stupid would join it. From 1961 to 1968, how-ever, the hostel went from a satisfactory new arrangement, par-tially adapted to contemporary needs, to a manifestly unsatisfac-tory state. First, the QC scheme gradually ceased to operate as originally intended, and, instead of gaining matriculation and going on to the university, an increasing number left with poor qualifications to go as non-graduates to colleges other than Mir-field, which, practically alone among theological colleges for a time, accepted only graduate students. This transformed the QC scheme into one which prepared men for the requirements of study for the General Ordination Examination; it was never intended to serve this purpose and was ill equipped to do so. Secondly, the scheme itself was gradually rendered unnecessary, as the new colleges of further education provided opportunities for men who had missed out at school to qualify for university entrance, and, eventually, as local education authorities made grants to students at colleges of further education. Thirdly, the number of undergraduate ordinands at the hostel dropped, as did the number of QCs, and the proportion of men who had no wish to be ordained was obliged to increase until the hostel became predominantly an ordinary hall of residence of the university as far as its student members were concerned. It had ceased to serve the function of preparing men for the ordained ministry, and finally in 1976 the building was sold to the university, when it became, not inappropriately, the home of the Department of Adult Education and Extra-Mural Studies.

With the steady decline of the hostel, the college lost its immediate associations with the University of Leeds and took students from other universities, but it was subject to other influences as well. For a while it appeared that the old link with Leeds might have been forged afresh, for ACCM ordained that ordinands who were graduates in subjects other than theology should read for a post-graduate university diploma in theology, and a few students from Mirfield were resident at the hostel for a year for this purpose in its last days. The short journey of 12 miles from Mirfield was easily made by road, however, and, before the hostel closed, the college had already found it unnecessary for its men to reside in Leeds.

The insistence by ACCM on university instruction breached the integrity of the college course, however, taking students away from the college and its own facilities, and placing an emphasis on something extrinsic to Mirfield. This moved the Mirfield scheme of training away from the closed model we described above, and towards the open model. The shift was increased in the late 1960s, when the first student was permitted to live with his wife outside the college, becoming, as it were, a 'day boy'. In ensuing years the number of married students increased, until they formed a substantial proportion of the college population. Thereafter the College of the Resurrection was simply one theological college among others, with its own particular character, but no longer serving the purposes for which it was founded.

The fate of this one college was the result, in part, of decisions taken and decisions not taken in the late 1940s, which then worked themselves out with an inevitable logic; in part it was the result of the Church's stress on academic theology; and in part it was the result of the Church's specific decision, for the Community of the Resurrection might well have been willing to close its college at the time of the national reorganisation of theological colleges in the early 1970s, but in ACCM's report and recommendations on the future of colleges it was scheduled to continue.

This leads us to make two impertinent, yet pertinent, observations in conclusion. Following the Second World War the whole situation regarding free higher education in England changed and it is not clear that the Community, if it wanted to continue training priests, should have carried on doing so in England. A strong case could have been made, and doubtless was made within the Community, for ministering in this way to the needs of deprived countries such as those in the West Indies and in southern Africa, since the lot of the educationally deprived classes in English society had been so substantially improved. But, granted that such a decision was not taken, and that the Community resolved to continue its work in England, the implications of the 1944 Education Act should have been apparent to the Community. The need which the college and its associated hostel were established to meet no longer existed, and this quickly became clear as the backgrounds of men embarking on their ordination training there ceased to be deprived, and instead were pious and devout, and merely partisan in religious terms. The QC scheme, on the other hand, inaugurated quite shortly after the War, met a real and an urgent need such as the Community had had in view in 1902. It was to remain a need for 20 years, until not only teaching but also financial support were made available by the State for those wishing to make good educational deficiencies after leaving school. It should have been embraced with all the enthusiasm of an earlier generation for the needs of the deprived. Unlike many other bodies, the Community had at its disposal all that was necessary: the physical plant, long corporate experience in ordination training, funds from which to make grants-in-aid to needy students, some of the personnel who would have been necessary for the teaching and money to employ additional staff. Had it been successful, the scheme would have set a clear precedent for the Church to insist that almost all ordinands should read for a degree, which was another firm conviction of the early members of the Community. Instead, 'pre-theological' schemes, such as those subsequently provided by Brasted Place and the Bernard Gilpin Society, opened the way for young non-graduates to be ordained, many of whom might have read for degrees if they had been given the appropriate training. But by the time the QC scheme had in fact become established the time had almost arrived for it to be closed.

By the middle of the 1960s, with the successful establishment of the Southwark Ordination Scheme in 1963, yet another new need had become clear: that of men wishing to prepare for ordination while continuing to work in secular occupations. Again the Community had at its disposal to a unique degree the necessary resources. It had buildings in the centre of a large industrial conurbation, it had experience, and it had capital donated for the express purpose of training for ordination men who otherwise might be prevented. Perhaps the Church authorities preferred an alternative scheme, but in any event the resources were not used for this purpose.

If a Yorkshire centre for training men for the Auxiliary Pastoral Ministry were, quite naturally, to find a home in Leeds University's Department of Adult Education, the old Hostel of the Resurrection, it would be ironic indeed.

CONCLUSION

The College of the Resurrection is no more than one example of the general trend in ordination training in the Church of England since the Second World War. We have described the trend, which is still continuing, as one which takes colleges away from a closed model of training and towards an open model. The combined effect of studies pursued outside a college, and men living out of college with their families, is that the centre of gravity in their training is no longer firmly within the college. This is seen nowhere more clearly than at Mirfield, where the pattern had been of a close, and relatively closed, family. It may be thought that the best of the old ways can be preserved and enriched by new developments, but we doubt whether the old pattern of college life can survive more than rare and exceptional breaches in its integrity. A principal's relationship to his students is wholly changed when instead of living together continuously as a tightly knit group a proportion of the students come into college as a businessman goes into the office; the guidance and instruction which comes naturally from the father of a family comes ill from the professor who heads a college. It is not unlike the changes experienced at Oxford and Cambridge colleges as increasing numbers of fellows chose to live out with their families, and to work at home, coming into college to teach and occasionally to dine.

We do not wish to say that the changes are bad. We wish to say only that they are very important changes which will have far-reaching consequences. In a predominantly open form of ordination training the theological colleges will play a radically different role; their place in the lives of ordinands will be much less central, and the colleges' main duty will be to co-ordinate training. Beyond that, however, as we have argued in this chapter, the changes may have profound implications for the whole conception of the ordained ministry and its future development.

6 The Training Process

We have seen something of the backgrounds from which men came to train for the Anglican ministry in the 1960s. We have seen how they came to be selected and to select themselves; we have seen some of the major variations amongst these ordinands; and we have seen a little of the kind of college in which the training takes place. But in what, precisely, does the training consist? We know that the men go in as laymen and come out as clergymen, but in just what ways do they change in the course of their training in terms of attitudes, values and so on? It was in order to attempt some answer to these questions that we took the group of about a hundred students who were about to enter theological college in 1966 and talked to them before they embarked on training and then at intervals of six months over the next two years. These hundred men were to have been the intake at five theological colleges in October 1966, but in the event only 80 arrived at college. The reasons of the other 20 for going in other directions were various, but since they were never interviewed a second time there was no opportunity to probe their accounts of their choices to go elsewhere.

What would one have expected to find happening over this period of two years? Well, the process to which the men are subjected is one of socialisation. Robert Merton, we have seen, has described socialisation (1957b, p. 287) as 'the process by which people selectively acquire the values and attitudes, the interests, skills and knowledge – in short, the culture – current in the groups of which they are, or seek to become, a member. It refers to the learning of social roles.' Thus, the doctor, for example, must learn in medical school not only to practise complex medical skills, but also to practise them within an even more complex network of social expectations. But is this still true of the clergyman, for whom there is no core of essential skills to be mastered? It is true that every theological college offers instruction in theology to the minimum level required to pass the General Ordination Examination, but, as we have argued above, it is not possible to maintain convincingly that theology is the necessary professional knowledge of the clergy (pp. 46 f). So we conclude that ordination training is simply socialisation for a new role. An exhaustive account of the various ways in which students change in the course of training would require a large number of biographies, but some of the more salient aspects of the process became clear in the course of our research. We assume, it will be noted, that what we called the closed model of training is the salient one in the Church of England, for the movement away from it has only been suggested here.

The bishops bear the ultimate responsibility for training men for ordination, as well as for selecting them and ordaining them, but the first responsibility is delegated to the theological colleges and their principals; so it is the colleges which are the agents of such changes as take place. Since, however, the students themselves also train and influence each other, it will be more helpful to view the theological college as a socialising 'milieu'. Within this milieu the student is exposed to two main sources of formative influence. The first is the official influence exerted by the college, and this itself acts in two separate ways. As a group, the staff under the principal are responsible for the teaching given at the college, for lectures and tutorials in theoretical subjects and for instruction in more practical matters. As individuals, however, they also fulfil the important function of acting as models or examples of priesthood, for they provide the group from which a student may select a 'significant other' on whom to model himself in the transition from layman to clergyman, and to whom he may refer his emergent image of himself as a clergyman. We have seen already (above, pp. 71 ff) that particular clergy known personally to the students have played an important part in the process of occupational choice; now once more it is particular clergy who are significant in the socialisation into clerical status (Mead 1934; cf. Merton 1957a, p. 302, and Hadden 1969, p. 213).

The second source of formative influence in the socialising milieu of the college is the student body. Students support each other through the gradual process of redefinition, and this group to which they belong represents the only source of roles which are unchanging while all others are in a state of transition; in other words, the student group acts as an agent of change in so far as shifts in self-identification are mutually reinforced, but at the same time it acts also as a reassuring membership group which makes the complex transition easier by remaining a centre of stability while all else is in a state of flux. This dual role of the group of college peers in the socialisation process is seen in the alternately serious and self-mocking ways in which, corporately, they view their approaching clerical status. Sometimes they take it very seriously and regard the future which lies before them with reverence and awe and humility. But these are relatively private sentiments, articulated publicly only in the formality of corporate devotion and worship, and although they are recognised it is the other side of the coin that shows in everyday conversation, where only the humorous aspects of doing something so outrageous as becoming a parson are likely to find expression. So the talk in theological colleges for the most part is irreverent and ribald banter, and often downright obscene, though visitors are spared the display of such impropriety. In some ways this levity is no more than a silly juvenile game in which all vie with each other to be 'unholier than thou'. In other ways, however, it is a necessary and healthy device whereby the men are preserved, or rather preserve themselves, from developing an oppressive over-earnest intenseness and sanctimoniousness; and it serves as a safety-valve to let off the steam which is inevitably generated in the confined space of an all-male community of ordinands.

Colleges vary, of course, and, while the obvious differences between them derive from differences in churchmanship, educational background, age and marital status of the students, there is a wider divergence in ethos which derives from this ironic aspect of the college culture. It can assume very different forms, and it is conspicuously absent from some colleges. The earnestness of the evangelical tradition, for instance, militates strongly against it in any form. The puritan will strive to extend the sober zeal of his devotions to every aspect of his daily life, so the evangelical college is marked by a kind of dull ardour in which the gravity of the men's calling is never allowed to be forgotten, but in which the unrelieved seriousness unavoidably shades into a rather strained and attenuated piety (see above pp. 101 & 133–4). The variations between evangelical colleges, therefore, tend to be theological only, some being more conservative than others, some more scholarly and some stridently evangelistic. The other colleges also differ theologically, of course, but they differ in other ways as well, and in ways which change from generation to generation.

The effects on training of these diffuse differences in ethos are impossible to chart. They operate in subtle ways. We should argue, however, that there is a major division between the evangelical colleges and the others, marked by the absence, in the more puritanical tradition, of the humorous, self-mocking aspect of the student's attitude to his forthcoming ordination.

The gradual shift from lay to clerical status as men pass through their theological colleges is further facilitated by the way in which colleges are stratified into groups of increasing seniority. In the Catholic seminary, as we have noted, the journey from layman to priest is marked by numerous *rites de passage*, moving from minor to major seminary, wearing different clothes, having different holidays, and being admitted to the various minor orders of ministry. But even the brief two years of Anglican training in the 1960s was capable of generating its own graduated structure. As well as the junior and senior years, in the latter of which more time is spent in practical training and instruction in pastoral and liturgical matters, the students are aware of the next generation of students, whom they see when they visit the college for interviews, and of the preceding generation, who often return for brief visits as newly ordained priests. This structure brings home to the student the fact that he is himself in transition from one state to another, and introduces a pattern of change into what would otherwise be a lengthy period of limbo in which he is no longer a layman but not yet a clergyman.

THE ORDINAND'S PERCEPTION OF HIS TRAINING

The man newly arrived at his college, or eagerly waiting to enter it, has relatively few opinions about the training on which he is about to embark. When they were asked for their views the ordinands were reticent, but beneath the reticence general attitudes were divided. The majority of them approached their college experience with a degree of submissiveness. They felt that the choice to be ordained had not yet finally been made and that the period of training would crystallise the decision. For these men entry into a theological college amounted to more than starting a training programme. It was to be an experience in its own right which might lead to any one of a number of outcomes, of which ordination was only the main one. It was natural that ordinands who approached their training with this attitude should be somewhat submissive, for they were waiting to see whether their decision to offer themselves for ordination would be confirmed, and trying to find out more clearly just what it might involve. We should not wish to exaggerate their uncertainty about ordination, but on the other hand it is important to recognise that some of the men entering their theological colleges did not feel that they had made an irrevocable decision, but, rather felt that they were approaching that vital choice. (To enter theological school before having attempted to make a decision about ordination is quite normal in American Protestant denominations, partly because the course leads to a qualification of value in itself; but this is unusual elsewhere [Dittes 1964].)

A sizable minority of the men about to enter training displayed no sign of humility or submissiveness in the face of the course of training. There is more than a grain of truth in the caricature of the red-faced Yorkshireman who announces bluntly that he is 'getting out of wool to go into the Church'. For those who are unshakably certain about ordination and think that they know what it will entail, the course at theological college is seen as rather like getting a couple of GCE subjects at 'A' level. Some of the older men in our group had this attitude, and for them the state of certainty had been a necessary condition for giving up a secure and well paid job. Some younger men, whose ideas had already assumed a dogmatic form, viewed ordination training as a chore to be got through as quickly as possible or even as an irritating delay to be suffered with as good a grace as they could muster. For the students who enjoyed this complete certainty and self-confidence the study of theology was the main part of training. Two years at college was going to afford a useful chance to learn.

Asked at this very early stage before they had begun training, 'Do you think that in general the content of the theological college course is all right?', the average response was one of satisfaction (Table 20). The men about to enter one of the five colleges concerned, and only one of them—St Chad's—were more critical, which is easily explained by the fact that they had already been ordinary undergraduate students of the college for three years and were therefore in a position to have heard the comments of older students in the postgraduate section of the college. Those students who subsequently proved to be of the puritan type discussed in Chapter 4 were a little less critical than the average and those of the antipuritan type a little more. A year later and then again two years after that the men were asked the same question, and they expressed greater dissatisfaction on each occasion, becoming more critical as their training progressed, in a continuous and uniform way. The two types of ordinand, however, continued to stand out quite clearly throughout, with the puritan type never becoming more than very moderately dissatisfied with his training, while the antipuritans finished their course extremely critical of it.

The adverse opinion expressed by this group of men is shared by other ordinands. In 1967 we examined the attitudes of a sample of men in training for the ministries of the several denominations which have colleges at Cambridge, under the auspices of the Cambridge Theological Colleges' Union. The answers there to the same question were almost exactly the same as the average of the replies at the five Anglican colleges over the three years of our study.

Of what were the students critical? And what does the criticism signify? Earlier in our studies we asked a much larger sample of ordinands to evaluate the usefulness of 12 separately named subjects which might have been included in their studies. As might be expected, this exercise was of only limited value, and one principal has subsequently commented that since almost none of his students had known what was meant by dogmatic theology they were unlikely to have known whether they would have preferred to be taught more of it or less. Following up leads from this earlier study, two points did, however, emerge as important. There was a general feeling among the ordinands that not enough attention was given to the relevant application of sociology and psychology; and, at a more general level, there was an almost universal feeling that more time should be devoted to practical training in the form of field courses, and less to purely academic studies. Some students favoured spending during their training a prolonged period, of months rather than weeks, on the staff of a parish church, but, although this desire for more practical activities was very widespread, the attitude of students to such activities as were provided already was distinctly ambivalent. They approved of them in principle and deplored both the limited range offered and the small amount of time devoted to them; but on the other hand the activities themselves were greeted with something less than enthusiasm when they actually occurred. This suggests that, while the ordinands feel the need to train for practical skills, they are at the same time unclear what skills might be appropriate. The experience of ordination training as being unsatisfactory, taken together with the absence of ideas for directions of change, underlines a point we have made already – namely, that the clergy are uneasy about having no practical role to play in society. So it is to the general attitudes of ordinands to the ministry that we turn next.

TOWARDS REALISTIC IDEAS

To say that the ministry in the 1960s was going through a period of change sounds like a cliché, but like many clichés it needs saying, for obviously it is significant for the training of new clergy. One might reasonably expect that the period of training, in these circumstances, would be one in which ordinands came to grips with the changes which were taking place and worked out their own ideas with regard to them.

In the 1950s the clergyman who worked outside the structure of the parochial ministry, with its incumbents and curates, though not a rarity, was comparatively inconspicuous; in the 1960s, however, much was said, informally, about specialist ministries, so it is strange that the widespread discussion about the future of the ministry going on at the time (see, for example, CA no. 1640, and Ellison 1968) should have paid so little attention to this aspect of the possible changes. In the recent past the parochial clergy, secure in their freehold, had laid great stress on their autonomy and there was little co-operation between neighbouring parishes (see below, p. 182). It is true that parishes were organised into deaneries, each with its own chapter, but in practice the deanery counted for very little and the trend in the 1960s was towards fewer beneficed clergy and more curates. Many clergy found themselves with jobs carrying much more responsibility than falls to the lot of the average curate, but without the security of tenure furnished by the traditional benefice. In the period from 1959 to 1968, for instance, the ratio of incumbents to curates fell from 3·5 : 1 to 2·8 : 1, which was a decline of nearly 20 per cent in only eight years (Table 21). On the positive side, the distinction between incumbents and curates was being rendered somewhat obsolete by the proliferation of curates-in-charge where once there had been incumbents, and so, gradually, the whole structure was becoming more fluid. A change which received much less attention was the increase in the numbers of men working outside this framework, either as 'auxiliaries', i.e. clergy who followed mainly secular occupations, or as chaplains in hospitals, educational establishments, industry, and so on. Over the same period of ten years the number of these men outside the parochial ministry had increased by nearly 60 per cent; and these changes were taking place at a time when, as we have seen, there was already evidence of a steady decline in church membership and attendance. Some in the Church saw the various changes in the ministry as ways of coming to grips with the situation. Others resented the changes and maintained that they would weaken the Church rather than strengthen it, arguing that what was needed was redoubled pastoral and evangelistic effort and greater personal holiness. We asked the men for their views on this matter and found that just over half favoured new approaches, most of the remainder seeing greater faithfulness within the existing set-up as preferable to innovation, and a few being uncertain. Moreover, opinions changed very little during the two years of training. After two years the same proportions looked for change through reforms, or for faithfulness to traditional patterns, as at the beginning of training, and, of the 70 men who were interviewed on three occasions, 50 held to their original view.

If ordinands were divided in their evaluations of the way in which the ministry was organised in the 1960s, they did no more than reflect opinions in the Church at large. A specific step lies ahead of the ordinand, however, for every individual clergyman has to work out how to conduct himself, regardless of the organisational structure within which he works. We have referred on a number of occasions to the several components of the clergyman's role, and have used Samuel Blizzard's list of the aspects of whole complex: teacher, organiser, preacher, administrator, priest and pastor. One point of interest is the distinction between the traditional roles which are backed by religious legitimation, and the more functional roles involved in the running of a parish, which are invested with no specifically religious meaning (see above pp. 109–13). This distinction has been treated as one which appears in two conflicting orders of priorities, for there is a functional order of priorities which is imposed by the man's situation in the organisation, and contrasted with it is a normative order of priorities which the religious tradition seems to demand. Both Sklare (1955), for Jewish rabbis, and Blizzard, for Protestant clergy, have argued that training for the ministry tends to inculcate the normative ordering of roles and to disparage the functional order of priorities. Both have drawn the conclusion that theological schools are systematically unfitting men for the active ministry, with the result that once they get into parishes they experience a chronic conflict between ideas and expectations into which they have been socialised and those which must obtain in the practical situation. As we have already noted, our findings do not support this theory. On the contrary, they point in quite another direction. At the beginning, in the middle and again at the end of their training we asked the men to rate each component of the clerical role for its importance, and Figure 14 shows how their responses fell along a continuum of attitudes at the beginning and at the end of their training. Both before and after training, the separation between the merely functional components of the role and those with religious significance is clearly apparent. What is less expected, however, is the way in which the importance attached to every one of the components increases over the period under review. All the increases except that for the 'priest' component are statistically significant and those for the 'organiser' and 'administrator' components are significant beyond the ·001 level. But the most interesting feature of the changes is that, while the normative components of the role, i.e. as teacher, preacher, priest, and pastor, are accorded greater importance at the end than at the beginning, the functional components, i.e. as organiser and administrator, enjoy an even greater increase in the importance ascribed to them. The result is that the gap between the two sets of role components narrows very considerably in the course of training. The general implication would seem to be that training reinforces the normative ideals of the ministry with which an ordinand begins training, but also that it mitigates the low evaluation of non-normative functions.

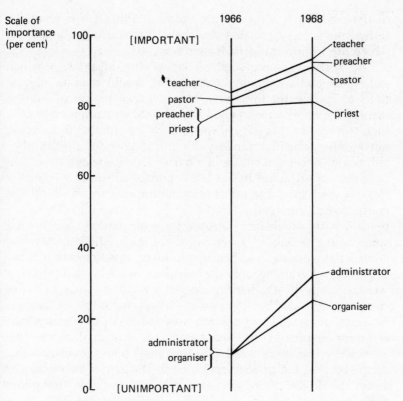

FIGURE 14   Importance of six role components

NB. In 1966 the top four components, on average, were rated as 7·5 times more important than the bottom two; in 1968 they were rated as only 3 times more important.

We suggest that ordination training, in this respect at least, develops in the ordinand a greater realism about the actual exigencies of life as a clergyman. Pure idealism, in other words, is tempered by an awareness that ideals have to be pursued in the context of running a church, with all the mundane responsibilities which that entails. This is to put a favourable interpretation on the changes, of course, which might be taken to indicate no more than that the men become reconciled to activities which they continue to judge as trivial and unpleasant. We favour the former interpretation, however, and see it as evidence that in the course of training an ordinand becomes more wedded to the traditional ideals of the ordained ministry while at the same time recognising that they have their unromantic aspects which are important in their own way.

The little we have seen so far of the ideas with which ordinands embark upon their training would tend to suggest that, to start with, they have only a vague notion of what is involved in being a clergyman. If this is so, we cannot expect the men to know at this stage if they might eventually opt for a job outside the parochial ministry, for it is almost certain that they will begin by being a curate in a parish. Nevertheless, the extent to which an ordinand has at least thought of working in one of the so-called specialist ministries, the importance of which was conspicuously increasing in the 1960s, is some measure of the realism with which he is approaching ordination. Mentioning some of the possibilities, we asked the men whether they had considered working in a specialist ministry and found that at the beginning of training only 24 had done so. After a year there were still only 26 who had considered it at all seriously, but after two years 51 said they thought it was a possibility. Of the possibilities mentioned, a chaplaincy in a university or school occurred most frequently, and four men spoke of it on all three occasions when they were asked. The next most popular option was a chaplaincy in the prison service or in the armed services, and again there were those who saw it as a possibility throughout their training. Immediately before ordination 14 men were thinking of some kind of educational chaplaincy, and 12 of a job in prisons or the services. The only other specialism mentioned at all frequently was the religious life, but no one persisted in this interest over the three years of the study.

The time spent at theological college results, then, in a certain realism entering into the ideas and plans of ordinands. In particular, they see the importance of routine duties of administration and organisation by the time they are nearing ordination, and a majority have at least given serious thought to the possibility of working in a specialist ministry after their first curacy. These are quite minor changes of view, however, and we should expect to find them simply because of the passage of time and the imminence of ordination. More interesting are those changes which may indicate that men are accommodating their ideas to what they think is normal for clergy. Such changes would indeed count as socialisation into the role of a clergyman, and it is to three areas of potential socialisation that we now turn.

TOWARDS APPROPRIATE ATTITUDES

The first area of interest is the involvement of the clergy in social affairs. We asked the men what they understood by the expression the 'social implications of the gospel', to make sure that they understood us to be interested in social involvement which was religiously motivated or which had religious significance, and then asked whether they thought that these social implications of the gospel were very important. At the beginning of training, 49 per cent thought them very important, 41 per cent fairly important, and 10 per cent of no importance. Their views gradually shifted in the course of their training, following a consistent but not dramatic pattern whereby both pros and cons gave place to a middle position: after two years 35 per cent thought the social implications of the gospel very important, 68 per cent thought them fairly important, and 7 per cent unimportant. Cautious support for social action in the name of religion would seem to be what theological-college training leads men to accept, unless, perhaps, what they would like to accept, is cautious social action. Caution on controversial issues would certainly appear to be a fair-enough way of characterising the Church of England, which has always favoured the avoidance of excess; and certainly these figures would support the view that training for ordination produces men whose over-interest or under-interest in social matters has been curbed, and who for the most part favour moderation.

Social concern, of course, can mean almost anything. In asking about politics we ventured into an explosive area, requiring in a man the kind of concern which is not afraid to be partisan. We asked, 'Do you think the clergy ought to involve themselves in politics?', and before asking that question we had already asked, 'How interested would you say you were in politics?' Figure 15 plots with a dotted line the degree of interest in politics which the students felt to be right for clergy, at three points during their training, and it shows with a continuous line the mean level of their own interest in politics which they expressed. There is not a great deal of variation; the most interesting point is that the ordinands consistently rate the level of political involvement proper for clergy as being higher than their own political interest, but that the gap narrows during training, so that their self-image at the end of training approximates more closely to what they think of as the norm for clergy than it did at

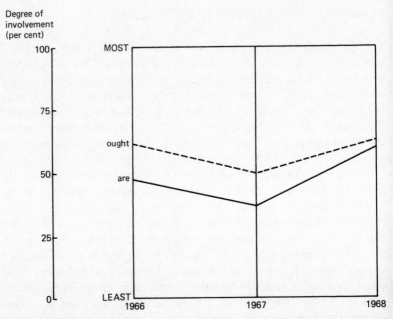

Degree of
involvement
(per cent)

FIGURE 15   'How involved *ought* clergy to be in politics?' and 'How interested
are you in politics?'

the beginning. Furthermore, the decline after one year, followed by an increase after another year, also calls for some
explanation. In the most general terms we should suggest that
the answer lies in the rather academic quality of ordination
training. The colleges are staffed by clergy who are qualified in
theology, doctrine, church history and so on, or else by men
thought to be good at teaching pastoral skills, and so the atmosphere created is one of scholarship and devotion. The politically
minded clergyman would be unlikely to find his way to a job on
the staff of a theological college. The general pattern conveyed
by Figure 15 masks certain important differences between the
individual colleges. Since these separate patterns help to shed
more light on the processes which we believe to be at work they
are presented in Figure 16. Looking first at the extent to which
the ordinands believe that clergy ought to be involved in politics,
Mirfield's different pattern is immediately striking. At each of
the other colleges (Queen's, Birmingham, is omitted, since it
provided too few students for the sample to be represented sep-

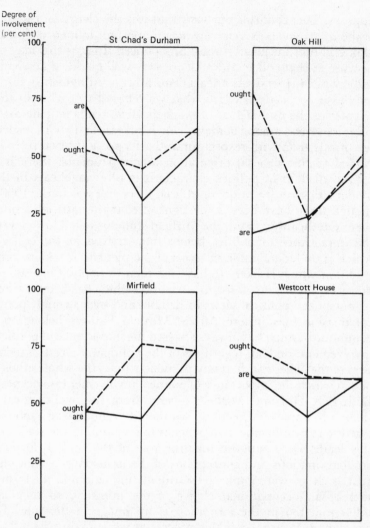

FIGURE 16 'How involved *ought* clergy to be in politics?' and 'How interested *are* you in politics?' – by college

arately) the level falls after one year. If we remember that the initial interviews were almost all conducted prior to entry into college, we see that the effect of nearly a year of training is to make ordinands attach less importance to the involvement of clergy in politics, except at Mirfield, where the reverse effect appears. This confirms our view that it is the clergy on the staff of the college who exercise the most important influence. It is at Oak Hill that the effect is most pronounced. In part this may be because at that college the staff are very well qualified academically, while the students are academically undistinguished, but it may also be partly because what we referred to earlier in this chapter as the dull ardour of evangelicalism tends to generate a submissiveness among students which has less to do with respect for priests than with respect for authority *per se* (but cf. p. 133). Added to this general orientation among students, there is a certain disdain of politics characteristic of evangelicals in the modern English tradition; or at least there still was in the 1960s, though there have been some signs of changing attitudes since then. On the other hand, the Mirfield students had a low view of the importance of politics before they arrived at the college, which is understandable in terms of the pietistic Anglo-catholic tradition which is likely to have led men to apply. Once there, however, they are exposed to a tradition which has been marked by outspoken political views in Britain, and by a strongly political mission in southern Africa. Mirfield Fathers belong to a community which has always stressed the importance of political involvement, and so, regardless of the political interest of members of the college staff at any particular time, the whole ethos is one in which the importance of political involvement is accepted. Both Oak Hill and Mirfield diverge from the overall means, though in opposite directions; we should argue that in each college the reason for the divergence is to be found in the staff, and this leads us to suppose that the role of the staff in forming student opinions and conceptions of the ministry is a vital one. Just as clergy were found to be strongly influential in the formation of an occupational choice of the ministry, so they are influential too in the formation of an image of the role of a clergyman. We shall see this process at work again presently.

If we turn to the level of interest in politics professed by the students, we find a pattern among the colleges which is not entirely dissimilar, but the exception is Oak Hill. After a year at any of the other colleges a student claims a lesser degree of interest in politics than he had before the start of training, and after a further year his interest increases again, approximating to the level of involvement he thinks right for the clergy. The Oak Hill student has a spectacular disinterest in political matters before training, and at the same time thinks that the clergy ought to be politically involved. After a year his interest rises somewhat, and coincides with a drastically revised view of what is proper for clergy; and after a further year both his own interest and his image of what is right for the clergy increase so that both become moderate. The pattern is an interesting one, but the feature we should suggest as most significant is the convergence, in the course of training, between what the student thinks a clergyman ought to do and what he himself feels inclined towards, in the matter of political interest.

The clergy may be poor, as we have remarked, but they enjoy an elevated position in the class structure even in modern Britain (see below, p. 182). We shall not embark on the question of the social class to which the clergy belong, for it would raise complex issues of definition which are irrelevant to the present discussion. What is highly relevant, however, is the prestige which these students may confidently expect when they emerge as clergymen. For the great majority, mentioned above (pp. 79–80), the new respect in which they will find themselves held will be quite marked, and it is interesting to know whether the two years of ordination training is a period of gradual redefinition, and whether on average they emerge thinking of themselves as belonging to a 'higher social class' than when they entered training. In fact the changes among the group of men whom we were studying were not particularly striking. Both before training and after, one quarter of the men said that they were 'working class'. Encouraged to use the crude labels of upper-middle and lower-middle class, the remainder of the men shifted their self-definition in the direction one would expect, the proportion saying that they were lower-middle class falling from 45 to 33 per cent, and therefore the proportion saying that they were upper-middle class rising by the same margin, from 30 to 42 per cent. The shift is noticeable and in the direction one would predict, but it is not spectacular.

There is some slight evidence, then, that ordination training turns out men who have, to a degree, been socialised into the new role in society which they are to occupy. But we doubt whether these changes which have been reported amount to something which may properly be called professional socialisation. For example, the quarter of the men who persisted in thinking of themselves, or at least in advertising themselves, as being working class are expressing an attitude which is unaffected by training. Or again, the convergence towards a middle view in the importance men attach to the social implications of the gospel may equally well be interpreted as the product of maturation as of socialisation. We do not wish to ignore the signs of convergence, however, and the way in which the gap between personal interest in politics and perception of what is normal for clergy narrowed over a period of two years is certainly worth remarking.

CHANGES IN RELIGIOUS VIEWS

Theological colleges exist, by title at least, to teach theology. Obviously this is only one part of their job, although we have seen that they came into being largely in response to changes in the educational system in the nineteenth century. The theology taught in the colleges up until the 1960s was a strange animal, however, which stood in a peculiar relationship to the theology taught in the universities, for the processes to which we referred in the last chapter had at that time not begun to make themselves felt. Unlike the Greek Orthodox Church, most of whose theologians are laymen, the churches of the West expect their theologians to be clergymen. And, what is more important here, they expect their clergymen to be theologians. Not all clergy are scholars, however, and still fewer are scholars with a penchant for theology, so the theology which was taught in the theological colleges as a basic requirement stood in relation to academic theology in somewhat the same way as New Testament Greek does to classical Greek. Theology of this kind, now as in the 1960s, is the medium through which are expressed the range of religious opinion and the entrenched positions of religious debate.

The bishops of the Church of England, as the ultimate authority which lies behind ordination training, require a student's knowledge of theology to be examined, and this is done by means of the General Ordination Examination. The progress a man makes in grasping the elements of theology, which is the only thing examined in a way open to inspection, is the one change in which we are not interested. It is the changes which take place in his religious views which concern us. The 1960s were a time when people talked of the 'new theology'. J. A. T. Robinson's *Honest to God* was published in 1963 and the row which ensued did much to bring further into prominence the writings of Bultmann, Bonhoeffer, Buber and others. Radical questioning of the literal truth of scripture and doctrine was nothing new in academic theology, nor were the writings of these scholars at all unknown. Radical theology, however, had begun to enjoy a popularity in the 1960s outside the charmed circle of university theologians. *Honest to God*, as a result of the publicity given to it by the mass media, boosted this rising popularity, and the movement, if that is what it was, culminated with the 'death-of-God theology'. Every religious controversy hits the clergy first, and hits them hardest, and the debate of the 1960s was no exception to this rule. It hit them first because it was of 'professional' concern to them. Academic theologians were familiar with the issues already, and the general public got wind of the debate only slowly; but the clergy, having been trained in a certain amount of theology, were quick to take an interest. It hit them hardest because it affected theological positions they had worked out for themselves and because it was to them that the laity looked for guidance. By the same token, these were matters of vital importance to ordinands. As we said above, the period of training is one when men may work out where they stand on issues. We asked the men the deliberately vague question, 'What do you think of the "new theology"?' and recorded their responses as either disagreement, agreement, or strong agreement. Before they entered college, 48 per cent disagreed with it, 17 per cent agreed, and 35 per cent agreed strongly. During training their opinions became gradually more favourable, and after two years only 25 per cent disagreed, 17 per cent agreed, and 58 per cent agreed strongly. (Table 24.) As one would expect, there was considerable variation between colleges. Oak Hill was the only college to which men went with an overwhelming weight of opinion in one direction, 80 per cent of its entrants saying that they 'disagreed'; the views of men going to the other colleges were very mixed. After two years, however, more than 80 per cent of the men at both Mirfield and Westcott House said that they strongly agreed with the new theology, and even at Oak Hill the hostility was much less marked, though still clearly apparent.

The main characteristic of the 'new theology' was its undogmatic, often anti-dogmatic, quality. Therefore, to say that one disagreed with it implied holding traditional beliefs and not being interested in newfangled ideas from which one judged that nothing but ill could come, and, conversely, agreement signified a willingness to question the meaning of beliefs rather than readiness to deny them. Of course, the new theology did involve certain denials for many of those who entertained it: for example, the resurrection and ascension of Jesus were regarded by many not as necessarily physical facts, but rather as a figurative way of expressing the belief that Jesus had triumphed over his enemies, instead of having been overcome by them, and was united with God. Because this openness to questioning and doubt is so central to the new theology, we should expect to find it sympathetically regarded by those men with an antipuritan type of vocation and very unsympathetically by puritans, for flexibility is one of the defining characteristics of the division. This was indeed so, the antipuritans being some five times more sympathetic than the puritans. Moreover, in the course of training the antipuritan group became even more favourably disposed towards the new theology, though we must see this in the context of a general shift in the same direction. Many who were opposed when they entered training, or at least lukewarm in their support, came to see something good in the movement simply because they learned more about it.

We have said that 'agreement' with the new theology did not imply a rejection of the traditional tenets of the Christian religion. This point can be underlined from our study, for, although the level of agreement with the new theology rose consistently on average over the two years of training the importance attached to four traditional doctrines did not follow a similarly simple pattern. The doctrines we selected were belief in the virgin birth of Christ, the bodily ascension, the inspiration of scripture, and the bodily resurrection of Christ, and we asked the ordinands to say whether each of these beliefs was for them very important, important, or not very important. After the first year of training they attached less importance, relatively, to these beliefs, but after a further year they again regarded them as being important. (Scoring the responses 0, 1, and 2, and scaling the mean scores from conservative to radical as 0 to 100, sympathy with the new theology went from 44 to 52 to 63 over two years, while importance of the four beliefs went from 43 to 35 to 48.) While the second year saw a further increase in sympathy for the new theology, it also saw a renewed importance being attached to these traditional beliefs. It would appear that what the men were doing over their two years in training was coming to appreciate the value of the ideas and intellectual attitudes embraced by what is called radical theology, while at the same time seeing the importance of traditional symbols of belief, albeit interpreted anew. This is hardly a simple process, and there is reason to think that those who are most intimately acquainted with modern theological ideas feel most acutely the gap between themselves and the laity, who, if they were privy to the mind of the theologians, would think that the new theology was very radical and suspect. Thus, in our inquiry at the Cambridge theological colleges of all denominations we found that there was a significant difference between the men who were reading theology in the university's Divinity School and those who were pursuing their studies, presumably at a somewhat lower level, within their denominational colleges. We asked them, 'How radical do you imagine you would be thought by an average group of laymen of your own denomination were they to know your views?', and, while 74 per cent of the Divinity School students said that they thought they would be considered radical or very radical, only 39 per cent of the others gave the same answer; while, conversely, only 9 per cent of the Divinity School students said they would be thought to be conservative or very conservative by the imaginary group of laymen, compared with 23 per cent of the others. Doubt and open-mindedness is clearly a complicated affair. It is difficult for someone to entertain ideas which entail a reformulation of traditional religious beliefs and at the same time maintain the importance of those beliefs, and the difficulty is nowhere more apparent than in the relationship between clergy and laity.

One of the chapters in Robinson's *Honest to God* is entitled 'The New Morality'. At the risk of oversimplifying, one might say that the major issue at stake was whether, for the Christian, there are absolute, universal moral precepts such as, 'Thou shalt not lie with mankind, as with womankind: it is an abomination' (Leviticus xviii 22), or whether there are only moral principles such as, 'Thou shalt love the Lord thy God . . . and thy neighbour as thyself', which the individual has to apply to particular situations as they arise. It is probably fair to say that as one absolute prohibition after another has dropped out of the general consciousness, and out of the law of the land, the case has become stronger for saying that such universal proscriptions have no validity. We asked the ordinands one question about morality, 'Do you think that sexual relations outside marriage are always wrong?' Before training, 58 per cent said yes, after one year 46 per cent, and after two years 43 per cent. The general pattern of change is towards a more open attitude in morality. As would be expected, there were marked discrepancies between various sub-groups. Only 29 per cent of the anti-puritan group said, when they were first questioned, that they thought sexual relations outside marriage always wrong, and by the end of training the proportion had dropped to 16 per cent; but 86 per cent of the puritans said yes in answer to the question and the proportion did not fall over time. Agreement at Oak Hill was more solid and more immovable still.

Before examining the possible implications of these patterns, there is one other issue which may usefully be considered, and that is the matter of 'churchmanship'. We invited students to identify themselves with one of six labels: Anglo-catholic, Prayer Book catholic, central Churchman, modernist, liberal evangelical, and conservative evangelical. Many did so only with very great reluctance, as we have already noted (see above, pp. 107–9), which confirms the general impression at the time that party labels were of declining importance. What is interesting for our purposes is the question of whether the theological colleges tend to diminish the importance of these differences, or whether they help to keep alive distinctions which otherwise would die out more rapidly. The colleges certainly attracted distinctive groups. Most of the men going to St Chad's said they were Prayer Book catholics; most of the Oak Hill students were conservative evangelicals; Mirfield men were either Anglo-catholic or Prayer Book catholic; those going to Westcott identified themselves predominantly as central Churchmen, with some Prayer Book catholics and some Anglo-catholics. It would be no distortion to say that St Chad's, Oak Hill, and Mirfield were party colleges. (It should be noted that some 'party colleges' were chosen deliberately, so that the range of churchmanship represented in this small, non-probability sample should approximate to the whole population of the theological colleges.) But what happens to these self-definitions in the course of two years of training? At the

catholic St Chad's and Mirfield there was little change, and at
Westcott there was a tendency for more men to identify themselves as central Churchmen. At Oak Hill, however, the tendency was for all men to adopt the 'conservative evangelical'
label, and by the end of two years there were only two men who
persisted in calling themselves liberal evangelicals. Considering
all the colleges together, the number of evangelicals remained
steady, while the proportion of catholics of either label dropped
after a year from 45 to 30 per cent, increasing again after a
further year to 35 per cent, which was still substantially below
the initial level. Clearly, it would be mistaken to say that
churchmanship in the 1960s was a thing of the past, but
throughout our researches the distinction between radicals and
conservatives stood out as of greater importance.

It seems to us that these various changes in religious views as
a result of ordination training can most accurately be summarised by saying that there are two patterns to be discerned.
Except at one college, the men consistently moved away from
entrenched dogmatic positions. They were not shifting from one
religious position to another, and certainly not from a variety of
ideas towards a consensus. If anything, there was greater variety
of opinion after two years of training and less reliance on
received formulas. The only single direction in which one could
say that all these men were travelling was away from the laity,
for, although there are no comparable data on English lay people, there is every reason to think that the same applies here as in
the United States. There the clergy appear to be becoming less
and less conservative, but lay people who move in the same
direction become more sporadic in their church attendance and
eventually stop going at all, with the result that church congregations are increasingly confined to the faithful, conservative few
(Stark and Glock 1968; Hadden 1969). At one college, however,
the evangelical Oak Hill, a different pattern emerges. The men
there emerge from training more, not less, conservative, and so
closer to the lay people whom they will serve rather than further
away. There is a marked, if not a dramatic, tendency for two
years of training at Oak Hill to produce a group of men ready for
ordination who share a single view and hold solidly to a party
line. A further point will further illustrate this pattern. In the
course of interviews we asked the men, 'Have you had what
could be called a conversion?' All the men who said yes were

Oak Hill students, and before they arrived at college 16 out of the group of 23 said that they had had a conversion experience and gave a date to it. They were all asked the same question again after they had been in training for nearly a year, and on that occasion 19 of the 21 men who were then at college said that they had been converted. Moreover, the additional three respondents who had joined the ranks of the converted all dated their conversion experiences prior to the earlier interview. We do not wish to imply that these men were lying, but suggest that training leads them to reinterpret earlier experiences in ways which conform to group norms, so that what is created is a body of men who agree on a set of fundamental ideas and who share a single perspective, i.e. who have been socialised into an identifiable sub-culture. This pattern is all the more striking when compared with the reverse process at the other colleges.

THE CHANGES INTERPRETED

We have set out to describe and explain the changes in a small number of attitudes and values which take place as ordinands pass through their period of training. The main problem is whether or not such changes as occur should properly be described as an example of professional socialisation. It constitutes a problem because the professional status of the clergy is problematical, and this is more than a technical quibble. If the ministry is indeed a profession, then it should be looking to the other professions for guidance in the right conduct of its affairs; if it is not a profession, such reference to doctors, lawyers and so on will lead nowhere but along false trails. From a narrowly sociological point of view, the danger is of citing the ministry as an example of something it is not, and of trying to understand it in wholly inappropriate terms. We have attempted to let the modest data speak for themselves. Does the picture which has emerged conform to what one would expect of professional socialisation? On the whole, we think not; but there are three ways in which the processes observed do approximate to it.

First, the progressively greater doubt about the satisfactoriness of the ministry which was expressed by ordinands as they went through training suggests a growing realism about the structure of the life they are about to enter, as they approach ordination and consider the opportunities which are likely to be open to them. The same increasing realism is seen in the greater interest they take in the various forms of specialist ministry as they get nearer to ordination. Having started training with only a vague picture in their minds of what the ministry might be all about, they become gradually more aware of the realities and their attitudes change appropriately. This increasing realism was most clearly apparent in the changing attitudes to the various components of the clerical role. When they arrived at college they dismissed the clergyman's role as the organiser of church activities and the administrator of church affairs as almost totally unimportant, but in this respect more than in any other they changed remarkably over the following two years until eventually they fully acknowledged these functional aspects of the role. They were never accorded an importance equal to the normative, traditional aspects of the role; but they were recognised, none the less, and no longer dismissed out of hand. So during training the image of the ministry became clearer as the ordinands' conceptions were marked by an increasing degree of realism. The second similarity to professional socialisation is seen in the way that ordinands adjust their own personal levels of political interest to what they perceive as normal for clergy. The actual levels are unimportant, but the adjustment is significant. The third way in which changes resemble those one would expect of entrants to a profession is in the redefinition by the students of their social class. The change was not spectacular, however, and there was a small but important group of men who maintained, or even switched to, the highly non-professional definition of themselves as working class.

These similarities exist, but they are not at all compelling. One must add that there was no reason to suppose that in any of these respects was ordination training designed to promote changes towards a professional clerical status. The approach of ordination forced an element of realism into the situation, and one could argue that these changes took place not so much because of the way in which training was organised as quite independently. No effort was made by colleges to simulate situations in which the men would find themselves having to act out a clerical role, so that they might gradually learn appropriate modes of behaviour. If anything, training is geared exclusively to the moment of ordination, on the implicit assumption that the 'job' will be learned by actually doing it. When the medical student goes on hospital wards, he or she learns how to act as a doctor and how to respond when treated as one by colleagues, by subordinate staff and by patients. At one of the theological colleges the students went once a week to visit patients in a neighbouring hospital, dressed more or less as clergymen. This had something like the effect of the medical student's ward round, but was regarded by the college as a source of general experience, not as having anything to do with teaching. There was no instruction before the visits and no discussion afterwards, and certainly no surveillance during the exercise. Since the skills involved are only those of personal relations, we should argue that the college was limited to providing experience, and could not give instruction. (Exercises in group dynamics were staged in the colleges very occasionally, by outside bodies, but the mumbo-jumbo of the human-relations industry had made few inroads into ordination training in the 1960s.) Nor was the exercise deliberately intended by the college as an opportunity for students to learn how to act as clergy. This was made clear by the conduct of a similar activity, prison-visiting, at the same college, for there the students dressed as students and behaved exactly as lay prison-visitors. It seems clear that at this college, and at others too, the periodic excursions of this nature were meant to provide opportunities for the students to meet problems they would encounter as clergy, but that its teaching value was regarded as inhering in the experiences themselves.

Oak Hill, the evangelical college, must be excepted from these comments. While the findings we have reported above made it appear similar to other colleges in being only very ambiguously like a professional training school, the organisation of the college, by comparison, was noticeably more professional. To a much greater extent than the other colleges, Oak Hill was geared to the acquisition of skills. The importance of learning to preach and to lead extempore prayers was stressed, and there were occasional trips for a Sunday afternoon's outdoor preaching when the men could learn to cope with apathy or even hostility while enjoying the moral support of a group of peers. Theology, too, was taught in an essentially practical way, as the equipment which the ordinand would require for his work. All the emphasis was placed on learning, and duplicated notes figured importantly as a teaching medium, together with definitive texts and basic primers in this and that. In many ways Oak Hill provided the practical training required by a religious professional, and this phrase is an apt one, for all the emphasis was on preparation for the life of a full-time church worker, with little notice being taken of the specifically clerical character of their ministry. The ordinands were being trained for particular tasks – namely, to reach the unconverted and to build up the life of a local church community – and the college aimed to equip its students to undertake these tasks with maximum efficiency.

The approach to the teaching of theology which we found in other colleges provides a comparison which illustrates a whole range of differences. Using methods more like those employed in universities (two of the colleges were, of course, associated with universities) they taught theology as a subject in its own right. It was to be pursued for its own intrinsic interest and for the new insights it might throw up, not as a body of useful facts to be stored away. The whole course of studies was suffused with the same non-practical ethos and could be epitomised better as 'religious education' than as occupational training. Such social-isation to the culture of the ministry as we have described was incidental to what the principals saw as their business, and it was provided by the students themselves and by the approach of ordination.

7 The Career Structure of the Clergy

So far we have tried to throw light on the clergy by examining the processes by which men come to be ordained, carefully avoiding any discussion of the ordained clergy themselves except in so far as it provides necessary background information. Before we use the processes at work among ordinands to draw together some conclusions for the ministry as a whole, however, we must consider the career upon which the ordinands are about to embark. This is essential to a completed picture of ordination training, for it will give some idea of what training leads to; and, furthermore, some of the factors we have discussed already, such as educational background, will be found to determine not just the course of ordination training but the whole career which awaits a man. We gave some hint of this when we referred to the influence on his subsequent career of the kind of school to which a man goes (see above, pp. 85–7), but it was no more than a hint, and here we shall consider the kinds of career which may be pursued, what proportion of men pursue each of them, and what influences the course of a career. Our account will be no more than a first sketch, since a full discussion of .all the complex factors involved would require a separate monograph, but it will provide a broad outline sufficient for present purposes.

THE SHAPE OF THE MINISTRY

The ecclesiastically informed reader must bear with us, and omitting this section go straight on to the next; those, however, who are unfamiliar with the Church of England can easily get lost without a basic guide to the range of posts which may be held by an Anglican clergymen, while anyone familiar with the Church cannot but find such a guide tedious.

Clerical posts in the Church of England fall under four broad headings: parochial appointments; preferred posts or dignitaries; positions in the non-parochial ministry; and posts held by men not normally exercising their orders. (We suspect that in the last sentence we have already introduced two terms which will be as unfamiliar to the average student of sociology as they are unavoidable.)

The parochial ministry

When a man first becomes a clergyman and is made a 'deacon' in the Church of England, he must be 'ordained to a title'. In practice this means that he becomes a curate in a parish, but a word of explanation will help to clarify some of the other positions which must be defined below. Most of the long-established posts in the Church of England are comprised of two elements: the spiritual and the temporal. In the case of the newly ordained clergyman, the spiritual, or purely religious, aspect is his being made a deacon, i.e. being given religious authority to perform certain functions in the Church; he can be given this authority, however, only on condition that some provision is made for his material, or temporal, support, and the 'title' to which he is ordained indicates the source of his income. In the great majority of instances a man's title is to a parish, where he is employed to assist the parish priest; but there are other titles, and, for example, he may be ordained to a 'college title' if he holds a college fellowship which provides for his temporal support. The distinction between the 'spiritualities' and the 'temporalities' of an ecclesiastical post is important, for, put crudely, it means that a man cannot simply 'be ordained' but must be ordained to a particular job which provides work and support; at the other end of the ecclesiastical scale, a man cannot simply be consecrated a bishop, either, but must at the same time be appointed to an episcopal see, which provides him with specific work and accompanying support (for technical definitions, see *The Oxford Dictionary of the Christian Church*). In the past, ministers of the Church had temporal authority, as well as temporal benefits, but the distinction between 'spiritualities' and 'temporalities' is important now only because certain commonly employed expressions have no meaning other than those which depend on different temporalities attached to posts.

These details notwithstanding, the first post held by most

clergy is that of *curate* in a parish, where he is responsible to the priest in charge of it. He may be given more or fewer responsibilities, but he is answerable to his parish priest, who is formally charged with responsibility for the parish.

Most clergy serve as curate in more than one parish (though they serve their 'title' only once), often moving to parishes in which they are given progressively more responsibility and autonomy in particular geographical areas or spheres of work.

The step beyond a curacy in the parochial ministry is taken when a man is made an *incumbent*, or given a 'benefice' of his own. Posts included under this heading are rector, vicar, perpetual curate, curate-in-charge and priest-in-charge, which differ only in the nature of the temporalities which used to be attached to these benefices. Church statistics often draw a broad distinction between beneficed and unbeneficed clergy, the former consisting of all incumbents and dignitaries whose incomes, i.e. benefices, are held in return for the performance of religious duties, while the latter group includes all other clergy who either perform no set religious duties or whose duties are not of the traditional parochial kind; but the distinction is now used less and less.

The dioceses of England, which have an average of about 350 clergy each, are the framework within which certain minor positions of responsibility and honour are open to incumbents and other clergy, apart from curates. The main ones are as follows.

First, there are the *rural deans*, who are appointed by the bishop to preside at meetings of the rural deaneries, or ruridecanal conferences. There may be 12 or 15 in a diocese. Secondly, there are three or four *proctors in Convocation* (or members of the House of Clergy in the General Synod) for each diocese. They are elected by all the beneficed clergy of the diocese. Thirdly, the *honorary canons* (or non-residentiary canons, or prebendaries), of whom there may be about 20 in a diocese, generally hold their title as long as they remain beneficed clergy within the diocese (unlike rural deans and proctors, who serve for only a limited period), but the position is solely honorific, entitling them to no more than a stall in the cathedral choir and the style 'The Revd Canon A. B.'. Fourthly, there are *diocesan directors* for certain areas of work, such as mission, industry, youth, and ordination training, who are appointed by the bishop and often combine this work with running a parish. Outside the diocesan structure there is a college of 36 *chaplains to the Queen*, each of whom, though usually an ordinary incumbent, may be thought to hold a position of considerable honour.

Dignitaries

Within each diocese there is a hierarchy of dignitaries, headed by the *diocesan bishop*. He is appointed by the Crown[8] and holds his appointment until he reaches the age of compulsory retirement at 70. Formally, the bishop is still elected by the dean and chapter, but since they receive only one nomination their role in the appointment is only a ritual one. The diocesan bishop is assisted by between one and three *suffragan bishops*, appointed by the Crown on the advice of the diocesan bishop. Often they take responsibility for a geographical area of the diocese. In some dioceses the bishop is helped also by one or two *assistant bishops*, usually bishops who have retired and live in the diocese, but they are strictly part-time bishops and are not salaried. About three *archdeacons*, appointed by the bishop, are responsible within particular areas of the diocese for the disciplinary supervision of the clergy and the temporal administration of ecclesiastical property.

The cathedral of each diocese is under the direction and control of a *dean* (or provost) who is appointed by the Crown and ranks next to the diocesan bishop; and the cathedral is staffed by three or four *canons* (or residentiary canons), who, with the dean, form the cathedral chapter; and there are usually, in addition, two or three minor canons with various titles and responsibilities (for instance, the precentor, who has some responsibility for the music), who are like curates to the cathedral.

Outside the diocesan structure are the cathedral-like Royal Peculiars. Senior appointments in these institutions, the chief of which are Westminster Abbey and St George's Chapel, Windsor, are believed to be made by the Sovereign without reference necessarily being made to the Prime Minister. They account for no more than 50 posts among the Church of England's 20,000 clergy, however, and positions in them are very similar to positions held in cathedrals.

The Diocese of Rochester is fairly typical of Anglican dioceses and will serve to illustrate the structure of the parochial and 'preferred' clergy, as those are called who have been raised above the rank of incumbent.

Bishop
Suffragan Bishop
Assistant Bishop

Cathedral
  Dean
  Canons, 3
  Honorary canons, 24
  Cathedral staff (priest vicar), 1

Archdeacons, 3
Proctors in Convocation, 3
Rural deans, 16

Clerical diocesan officers
  Director of Education
  Director of Ordinands (Suffragan Bishop)
  Director of Post-Ordination Training
  Warden of Readers' Association
  Clerical Registrar
  Missionary and Ecumenical Council (? Secretary)
  Industrial chaplains, 3

Clergy (1976), 259
Church workers (full-time or salaried) (1975), 278
Laymen on electoral rolls (1974), 47,400
Population of diocese (1971), 1,136,000

The non-parochial ministry

Clergy are employed, *qua* clergy, in a multiplicity of posts outside the parochial structure. In education they are found, almost as a hangover from earlier generations, in Oxford and Cambridge colleges, and on the staffs of public schools and specifically Anglican independent schools. Of course, they hold positions in theological colleges, and, also in the educational sector, many schools and colleges and universities have clergy attached to them as chaplains rather than as members of the ordinary teaching staff. The post of chaplain exists in many institutions, most notably in the armed forces, prisons, hospitals, convents and embassies, but there are also chaplaincies to specific groups of people too, such as chaplains to the deaf, and to the blind. Some organisations, such as the Missions to Seamen, employ clergy for pastoral work, while others, such as Christian Aid, the headquarters of the missionary societies, and the British Council of Churches, provide posts which are not specifically clerical but are usually held by clergy. The Religious communities of men represent another set of non-parochial positions which clergy may occupy; and, finally, there are the many pastoral posts in Anglican dioceses overseas.

The rest

Lastly, there are the clergy who remain clergy in the sense that they have not renounced their orders, but who do not act as clergy: men who do not actively exercise a ministry, or do so only to a limited extent. Under this heading may be included fully retired parochial clergy as well as men who have quit the ministry, either permanently or for a time, to pursue wholly secular avocations. Some of these men may still hold a bishop's licence to preach and to officiate at services from time to time, for such activities can only be performed by men properly licensed as well as validly ordained, but this qualification is of little practical significance.

The structure of the Church of England is broadly similar to that of other episcopal churches in Western Christendom. The reader more familiar with the Roman Catholic Church will note two major differences in the Church of England: first, the Religious orders account for a tiny proportion of the clergy, and, secondly, the parochial clergy are not trained in the diocese from which they come and after ordination they are free to move from diocese to diocese, the envy of many a Catholic colleague, for this means that they are not wholly dependent on the bishop who ordained them.

CURACIES

The overwhelming majority of men go to a parish to serve their title as soon as they are ordained, but not all do. In a sample of clergy ordained between 1934 and 1969 (see Appendix I), 3·5 per cent of the total group of 568 never served as curates, a handful in each generation serving their titles to a college or to a bishop as his domestic chaplain and secretary; 53 per cent of men serve just one curacy before going on to a parish of their own or to some other post; 34 per cent serve two curacies, leaving less than 10 per cent who are curates in three or more different parishes. This pattern remained stable between 1934 and 1969; there is no evidence that ordinands of today may expect to serve more or fewer curacies than did men in the 1930s; and, furthermore, those who go on to be rural deans and honorary canons follow the same general pattern. The pattern is not quite the same, however, for those who are to become bishops. Of the bishops in the 1930s, 25 per cent had never been curates, 55 per cent had served one curacy, and only 20 per cent had served more than one; of the present bench, 6 per cent have not been curates, 80 per cent have served one curacy, and 14 per cent more than one.

The pattern is reflected in the total length of time for which men serve as curates before going on to some other kind of post. The percentages are as follows.

				Years served						
None	*1*	*2*	*3*	*4*	*5*	*6*	*7*	*8*	*9+*
Percentage of clergy after curacies	3·5	4	11·5	20	17	14	10	7	5	8

It is more difficult to make general remarks about the subsequent careers of recently ordained clergy, since obviously they are still in mid-career. If we consider the whole sample of 568, however, the recurrence of one particular pattern is striking: there is a regular association between the kind of higher education a man has received and the highest post he reaches in the course of his career. Men from Oxford and Cambridge are under-represented in the groups who reach only moderate positions of preferment as compared with non-graduates and graduates of the provincial universities, while they are over-represented in the groups which achieve higher status. The data can most clearly be presented in tabular form, as follows.

	Highest position reached (%)			
	Incumbent	*Rural dean*	*Hon. canon*	*Canon*
Oxford/Cambridge	28	32	48	58
Provincial	30	35	30	17
Non-graduate	37	22	13	8
N =	(371)	(37)	(40)	(12)

Note. The columns do not sum to 100, because for the sake of simplicity we have excluded the category of men with higher degrees, i.e. BD, PhD, and so on.

The pattern is clearly seen in the way in which the figures in the top row increase from left to right, while in the bottom row and the left-hand column the figures fall from left to right and from top to bottom respectively. Thus, the trend seen in an earlier discussion about bias in selection is repeated here: not only do graduates account for a higher proportion of the men holding posts at each successively higher level of preferment than do non-graduates, but, in addition, graduates of Oxford and Cambridge are preferred above graduates of other universities.

To pursue the matter of higher education a little further, for the sake of completeness at this point, we find that there has been a significant trend from the 1930s to the 1970s. It has been remarked above that the proportion of non-graduates among those ordained has increased consistently, and in this sample it has increased at the expense of all graduates from 22 per cent in 1934 to 55 per cent in 1969. The way in which higher education affects a man's chances of being raised to the bench of bishops has changed correspondingly, as the following figures show.

Higher education	*All bishops 1930* (%)	*All bishops 1973–4* (%)	*Diocesan bishops only 1975–6* (%)	*All clergy 1934–69* (%)
Oxford/Cambridge	55	70	71	53
Provincial	2	18	5	29
Higher degrees	43	7	17	7
Non-graduates	0	5	7	31

Ignoring the group of bishops with higher degrees (for they represent a special problem discussed above, p. 33), two things are striking. First, graduates of universities other than Oxford or

Cambridge are more fully represented on today's bench of bishops than they were on 1930's; but, on the other hand, they are still grossly under-represented, and if we consider only diocesan bishops the under-representation is truly remarkable. Secondly, non-graduates are no longer without their representatives among the episcopate, as was the case in 1930, and, indeed, among the diocesan bishops there are more men with no degree at all than men with only first degrees from provincial universities, although it has to be remembered that we are talking in terms of only two or three men.

As we have said, comparisons of 'highest preferment reached' are difficult when only a modest proportion of the sample have completed their careers. What admits of fuller examination, however, is the posts to which some men rather than others go after an initial period serving curacies, and here we encounter changes over the past 40 years which are interesting though not dramatic.

The majority of men, on finishing an initial period in curacies, become incumbents; or perhaps it would be more correct to say that a majority of men complete their period in curacies when they are offered livings. Of our sample of 568, 61·8 per cent proceeded thus to the next step within the parochial ministry, but the proportion did not remain the same from 1934 through to 1969. Whereas of those ordained in 1934 53 per cent went from a curacy to an incumbency, of those ordained in the 1950s and 1960s well over 60 per cent, the precise figure varying between 62 and 68 per cent, made the same move. Many possible openings exist, but we need to know where the remainder went, who did not go from curacy to benefice, in the earlier period, and where the corresponding smaller group have gone latterly. The answer is that a roughly constant 20 per cent go to a very wide variety of posts, which change on what appears to be an entirely haphazard basis. The increase in the proportion going to incumbencies is accounted for by, first, a marked decline in the proportion who go to work overseas, and, secondly, the disappearance of the group who went from curacies to chaplaincies in the armed forces in the period leading up to the Second World War. The second change can be discounted readily enough, but the change from 15 per cent or more young clergy going out to ministries abroad in the 1930s to 5 per cent or less doing so in the present generation is worth remarking upon. There is nothing surprising in it, of course, for the Kiplingesque duty has receded as more emphasis has been put on the 'indigenisation' of the ministries in national Anglican churches, but nevertheless the change needs to be noted.

Apart from this change, what is most striking is that, despite year-to-year fluctuations in the numbers of men ordained, and despite the attempts to rearrange the parochial system, and the relationship between beneficed and unbeneficed parochial clergy, the proportion of men proceeding from curacy to benefice has remained extremely stable, as has the number of curacies served and the average period spent serving them.

There is reason to suppose that the immediate 'post-curacy' job is of considerable significance for a man's subsequent career, however, and this becomes clear when we compare the 'post-curacy' jobs of men who finally reached various levels of preferment. Of the 371 men in our sample whose highest position was that of incumbent, 77 per cent went from curacy to incumbency. Of the 40 who eventually became honorary canons, only 63 per cent made the same move, and, of the 210 bishops who made up the benches of 1930 and 1973, rather less than 40 per cent went to benefices from their initial periods of curacy. (There were only 12 men in our sample who became, as their highest preferment, residentiary canons, and, although the figure is too low to yield a reliable datum, it is worth noting the fact that only two of them, or 17 per cent, went from curacy to benefice.) Those who are to be high flyers, it would seem, are less likely to follow the conventional path through the parochial ministry.

PARSONS' CAREERS

These overall statistics are too unspecific to be very informative. Because the shapes of careers vary so much, we need to have a picture of the major paths which may be followed. When the completed careers of the samples of men ordained in 1934 and 1939 are compared with the uncompleted careers of the samples of those who set out on their ministries in 1954 and 1959, making allowance for predictable preferment and for the war service of the older men, the patterns are remarkably stable.[9] It is possible to distinguish 11 types of career pattern, distributed as follows among 100 men ordained to the ministry of the Church of England in the middle of the twentieth century.

1. *Unadorned parochial*. 39 will spend their lives in the parochial ministry and retire as incumbents, having never been anything else, save curates.
2. *Unadorned, interrupted parochial*. 17 will finish as beneficed clergy, having spent one quite short period, and occasionally two periods, working abroad or in a chaplaincy, and otherwise having been only curates.
3. *Parochial with minor honours*. 17 will be curates, incumbents, and at some point will be rural deans, honorary canons, or hold some equivalent minor position of honour and responsibility.
4. *Parochial, interrupted and with minor honours*. 3 will be curates and incumbents, and will enjoy a position of minor importance, their careers being interrupted at some point by a short period or very occasionally two such periods, of work abroad or in a chaplaincy.
5. *Senior honours*. 2 will become canons or archdeacons, spending part of their ministries in parishes, but commonly with excursions into education and a variety of other specialist ministries.
6. *Preferred*. 3 will be made deans or raised to the episcopate (we discuss the routes to preferment in the next section).
7. *Ministries abroad*. 4 spend most or all their working lives, after being curates in home parishes, in parochial work overseas.
8. *Specialist ministries*. 4, after initial curacies, spend all or most of their lives in a chaplaincy or a specialist ministry of some description, with education being the most likely option.
9. *Varia*. 5 will go from job to job in a way which is entirely idiosyncratic.
10. *Drop-outs*. 4 will maintain clerical connections while spending most of their working lives in secular jobs, or drop out altogether.
11. *Disappearances*. 2 will accountably disappear from published records, through premature death or misfortune.

We want to make only two comments on this variety of patterns, which for the most part speaks for itself. In earlier chapters we have commented on the increasing number of men who seek out positions other than in the parochial ministry (p. 151 above), while here we have said that specialist ministries remain restricted to something of the order of 4 per cent of men ordained. This is a glaring discrepancy and it is highly relevant to our general discussion. If the figures just given were a wholly accurate indication of the present state of affairs, then our earlier remarks would have to be disregarded; but the matter is not simple, for the movement away from the parishes to which we drew attention is of only recent origin, and it cannot be expected to show up yet in the empirical evidence about careers which is available, since we have no biographical information on the men ordained since 1969.[10] On the other hand, we readily grant that our remarks contain some element, which is a conscious element, of exaggeration, for those who quit the ministry altogether, at least, are accorded public attention out of all proportion to their numbers, going out with a bang rather than a whimper. We shall return to this phenomenon in Chapter 8. What should not be allowed to escape notice, however, is the way in which exits from the ministry have not so much increased as become more apparent. In the 1930s, when the Church had much wider influence, it was able to offer a whole range of jobs for clergy who were discontented with the lot of parish priest. The field of education and work in slum settlements are no more than obvious examples of work to which men were able to go without in any way questioning the general 'validity' of the ordained ministry as a way of life. Indeed, it cannot be said too strongly that the men of today (for we are not concerned with women) who compete fiercely for posts in the social services would have been forced to enter the ministry in the 1930s, or do a different kind of work, for there were no opportunities for 'social case-work' except those afforded by the ministry. Furthermore, it was considered entirely normal for a young clergyman to work outside the parochial system for a period, and subsequently to re-enter it. Not so today, when the pressures are to do 'the' work of a clergyman. We are inclined to think that in a few years a trend towards exclusively parochial careers, already apparent in the episcopate, as will be seen below, will begin to manifest itself. Social pressures within the Church and within the ministry itself will influence the non-conformist to quit before ordination, as happens so often already, or to seek permanent jobs outside the ministry.

The other comment which needs to be made is that the much-discussed erosion of the 'parson's freehold' appears to do nothing at all to affect adversely the parochial career structure. It was thought that to reduce, by even the slightest degree, the almost absolute freedom of action and of tenure enjoyed by an incumbent within his parish, would alter the character of the parochial ministry and render it a much less attractive vocation. In practice, such minor limitation of an incumbent's freehold as there has been has had little effect; it is rather the sheer impecuniosity of the average rector which makes an incumbency less attractive. On the other hand, the parson was never as free from his bishop's control as is sometimes pretended. It is not true that the bishop was powerless without initiating the unpleasant business of ecclesiastical court proceedings: as some clergy found to their cost, it was a severe penalty to be deprived of curates and never to have the bishop conduct confirmation services in their churches. What the general shift from the parson's position as 'freeholder of a benefice' to 'Church's employee' does erode, however, and does effectively discourage, is the mentality, among parsons, of arrogant autonomy and autocracy, which freehold was inclined to engender and support.

BISHOPS' CAREERS

Our comments in Chapter 2 notwithstanding (pp. 31–4), the clergy as a whole are an elite group. Despite the decline of educational standards in recent decades, the clergy as a whole are still overwhelmingly graduates, and fully 40 per cent of them have been to Oxford or Cambridge or have taken higher degrees. No occupational group has so high a proportion of men with this elite educational background. There is no gainsaying their poverty, and we have been at pains to emphasise it, but the paradoxical fact is that the clergyman occupies a position in society which gives him automatic access to very considerable power and influence. If his position has been eclipsed, it has been eclipsed along with a traditionally ordered society in which social 'quality' counted, and in which there was much which money alone could not buy. That traditional society may be passing, but it has not passed yet, and the clergy, together with impoverished county families, still enjoy a social power out of all proportions to their cash value. This is not to say that every parson exploits his position to the full. There are very many insignificant and powerless clergymen, just as there are powerless sons of families which a generation ago would have been rightly judged to be important and powerful. The clergy are an elite, however, because they occupy positions which, if they have the wit and the will to do so, they can use to enormous effect. The members of no occupational group have the same opportunity, or the leisure, to use the mass media of communication, and if the clergy are sometimes mocked they are nevertheless heard. Furthermore, by virtue of nothing more than simply being a clergyman, a man is counted as 'respectable' beyond any question, and he need fear exclusion from no club or group or society or dinner-table of his choice. No one will ask if he is black, or a Jew, or the son of a grocer; any of those misfortunes may damn a doctor, but it is overlooked in a clergyman.

In some respects the elite status which a clergyman can enjoy is the relic of a bygone age, but that renders it no less real. So long as people in general labour under the misapprehension that the clergy, by social origin and by education, are uniformly from a superior stratum of society, the clergy themselves can continue to act as though it were true. Combined with this, a style of life which makes them almost wholly masters of their time, and which almost certainly brings them into contact with high and low alike at the critical periods of birth, marriage, bereavement and great anxiety, means that the clergy of the Church of England must continue to be regarded as an elite in society, and so what once they were: part of the ruling class. They belong, therefore, to the cream of society.

If the clergy are part of the cream, the bishops are most certainly part of the *crème de la crème*. They come from the most privileged of homes and, if no longer princes except in the Church, they rank beside government ministers and High Court judges, and have immediate access, granted as of right, to every privilege our culture has to offer. The top rank of every occupational group, save perhaps the armed forces and the Law, are left standing by the presence of The Rt Revd the Lord Bishop of anywhere. And of course it is the standing of their own highest rank which does so much for the clergy as a whole, so long as a credible proportion of them continue to come from the public schools and from Oxford and Cambridge, which, as we have seen, is most certainly the case.

How, then, do men become bishops? What clerical careers lead to a bishopric? Three things are of particular interest in bishops' careers: what jobs they did after their initial curacies; what posts they held immediately prior to becoming bishops; and whether involvement in education figures in their earlier careers. The last point is of concern because it is often thought that a man stands a better chance of becoming a bishop if he has some kind of academic background, either of a purely academic kind or from involvement in ordination training. It is often put in a more partisan way, and alleged that too few bishops have first-hand experience of the kind of parochial work which, as bishops, it will be their business to guide and oversee, being drawn from universities and theological colleges rather than from the dioceses.

We referred to the first point when we remarked that, while more than 60 per cent of our sample of clergy went from curacies to a benefice, less than 40 per cent of bishops did so. This is part of a wider pattern among bishops, however, which has changed over the recent years.

Of the 1930 bench of bishops, 32 per cent went from initial curacies to benefices, 20 per cent went to an educational post, and 48 per cent went to something other than either of those two jobs. Of the 1973 bench, many more, 44 per cent instead of 32 per cent, went to benefices; and more went to an educational post, 26 per cent instead of 20 per cent; but a great many fewer, 30 per cent instead of 48 per cent, went elsewhere. This seems to point to the pattern mentioned in our last section, whereby more emphasis is laid on conventional parochial careers today than heretofore. The 'educational hypothesis' is also borne out, for while only 5 per cent of clergy as a whole go from curacy to education, we find that 20 to 26 per cent of men who are to become bishops make that their first move; it would seem to be a bishop's move: one square forward and one to the side.

The pattern of posts held by men immediately before being elevated to the episcopate has also changed from 1930 to 1973. The proportion coming from a parish has fallen from 17 to 13 per cent; the proportion coming from an educational post has dropped from 35 to 23 per cent; while the proportion coming from canonries, archdeaconries and deaneries – coming, in other words, from preferments within the parochial–diocesan structure – has risen from 37 to 48 per cent. Those who are made bishops from other career backgrounds has remained at 11 per cent.

The swing, therefore, is towards the placing of greater importance on the parochial ministry, whether one considers the job to which men go after serving their curacies or the post held immediately prior to being made a bishop. Educational posts, however, do remain a very significant part of the backgrounds of those who achieve episcopal status. If one looks at total biographies, and takes account of an intermediate period in education, as well as of the incidence of educational posts at the beginning of careers and at penultimate stages, a much greater degree of continuity emerges.

Careers	*1930* (%)	*1973* (%)
Purely parochial/diocesan	56·4	58·3
Including an element of education	32·5	33·3
Other pre-episcopal careers	11·1	8·4
	100·0	100·0
N =	(126)	(84)

If the appointments secretaries to successive prime ministers have aimed at stability, they must be congratulated on the level of success they have achieved. And, furthermore, those who complain that the bishops are out of touch with parochial work are making an unjustified complaint, since consistently 55–60 per cent of those made bishops come up through the dioceses, untainted by the academy.

It is not our business to comment on the relative merits of preferment through educational experience and preferment from a purely pastoral career. It could be maintained, however, that the 'pastoral route' is the safer of the two. We have not examined the livings from which men are raised to the episcopate, but it is generally thought – and we have no reason to doubt it – that certain parishes are 'jumping-off points' for bishops. These parishes, of which Leeds Parish Church is an example, are livings to which men are appointed, in no small part, because they are thought by the bishop or the Crown to be *episcopabile*, and the incumbents of these rather special benefices, together with the principals of theological colleges, may be thought of as constituting a permanent pool of men who are possible candidates for vacant sees. The difference between them is that, unlike these special incumbents, principals of theological colleges are appointed because they are possessed of pastoral or scholarly gifts which fit them for the job, and not because they are thought to be the material of which bishops are made. So there is a sense in which the Vicar of Leeds may be thought to have been 'tried' for his suitability as a bishop in a sense which may not be true, for example, of the Principal of Westcott House.

There are many other factors besides these which may be influential in the making of bishops (for example, to whom a man is married) but with only 43 diocesan bishops and not many more suffragans, the numbers involved are not large enough to permit generalisations about such complex matters.

CONCLUSION

Considering that we live in a period of great change, the career structure of the Church of England appears to be very stable indeed. It could be described as static, of course, and the epithet would denote a criticism, but such evaluations as we propose to make are a part of the next, and concluding, chapter.

8 Becoming Marginal

We have now given a broad picture of ordination training in the 1960s. It has certain features which we want to bring out in this concluding chapter, and there are certain trends which it is important that we note. But we shall do more than add a comment. The first chapter attempted to place the twentieth-century Anglican ministry within the larger context of the social history in which it grew up, and now we shall look at it again from a wider perspective. We shall suggest a way of understanding the changes of the past which we hope will make the present more comprehensible and forewarn of the future.

But, first, what has happened since the years when this study was in progress, for it began in 1961 and ended before the 1960s had ended? The most obvious development has been the decline in ordination training. In 1961 the *Church of England Yearbook* listed 26 theological colleges and gave their total accommodation as 1663 places. The 1977 edition listed only 15 colleges, with total accommodation for 769 ordinands. St Aidan's College, Birkenhead, founded in 1846, closed in 1969; Bishops' College, Cheshunt, was founded in 1909 and closed in 1969; Ely, which was founded in 1874, closed in 1964; Kelham closed in 1972; Lichfield, founded in 1857, closed in 1972. Most of the colleges which closed had been training men for the ministry for many years, but some others had been founded only recently. Rochester opened in 1959 and closed in 1970; Worcester Ordination College was founded to train older men in 1952, and it closed in 1969. The number of deacons being ordained each year reached a post-war peak of 636 in 1963, but by 1976 the number had dropped to 273. At the moment the numbers are rising very slightly, but we believe this to be only a temporary phenomenon, connected, perhaps, with national problems of employment; it may be a pale reflection of the stampede for places to train as accountants and lawyers and other seemingly safe jobs. Fundamentally to challenge our general thesis the annual rate of ordinations would need to return to 500, and then go on to 1000.

Anyone who doubts this should go back to look again at the figures set out on p. 30. But, of course, any such development is entirely out of the question. The Church has too little money to pay its depleted number of clergy a decent living wage, let alone pay a professional salary to more than three times the present number. Any substantial increase in the number of clergy necessarily implies a radical alteration to the way in which the Church of England is organised, and we shall have something to say of this possibility later in the chapter.

There is no point in dressing up this decline and calling it a change in policy, because the Church has shown no sign of wishing to change the pattern of its ministry.

The second development might have represented a decided change of direction, but in fact it has been undertaken as no more than an effort to make good deficiencies in numbers with a second-rate substitute. This has been the founding of schemes in the Southwark diocese and in the north-west of England to train men for the Auxiliary Pastoral Ministry (APM). Men are said to work in the APM when they have been ordained without the normal full-time training and continue to earn their living in a secular occupation while serving in a parish on a part-time basis. The inclusion of the word 'auxiliary' serves to make it plain that the Church, in ordaining men on these terms, does not wish to accept as normal anything other than the traditional full-time ministry. The development is no less significant for that, of course, and many other innovations began life as temporary arrangements only to find themselves recognised as normal in time. What we must notice about the APM, however, is that under its auspices men are being inducted directly to a style of ministry which exists already in the practice of clergy who have quit the parochial ministry and then, as teachers or social workers or whatever, help in parishes at weekends. In other words, the men who enter the APM serve to swell the numbers of clergy who are not part of the Church's normal structure.

A third development over the past 20 years has affected the normal structure of the Church's ministry itself. This is the spread of group ministries and team ministries. The terms are used rather loosely to refer to one thing here and to another there, but in every form they serve to erode the traditional pattern of autonomous parishes with their own incumbents, sometimes assisted by a staff which includes one or more curates. It is a trend with which we are familiar enough in the practice of medicine and elsewhere, but it is far from being the same phenomenon. The formation of groups for professional practice invariably takes place for the personal, or the professional, convenience of practitioners, and in the most flourishing practices. Vigorous parishes, by contrast, do not form groups and become teams by the addition of extra curates to undertake specialist ministries. Typically, group ministries are instituted to eke out an inadequate supply of clergy in areas where individual congregations are too small to justify the appointment of separate incumbents. Ecclesiastical groups, that is, are formed from weakness, while professional groups begin from strength. Nor is this all. A professional practice exists to supply services, and, if the services can be rendered with equal or greater efficiency by a different organisation, that is all to the good. A parish exists for no extrinsic purpose but only as an end in itself. It may be true that originally parishes were set up to administer the services of the Church to people in convenient groups, but the measure of a successful parish is no longer the number of people who can be served efficiently, but, rather, the number who can be induced to require such services. An Anglican parish is no more than the people who live in a specified area, and so, if the form of organisation by which the people are served tends to erode or compromise their self-awareness as a community, then *ipso facto* it serves them inadequately. There is an assumption built into that analysis which we shall examine below, since it is already called into question, but it can stand for the moment. The point is that many Anglican parishes exist as natural communities, and, indeed, are redrawn whenever possible so as to remain conterminous with the shifting boundaries of natural communities. Often the church, as the oldest surviving building, is the most essential symbol of the community. The vicar or rector is also a symbol of the community's integrity, so when the community is asked to share three clergymen with five other communities an absolutely vital element in the traditional pattern of ministry has been removed. No longer is it possible for a clergyman to identify himself with a parish, or for the parish to identify itself in the person of its own parson. In so far as one of the services rendered by the Church is a mode of community identification, the introduction of group ministries cannot fail to lessen the Church's effectiveness.

Other developments, besides these, could be indicated, but this short list will suffice to suggest the general direction of changes. We should argue that this direction can be discerned without any ambiguity. The changes are all in the direction of the decline of established institutions in the Church, and the decline is not mitigated by the emergence of new institutions in embryo.

The positive signs of decline are clear enough in trends in the supply of ordinands. In sketching the background to the present situation we saw that the decline in terms of the population of the country as a whole has been slow but inexorable. The absolute decline since the early 1960s is a phenomenon in its own right, however, for at no time in the last hundred years has anything comparable happened except in times of war (see above, Figure 1). The negative signs are to be found in the fate which is being allowed to meet the parochial structure. The retention of (indeed, the desperate hanging on to) dead or dying parishes, which are then merged into larger units while being left with nominally separate lives, has been an understandable strategy. To have abolished parishes would have been a cruel betrayal of the faithful few left in each. But in retaining the old parishes, and at the same time the full-time ministry, the Church allowed itself to be caught between two stools – stools which, moreover, were moving ever further apart. And this is where the APM is so significant an innovation. Parishes might have been kept if they had been deemed that important, so long as it was realised that they might have to do without their own incumbent, and in time, perhaps, without an ancient church building. Men ordained to the APM might have served parishes for which no clergyman was available, or for which no money was available to pay a clergyman, but these new clergy have not been so used. On the contrary, the Church has set its face firmly against replacing full-time with part-time clergy, and declared such a policy to be unacceptable. Instead it has retained parishes which it has ever fewer men to staff, associating the part-time clergy with parishes which already have incumbents.

So on the one hand there has been a dramatic fall in the number of clergy to staff the existing parochial structure, while on the other there has been a refusal to modify the parochial structure in any way which would make its operation compatible with a much reduced level of clerical staffing. The problem of the

full-time parochial ministry thus reduces itself to a comparatively simple one of input and output. Fewer clergy are available
to put into the system, but the demands for personnel are not
diminished.

Why has the supply of ordinands declined? The answer, we
believe, is twofold. Far and away the most important reason is
the decline in Church membership and Church practice. It
would be wholly unrealistic to expect the number of men entering the ministry to increase when practically every other statistic
of Church life is in decline. This answer to the problem is so
staggeringly simple and obvious that it fails to command notice.
The second reason is closely associated with the first, and that is
the extremely poor rewards received by the clergy, both in financial terms and also in terms of occupational prestige. Without
going as far as to say that the second reason is entirely derived
from the first, for it is much more complex than that, we should
nevertheless maintain that it is difficult in the extreme to
imagine that it is possible to increase the rewards of the ministry
during a period of Church decline.

THREE SECULARISATIONS

It will help to make sense of these present changes, and to understand what is at present happening to the clergy and their training, if we look at the problem again in the wide historical perspective employed in our opening chapter. It was suggested there
that we can use the term 'secularisation' to refer to a process
whereby the Church and its clergy lose control of some aspect or
aspects of the non-religious affairs of a society. This does not
necessarily imply that as part of the process the people of the
society become 'less religious'. That would be exceedingly difficult to show by any methods known to us, and in any case the
available evidence would tend to suggest that quite the reverse
tends to happen, i.e. it seems that at the end of periods of dramatic secularisation, in the sense in which we are using the word,
people are more religious rather than less.

The first secularisation in England took place in the Tudor
period. Before it, the clergy, a complex society in itself, was an
Estate of the realm. Its members discharged all manner of duties
entirely unrelated to Church affairs and in so doing they brought

under the effective control of the Church many areas of social life
and a substantial proportion of the nation's wealth. Before the
first secularisation it would have been necessary, if you were
interviewed by, say, the Bishop of Durham, to know in what
capacity he was seeing you, for just as easily as being your
religious superior he might be your political or judicial or financial or even military superior. All that was changed by the first
secularisation at the end of the mediaeval period of English history. The only non-religious aspect of social life over which the
Church retained control was education.

And so it remained for 300 years, and the Church's place in
society did not alter substantially. The Victorian era saw the
second secularisation. In 1837 the clergy had a clear place in a
social-class structure which rested on the base of landed property, and their side was that of the owners. Some had property of
their own, but most were simply associated with property and
supported by property. Educational establishments of all kinds
were under the control of the Church, from Oxford and Cambridge to the parish school. The second secularisation removed
the clergy and the Church from influence. The landed gentry, to
which they had belonged, albeit parasitically, were eclipsed by
the rise of finance capitalism, and education was freed from the
control of religion. Whereas in 1837 the clergyman you met
might have been a don or a magistrate, from 1901 onwards
ecclesiastical status was the only status he possessed. After the
second secularisation the Church was a wholly subordinate
organisation in society, able to influence the affairs of State only
through its individual members (we ignore the presence of
bishops in the House of Lords, since it is simply an anachronism,
if a charming one). The Church of England had become qualita-
tively indistinguishable from the Boy Scouts or the British Leg-
ion, though of course neither existed in 1901. It remained the
Established Church in name, but its Establishment no longer
rested on a basis of temporal power and effectively it was one
denomination among several. Two secularisations, then, have
limited the influence of the Church. First the clergy were
excluded from the control of all institutions save education, and
then they were excluded from that too, being left only as clergy.
Now we are in the middle of the third secularisation. The
Church is being transformed from its position as an important
and central voluntary organisation to one on the margins of
social life; simultaneously the clergy are being squeezed out of

the occupational structure of society. We have already argued that the ordained ministry never was an occupation in the first place. The mediaeval cleric was a man of learning or of piety and might have been found engaged in almost any non-menial occupation; at the height of the post-Reformation period, in the reign of George III, the parson was a man of culture who no more thought of himself as following an occupation than did the squire. Now, everyone must follow an occupation, and so we have laboured for many years to assimilate the status of a clergyman into the structure of occupations only to find that it cannot be done. The man (or woman) who organises and administers the affairs of a religious group, whether locally or nationally, may be said to follow a religious occupation, but that is only a subsidiary part of what the role of a clergyman is conceived as being properly about. But the fact that such flexible conditions of entry into the clergy can be allowed is itself sufficient to throw doubt on the occupational nature of the group. What occupation sets strict standards of academic competence and requires of its entrants a university degree and also a three-year course of postgraduate studies, only to admit nearly half its entrants with vastly reduced levels of qualification who have followed drastically curtailed studies? The additional damage which has been done to the occupational image of the clergy since the Church ordained part-time clergy is slight.

We have shown that if you remove 'late vocations' from the group of men approaching ordination you find that ordinands are very similar to men entering professions. They come from similar backgrounds, they reach their decision to enter the ministry at the same time and by the same process, and they face hurdles of qualification which are very similar indeed. The normal group of ordinands could just as easily be candidates for a life in medicine or architecture as in the Church. But the late group presents a very different picture indeed. It is not just that its members are older, but in addition they conform more closely to the general population in almost every way. The normal group show every sign of being an elite in the making, but the late group come from a lower range of positions within the British class structure, with all that that implies for their fathers' occupations, their schooling and higher education, their family backgrounds, and so on. And yet they enter the ministry on the same terms as men of the normal group. In the short run the terms are more favourable, if anything, since being older they may expect to progress from a curacy to an incumbency rather more quickly. If in the long run they have lower chances of being preferred to high office, that is at least as much because they will not have accumulated as many years' experience in the ministry as because their antecedents are inferior to those of their normal-group counterparts.

The normal group of ordinands are thus normal in far more significant ways than just their age at ordination. They are normal in the sense that they are almost wholly comparable with the entrants to a profession. The late group, paradoxically enough, are far more normal than the normal group, except in this highly partisan sense of being comparable with a profession. But their presence clearly demonstrates that there is nothing mandatory about the so-called normal pattern, that it is, indeed, quite arbitrary. And it demonstrates too that the ministry exists as an occupation only because the Church has not yet caught up with the changes which have taken place in society at large. It is suffering from what is called 'cultural lag'.

We contend that the very concept of priesthood or ministry as a calling from which men may legitimately expect financial support is dying fast. When the ministry became only that, i.e. when the clergy were stripped of their non-religious social functions, its days were over. Very soon the ministry will have dropped out altogether from our society's occupational structure. The movement in this direction within the Church can be seen already. All contemporary thinking applies the notions of priesthood and ministry to the Church as a whole, shifting them away from the clergy to the laity. This does not mean that there is no future for full-time employees of the Church. It does mean, however, that the combination, in the status of clergy, of full-time renumerated service and religiously defined ministry has dissolved. The existing clergy themselves are left saying, with the group of French priests we quoted in Chapter 2, 'it is necessary for us to rid ourselves of this clerical status before we can begin to work out anew how best we can fulfil the mission of the Church'.

TRAINING FOR WHAT?

The doubt about the occupational, let alone professional, character of the ministry was underlined by what we reported of the changes in attitudes and values during training. In certain rudimentary ways they resemble the changes associated with professional socialisation and at a stretch they could be so interpreted. The divergences are more interesting, however, for they seem to derive from the essentially symbolic, non-functional nature of the role for which the men are preparing.

The pattern of changes at Oak Hill was markedly different from what was found at the other colleges, and closer to what one would associate with professional socialisation. It was at Oak Hill too that the great majority of students showed evidence of the puritan type of vocation, which we described in Chapter 4, distinguishing it from the antipuritan type. It is reasonable that a more professional kind of training should be associated with this puritan type of vocation. The college which recruits men who are certain of their religious faith and who are convinced that they have received directly from God a call to the ministry is likely to effect only modest changes among its students, and to be concerned principally with the inculcation of appropriate practical skills and useful knowledge. The men have clearly formulated ideas of their duty to preach the Word of God when they arrive at college, and the college holds this to be the main task of the ministry; so training may be expected to reinforce these ideas and to cultivate the sense of being men called and set apart. The overriding belief of puritan religion is that men are called by God to turn from the world to a life of holiness, and the minister's task is that of preaching the call of God and caring for the spiritual well-being of those who have so turned. He is the minister of the call to be separate from the world, and so his training is a training for separation. In his view the Church should be marginal to society, set apart somewhat, and so his own training must help him to become firmly established in a world on the margins in order that he may call others thence.

By contrast, the pattern of changes found at the colleges other than Oak Hill followed closely what would be expected of a training appropriate to the antipuritan type of vocation, even though fewer than half the men at the colleges belonged to this category. The men tended to have an increasing interest in politics and also increasingly to think that the clergy should be involved in politics, and yet these views were not derived from religious premises. The contrast of a comparatively low interest in religious affairs and high interest in secular ones would seem to be reflected in such changes as we have noted if the interpretation of the antipuritan type of vocation we have offered is correct. Similarly, the progressive openness to doubt about religious doctrines combined with a sustained conviction of the importance of the beliefs also reflects the same style of religious commitment. The changes in the ways in which men defined their churchmanship are also explicable in terms of the two types of vocation, the highly religious puritans becoming more solidly identified with their churchmanship label while the rest followed a more antipuritan pattern in becoming less partisan and less concerned with religious differentiae.

CONSERVATIVES AND RADICALS

This pattern of two types of vocation, underlined by divergent patterns of ordination training, suggests that a broad distinction between conservatives and radicals is becoming salient. Such party alignments as survive have meaning only within this framework, for the conservative group in the 1960s was composed mainly, though not exclusively, of evangelicals, while radicals tended to derogate all distinctions of churchmanship.

The antipuritan type of vocation characterised only a third of the ordinands whom we were studying, but we should argue that antipuritanism as a religious style was the dominant direction in which the Church was heading at that time. There is a sense in which this remains true, as we shall maintain in conclusion, but it needs to be qualified if our analysis of the trends in theological education and ordination training in the 1970s is accurate. Before we add these qualifications, however, it must be recognised that antipuritanism, as we have called the radical option, is still the trend which the 'best' thinking in the Church advocates; and the deepest currents of secular society, which force the Church into decline and on to the margins of society, are still pushing in that direction. Thus, we find academic theology moving away from supernaturalist conceptions of God and from doctrines about Jesus which say that he was a different sort of person from the rest of us; an attitude to mission develops which maintains staunchly that Christians must stop assuming that the religious insights of other faiths are one bit inferior to their own; the World Council of Churches issues one document after another instructing its member churches that the Christian duty of Europe and North America to the Third World lies in the pursuit of justice through political and, if necessary, military means, and not in the conversion of heathen peoples to lives of individual holiness; Christian spokesmen say in public pronouncements that the art and literature worthy of Christian approval must be good in its own terms, not judged by reference to its 'religious' content. Wherever one looks one sees evidence to suggest that in the long term the direction in which the Church is heading is best described as one which leads away from the doctrine *Extra ecclesiam nulla salus* and the religious imperialism which has gone with it, and towards a much more immanentist belief in God, as working in the secular affairs of the world and served by an invisible Church.

This line of thought, in all its manifestations, undermines the distinctions between the Christian and the non-Christian, between the Church and the world, because it sees God at work outside the Church, sees the structures of the Church as in many ways working against the will of God, and because it sees the very drawing of a line between 'us' and 'them' as contrary to the idea of a God who creates and redeems the whole world. When this line of thought finds the Church, as it is presently established, visibly in decline, it is not filled with horror or even with regret, for it looks for a Christian universalism which will be wider than the Church as defined by an organisation.

This radical attitude is still widespread. It is espoused by more rather than by fewer Church leaders in the 1970s than in the 1960s, but it is less strident in its tone and less iconoclastic in its mood. The radicals no longer seek to alter the Church in a moment; after the first flush of enthusiasm they seem resigned to more conventional Church membership and Church leadership, at least for the present. Adopting a gradualist strategy, they advocate modest changes here and there, but for the most part they press on with their radical ideas and plans rather quietly, as a series of initiatives outside the Church, or perhaps along lines parallel with conventional Church life but separate from it. They have ceased to challenge conventional religiosity, and instead they prefer to tolerate it while they puzzle over the problem of what forms the new religiosity should assume when its hour at last comes.

Conservatism, meanwhile, still partly in reaction to the

aggressive radicalism of an earlier decade, but partly in an independent resurgence of traditional religious sentiment, seeks to pull the Church back to the old patterns and to breathe new life into them. It believes that God's work may be identified with the visible Church, and so looks for ways in which the organisation may be restyled so as to survive and to expand in the face of whatever social developments may occur. Conservatism is open to new ideas, and, latterly, together with other parts of the Church and with parts of all the major churches, it has shown itself open to more than just ideas: it is open to the Spirit. The charismatic movement is perhaps the most important single post-war movement to cut across every denominational boundary and, linking Anglicans, Baptists and Roman Catholics in England with Methodists in Africa and Catholics in South America, to bring to life an evangelical experience of individual spiritual rebirth which unites substantial numbers of Christian people who formerly were divided. Like the puritanism we have described, it is not limited to those brought up as evangelicals, and, indeed, it seems to hit hardest those whose previous experience has been in religious traditions which systematically suppress enthusiasm. The Charismatic movement is important and widespread; but it is not of massive proportions. Of the 24 or 25 Anglican congregations in the city of Leeds, for example, it has affected three; quite often its effect is utterly to transform moribund churches into flourishing concerns; and its effects are felt by individuals, too, even where it does not have an impact on a whole congregation at once. But it is not a unitary movement, and its appearances in Leeds and in Latin America are of widely different significance, and call for very different interpretations. Except in the Third World, and among recent immigrants from the Third World, the Charismatic movement, we should argue, is part of the conservatism we have just identified, remarkable only for its capacity to affect so powerfully a substantial minority of people in those churches traditionally immune to revivalist fervour.

Conservatism also embraces and includes new ideas and techniques. Thus we saw that at Oak Hill there was less aversion to the 'new theology' at the end of training than there had been at the beginning, but we should suggest that the reason was that it was redefined from being a threat to traditional faith and seen instead as a device by which some who had been estranged from the Church could be brought within the fold. Oak Hill's faith was left unmodified, and merely given a new 'program emphasis', an additional line of patter by which it might be sold, since it is 'Jesus Christ the same yesterday, and today, and for ever' who is preached. No holds are barred when the conservative wrestles with doubt, and the new theology is discovered as a good hold to use with some unbelievers.

The decade of the 1970s is, however, seeing the traditional evangelical conservatism strengthened not only by the Charismatic movement and by the introduction of new ideas and new techniques, for conservatism as a general trend is being strengthened also by the 'professionalising' tendency which in Chapter 6 we suggested is currently affecting ordination training. The colleges which were antipuritan in ethos in the 1960s now tend to be not specifically puritan, but more generally conservative, because of the emphasis on a quasi-professional form of training. The work of training ordinands, too, is undertaken by a somewhat different sort of man, for the colleges now tend to seek well qualified theologians and men equipped to teach special techniques and skills, while fewer antipuritans, or men of 'advanced' ideas, are found staffing the colleges. Specialism and qualification are now the order of the day in theological colleges. Where formerly a clergyman who was thought to be a 'man of prayer' might have been appointed, the college now finds someone who holds the new diploma in 'Christian spirituality' offered by the General Theological Seminary in New York; instead of finding a man with long experience in a parish to teach what was called pastoralia, the college will appoint someone with a postgraduate qualification in 'pastoral studies'.

All in all, the new conservatism is an impressive phenomenon.

The radicalism which was so prevalent in ordination training in the 1960s, but which now tends to plough a more lonely furrow, nevertheless merits careful attention. As we have said, it is consistent with the changes which seem to be overtaking the Church, but what is striking is that it must prove to be an unstable influence within the Church as it has traditionally been organised. To put it another way, antipuritanism as a type of vocation appeared to be digging its own grave. The men who were characterised by it had a highly ambivalent attitude towards organised religion, and yet by virtue of being ordinands at all they were clearly committed to the institution of the

Church; so their position was a highly anomalous one. B. R. Wilson (1966, p. 76) was expressing the same problem in describing some clergy as being

> uncertain of their own faith, uncertain of the 'position' of their Church on many matters, and unsure whether they agree with that position. The more advanced among them sometimes suggest that simpler men believe the right things for the wrong reasons. They themselves are institutionally entrenched but intellectually foot-loose.

Yet this is hardly adequate as an account of their dilemma, for it is plain that they were more than just intellectually footloose. More to the point, today's radicals, in common with those ordinands of the 1960s, find themselves secure within the organisation of the Church, but without belief in its adequacy, either at present or in potential. They are marginal to the Church by their own deliberate intention, because of their belief that the Church is marginal to society. It is understandable that people should ask whether their position in the ministry is viable, for a layman who held similar views might be forgiven for ceasing to go to church, while these are clergy whose presence is required as of obligation. A few years ago, when the colleges contained substantial numbers of these men and were staffed by clergy of the same ilk, one suspected that the future of the Church of England's ordained ministry might have proved to be a short one.

Now the situation has changed again.

Let us look at the matter bluntly. We recognise that the practising laity of the Church of England are overwhelmingly conservative. Those whose ideas are radical in religious matters find church attendance uncongenial and do not bother. So a decreasing number of people go to church, filling a small number of town churches, usually in the suburbs, and constituting a tiny handful who are almost lost in the great majority of churches. Most of the clergy who minister to them in the churches are conservative too, especially those who run the large and successful churches. Then there is a radical school of thought, espoused by some clergy and by a very few lay people, which is extremely vocal and influential out of all proportion to its numbers within the Church. This school of thought is largely responsible for framing the policies of the Church, for its views on national and international political and social affairs, and for developments in its theology, though this is less true of the Church of England than of British Methodism, for example. For a period it was influential in shaping ordination training in the theological colleges. Almost none of the clergy who belong to this school of thought are to be found in the parishes, however, for either they go into secular occupations or else they move into Church administration at a diocesan or national level or go into some other non-parochial job. In other words, there is a rift between the comparatively silent conservative majority in the parishes and the vocal radical minority, who for their part would not be caught within a hundred yards of a parochial ministry if they could avoid it.

The rift between the radical minority and the conservative majority in the Church is never more apparent than when a radical ventures into a parish, or when a conservative becomes vocal in the solemn conclaves of the church assemblies.

The amply publicised career of the Revd Nicolas Stacey at Woolwich parish church in the course of the 1960s is but one example of the radical's fate in a parish, while countless stories of failed experiments in radical ways of organising local churches have gone untold. There is no specially obvious example of a frank conservative being greeted by the frowns of Church leaders, but the response was common enough in the Church Assembly in the 1960s; and we guess that Mrs Mary Whitehouse would get a much less warm response from today's General Synod than she would undoubtedly be given by the average thriving congregation. The Church of England is not wholly undemocratic, however, and so many of the more radical policies which find their way to the floor of the General Synod from influential committees, or, indeed, from the bishops, go no further. A notable example in the 1960s was the predictable failure of the scheme for Anglican–Methodist reunion when put to the vote. The comparatively silent majority finds its conservative voice elsewhere, too, and not least in the religious press. In the 1970s, however, it is being heeded much more. The 'Festival of Light' and then the archbishops' 'Call to the Nation' in the autumn of 1975 both met with popular response; one must note, however, that neither initiative was the child of an official Church committee.

Our general thesis does not, however, concern the choice between the conservative and the radical tendencies in the Church,
interesting though that is. Our general thesis is that each of these
tendencies equally, if in its own way, demonstrates that the
institutional Church is becoming marginal to our society. The
third secularisation is in operation, and the familiar figure of the
clergyman of the Church of England is inevitably disappearing,
and with him the whole clerical model of a previous era. The two
tendencies are important for the purposes of this volume because
they indicate, and are indicated by, two directions which ordination training might take. For the moment at least, that choice
seems to have been taken.

The radical and conservative tendencies point also in contrary
directions as regards Church organisation, though again we
doubt if either form of polity will be less marginal than the other
to the secular society of the West. As church attendances fall, the
place of the church in the local community becomes progressively less central and the clergyman more and more works
within the confines of his own religious organisation. The pressure which restricts the clergyman's influence to the local church
is reinforced by the long process which has displaced him from
any official standing outside ecclesiastical circles.

The ordinand with a puritan type of vocation finds this
development entirely congenial. It serves to separate the Church
from the world, and it helps to dissolve the old links of the
Established Church with the secular community which resulted
in compromises which were distasteful and regarded as poten-
tially harmful to the work of Christ. If the vicar is no longer seen
as a public figure, that is all to the good, for too often in the past
official status prevented him from speaking out in the name of
Christ. The puritan may deplore the loss of Christian standards
and values in the country, but he welcomes the advent of
churches which contain only those who have a strong commitment to Christ and an unquestioning faith in God. It is better to
be marginal to society than to be implicated in its unregenerate
structures, for a good society is one composed of good individuals and there are no short cuts to lives of personal holiness.

Those who are conservative in the more general sense may
greet this retreat from the local community to within the confines
of the local church with something less than enthusiasm, but
modern trends in ordination training certainly point towards a

congregational mentality. What is of greater significance is that the role of academic specialisation in theology and allied subjects in this modern trend lends dignity to a process which otherwise would be seen in terms of a retreat into sectarianism. It lends it extra impetus, too, since the trend has all the appearances of falling in line with the dominant secular trend towards increasing specialisation.

In churches which are shrinking, those who remain want a conservative church. The latest sign of this obvious phenomenon is the secession of those parts of the American Episcopal Church which are unable to accept the ordination of women to the priesthood. Like the Roman Catholic followers of Archbishop Lefebvre, these seceders join other conservatives in pressing towards a congregational form of Church order, distasteful though they might find the idea in theory.

Of the forms of training we examined in the 1960s, that offered by Oak Hill was best suited to preparing men to serve churches under new conditions in which the emphasis might be firmly on the congregation; but it was narrowly evangelical. Other colleges might adopt the American style of emphasis on counselling and group dynamics, or on prayer and spirituality, which might equally form the basis of a welcoming and supportive local community group. The modern professionalising tendency does something of the kind. Though it lacks the clear objectives of evangelicalism, it finds its principal organisational concern to be with the local church, and may yield an effective training for conditions which focus exclusively on the local church.

It should be noted, moreover, that in days of continuing economic stringency it is only the locally based church which might not only survive, but positively burgeon. After all, if only 20 members of a congregation give 5 per cent of their salaries to the church, that is enough to support a minister at the same level his people enjoy. In the more congregational kind of parish, which must be a real possibility for the Church of England, the minister would share most of his religious duties with the people, and truly would become the religious professional, in the oldest sense of the word. He would not be a clergyman in the old sense, for his standing in the community would be little different from that of the full-time leader of any other sectional interest. But he would have a range of skills which would equip him to run a 'successful church'.

Those who conform to what we have described as the anti-puritan type, and in general to the radical tendency within the Church, find it depressing and claustrophobic when the Church is closed in on itself. The radical believes that his religion is about much more than church affairs and individual ethics, and if the world will not come to the Church then he must go to the world. He prefers to work in a hospital chaplaincy, or in a college, or in any other context which brings him into everyday contact with a wide cross-section of the community, but which, by the same token, frees him from the exclusive life of a self-selected congregation. What is more, the training which was being given in theological colleges in the 1960s prepared him for such an approach. He was encouraged to be open to questions which the people in an average congregation would consider to be, at best, irrelevant to their Christianity; at worst, a betrayal of faith. But the position for which he was prepared, that of the local clergyman, known to all and regarded as a man of learning and culture, ranked beside and doctor and the lawyer in the public eye, was rapidly ceasing to exist even ten years ago. It was only ever possible because the clergyman's religious duties formed the basis for a much wider social position which had little or nothing to do with the Church. But now the running of a church is all that is left: for the radical, however, it is definitely not enough.

It is of the essence of religion that it concerns the whole of a person's life. A religion which impinges on only a section of human life is a contradiction in terms, and yet in our society most of our affairs seem to have no need of the hypothesis of religion. Business has its own ethics, science fought hard to be free of religious restraint, and so one could go on. Where once the Church taught on scriptural authority that abortion was wrong, and ensured that its teaching was embodied in law, it now sets up a commission to investigate the matter, and seeks the professional and scientific authority of medicine and psychology and sociology before it can formulate any religious teaching. To the conservative such a situation is intolerable, and he seeks to defend his religion against any further encroachments. If the whole of society is not under the sway of religion, he will retreat into a corner marked 'The Church', where it is still supreme; supported by the community of believers, he lives as a stranger that part of his life which he cannot avoid spending in secular society, at home only among the faithful. The radical finds the partial role, which is the only one left to the Church, no less intolerable. His response is different, though, and, rather than build the walls round the sacred higher, he pulls them down altogether, in order that he may include the whole world in the sacred.

The sociological analysis which we have outlined here suggests that, at least in the short term, the future of the Church will be with the conservatives. It is they who have already adjusted the traditional parish to the conditions of modern society, or are rapidly doing so. As will be apparent, however, we are persuaded that their short-term success will be short-lived. The ravages of institutionalisation will be felt again, and where there is an enthusiastic first generation today there will be a passive second generation tomorrow. Those who wish to know what kind of congregation we anticipate seeing in England a generation hence should examine an average congregation of a mainline denomination in contemporary New Jersey or southern California. A remarkably similar pattern is already beginning to emerge within the heart of an Established Church in Europe, the Church of England.

In the longer term, however, we believe the future will be with the radicals. In the 1960s their work seemed to be one of setting out to destroy all the traditional structures of Christian doctrine and polity, which were crumbling already. But they were doing more than this, for they were also searching for ways of making the religious vision of the Christian tradition accessible to those outside the narrow confines of the Church. It was clear in the 1960s that they would not bring to life again the Church as it has been known, and it is as clear today that they will not; indeed, their present restraint and withdrawal from the centre of the stage suggests that they recognise that as yet they have no blueprint for the Church of the future. Theirs, however, is the search for a way in which the good news proclaimed by Jesus Christ may again be addressed to the whole of God's creation; it is they who seek to address people as they are, rather than as a failing Church has brainwashed them into being.

The first secularisation took holiness out of the cloister and saved a life in the world from being second best. The second found truth outside the divinity schools and saved science from being merely secular learning. The third is searching for God outside the religious club, so that godliness may be saved from being the hobby of a few.

Appendix I: Sources of Data

The data we have drawn on in the course of this volume came from six separate studies conducted by the authors, Robert Towler (RCT) and A. P. M. Coxon (APMC), working independently. For the sake of clarity we list them here.

1. Leeds (APMC). A study at the Hostel of the Resurrection, Leeds, carried out in the early 1960s, including sociometric tests, questionnaires administered in interviews, the Melvin–Eysenck (Radicalism–Conservatism/Tender-mindedness–Tough-mindedness) test, the Allport–Vernon–Lindsey Study of Values, and student diaries.
2. Cheshunt (APMC). A study at the Bishops' College, Cheshunt, carried out in the Advent Term 1962 and the Trinity Term 1963, which included items similar to those employed at Leeds.
3. 1962 survey (APMC). A questionnaire, administered via college principals and returned by post, completed by 93·56 per cent of a 30 per cent random sample (stratified, with a uniform working sampling fraction of 30 per cent, by college) of all ordinands in training in English theological colleges of the Church of England in November 1962. Non-response was accounted for almost entirely by the refusal of students at Lincoln Theological College to co-operate.
4. 1966 study (RCT). A study of the intake in October 1966 of men to St Chad's College (Durham), Oak Hill College (London), The Queen's College (Birmingham), the College of the Resurrection (Mirfield, Yorks) and Westcott House (Cambridge), including questionnaires administered in interviews, Richardson's version of the Allport–Vernon–Lindsey Study of Values, sections of the Theological Schools Inventory, and the Eysenck Personality Inventory; interviews in March–September 1966, October–November 1966, February–March 1967, October–November 1967, and February–March 1968.

5. Theological Colleges' Union (RCT). A questionnaire completed in 1967 by 94 per cent of a 50 per cent random sample (stratified by college) of ordinands in residence at the seven colleges of the TCU at Cambridge.

Complete information, including copies of the questionnaires, is available in the authors' PhD theses, the University of Leeds, 1965 and 1970.

6. Clergy careers (RCT) An analysis of the life histories published in *Crockford's Clerical Directory* between 1930 and 1975–6 of
(i) 10 per cent random samples of the names appearing in the ordination lists published in *The Times* in 1934, 1939, 1944, 1949, 1954, 1959, 1964 and 1969;
(ii) all diocesan and suffragan bishops of the Church of England listed in *Crockford* in 1930 and 1973–4.

More complete information may be obtained from Towler, and will be available in a forthcoming article.

Appendix II: Statistical Tables and Additional Figures

TABLE 1 Comparative distributions of Anglican ordinands' first thoughts of ordination

| Age | | Percentage distributions | | |
	Survey 1962	Leeds 1962	Cheshunt 1962	Canada 1959
Less than 10	5·6	9·1	7·4	7·7
10–13	12·2	22·7	9·3	}15·8
14–15	17·5	25·0	18·5	
16–17	21·4	25·0	9·3	}76·5
18 and older	43·3	18·2	55·5	
	100·0	100·0	100·0	100·0
	485	44	54	196

Notes
1. The Canadian figures (CC 1959) derive from a study in which questionnaires were distributed to all known ordinands from January to March 1959; the response rate was 52·6 per cent, although 'a substantial number of those in pre-theology did not reply'.
2. Details of the small-scale studies at Leeds and Cheshunt will be found in Appendix I. The age ranges of ordinands at these colleges differ considerably: for Leeds in 1961 the mean age of first-year students was 21, for Cheshunt it was 31. Since the mean age of Cheshunt students was beyond the highest point of the range for Leeds students, the relatively disproportionate frequencies are only to be expected.
3. See also Leiffer (1959, p. 87), and Fichter (1961, p. 16).

TABLE 2 Comparative ages of first thoughts of occupational choice: normal-group Anglican ordinands, doctors, and nurses

Age	Cumulative percentages		
	1965 study	*Doctors*	*Nurses*
Less than 10	4·0	24·0	53·0
10–13	46·0	51·0	71·2
14–15	72·0	69·0	86·4
16–17	88·0	86·0	98·5
18 and older	100·0	100·0	100·0

Notes

1. The figures for ordinands are from the 1965 study (see Appendix I) and differ from those on which Table 1 was based. The 1962 survey used questionnaires which asked, 'At what age did you first think of being ordained?'; the 1965 study used interviews in which questions were asked in the following order: 'How old were you when you decided definitely to be ordained?', 'For how long had you been thinking about it?', and 'How young were you when you first thought of it?'

2. The data on nurses are from Katz and Martin 1962, p. 151, the data on doctors from Rogoff 1957.

3. The discrepancies between the proportions, for the three occupations, of first thoughts by the age of 10 is one for which we can offer no explanation other than that tentatively suggested on p. 63. It is not of importance for the present study, but might usefully be pursued by psychologists.

TABLE 3 Comparative ages of definite decision on occupational choice: normal-group Anglican ordinands, doctors, and nurses

Age	Cumulative percentages			
	Survey 1962	1965 study	Doctors	Nurses
Less than 14	0·4	3·8	7·8	12·2
14–15	4·6	11·5	17·6	30·0
16–17	26·7	32·7	43·2	87·3
18–20	77·9	67·3	84·6	99·5
21–22	93·9	94·2	94·9	100·0
23 and older	100·0	100·0	100·0	100·0

Notes
1. The criterion for the 1962 survey was age of applying to CACTM to be considered for training.
2. The criterion for the 1965 study was the question, 'How old were you when you decided definitely to be ordained?' – see Table 2, note 1.
3. Figures for doctors and nurses from Katz and Martin 1962 and Rogoff 1957.

TABLE 4 Influences on the decision to train for the Ministry (N = 494)

Influence	Very important	Fairly important	Minor importance	No importance, inapplicable
Mother	8·5	21·3	24·7	45·5
Father	7·3	18·8	18·4	55·5
Wife/fiancée	15·2	4·7	2·0	78·1
Other relatives	2·8	4·3	11·9	81·0
Clergy known personally	39·9	31·8	14·8	13·5
Clergy heard/read about	3·6	12·8	14·8	68·8
Ordinands known	5·1	12·1	14·6	68·2
Friends not ordained	8·5	18·0	20·0	53·5
Headmasters, teachers	5·7	9·3	16·0	69·0
Books, films	5·9	12·7	13·8	67·6
Other	26·5	5·5	1·4	66·6

Note. Not only are 'clergy known personally' rated as a very important influence more often than is any other influence, but they are reckoned as of no importance less often than any other; 'mother' is next in infrequency of being rated as of no importance. Thus the frequencies of negative evaluation are not without interest.

TABLE 5   Parental and uxoral attitude at time when decision to be ordained was made (N = 494)

| Type of attitude | Percentages | | |
	Father	Mother	Wife
Strong encouragement	12·1	17·0	13·8
Moderate encouragement	11·8	14·2	2·2
'Completely left it to me to decide'	40·5	42·3	3·9
Slight opposition	11·9	10·5	0·4
Strong opposition	6·3	4·5	0·2
Inapplicable or unclassifiable	17·4	11·5	79·5

TABLE 6   Parental and uxoral attitudes to decision at time of study (N = 494)

| Type of attitude | Percentages | | |
	Father	Mother	Wife
Strong encouragement	38·3	46·0	25·9
Moderate encouragement	18·4	25·7	0·4
Completely impartial	16·8	10·9	0·2
Slight opposition	2·6	2·4	0·2
Strong opposition	1·6	0·4	0·2
Inapplicable or unclassifiable	22·3	14·6	73·1

TABLE 7   Initial and present attitudes of parents and wives (N = 494)

| Response type | Percentages | | |
	Father	Mother	Wife
Consistent	26·3	28·1	14·2
Changed	50·2	55·3	6·3
Unclassifiable or inapplicable	23·5	16·6	79·5

TABLE 8   Types of change in parental and uxoral attitudes to decision (N = 494)

Type of change	Percentages		
	Father	Mother	Wife
To more positive attitude	49·2	54·7	6·3
Consistent	26·3	28·1	14·2
To more negative attitude	1·0	0·6	0·0
Unclassifiable or inapplicable	23·5	16·6	79·5

TABLE 9   Registrar-General's Office 'social class' distributions for ordinands (N = 471) and the general population

'Social class'	General population (%)	Ordinands (%)			Deviations from base (%)		
		Total	Normal	Late	Total	Normal	Late
I Professional	3·9	19·3	26·4	11·3	+15·4	+22·5	+7·4
II Intermediate	14·4	31·2	35·2	26·7	+16·8	+20·8	+12·3
III Skilled	49·8	41·2	31·6	52·0	−8·6	−18·2	+2·2
IV Partly skilled	19·9	6·6	5·2	8·2	−13·3	−14·7	−11·7
V Unskilled	8·6	1·7	1·6	1·8	−6·9	−7·0	−6·8
Not classified	3·5	−3·5	−3·5	−3·5	−3·5	−3·5	−3·5

Notes
1. Figures for ordinands are from the 1962 survey.
2. General population distribution from the 1961 Census *General Report*, .p. 193, Table 55.

TABLE 10   School-leaving age of ordinands (N = 493; 1 unclassifiable) and for the general population (N = 7,275)

Age	General population (%)	Ordinands (%)			Deviations from base (%)		
		Total	Normal	Late	Total	Normal	Late
15 or less	72	17	4	32	−55	−68	−40
16	15	15	5	27	0	−10	+12
17	5	16	11	22	+11	+6	+17
18 or more	8	52	80	19	+44	+72	+11

Notes
1. Figures for ordinands are from the 1962 survey.
2. Population figures are from the *Crowther Report* (Report of the Advisory Committee for Education, England, 15–18, 1960, London, HMSO), as they are for Tables 11 and 12.

TABLE 11   Types of school attended by ordinands (N = 488; 6 educated abroad) and by the general population (N =7,275)

School type	General population (%)	Ordinands (%)			Deviations from base (%)		
		Total	Normal	Late	Total	Normal	Late
Public/independent	3·45	36·68	44·53	28·52	+33·23	+41·08	+25·06
Grammar	19·82	45·08	51·17	39·04	+25·26	+31·35	+19·22
Other	75·73	18·24	4·30	32·45	−58·49	−72·43	−43·28

Notes
1. The figures from the survey conducted by Windross in the 1970s are:
   public schools 24 per cent, grammar schools 50 per cent, other 20 per cent.
2. See Table 10, note 2.

TABLE 12   Age of school-leaving by type of school attended – deviations of ordinand distributions from the general population distributions

Age	Normal-group ordinands (N = 261)		Late-group ordinands (N = 228)	
	Public/ independent	*Grammar*	*Public/ independent*	*Grammar*
15 or less	0	−11	+6	+1
16	−11	−41	+8	−8
17	−12	−6	+9	+13
18 or more	+23	+58	−23	−6
Abs. dev.	*46*	*116*	*64*	*28*

Notes
1. Abs. dev.: the 'absolute deviation' is a somewhat crude approximation to the mean deviation, and here serves as a measure of relative dispersion from the base, which is referred to discursively in the text.
2. See Table 10, note 2.

TABLE 13   Mean scores for ordinands and for general population on 12 variables

Variables	General population	1965 study
1. Theoretical interest	32·8	24·9
2. Economic interest	30·3	24·7
3. Aesthetic interest	24·3	24·3
4. Social interest	38·9	40·4
5. Political interest	26·4	22·9
6. Religious interest	27·2	42·9
7. Natural vocation	50·2	46·3
8. Supernatural vocation	49·4	55·1
9. Concept of the call	49·9	56·2
10. Flexibility	53·2	50·7
11. Neuroticism	10·5	10·4
12. Extroversion	14·2	14·0

Sources
1. General-population figures for variables 1–6 in Richardson 1965, p. 15, Table 7.
2. Means for variables 7–10, for the sake of comparison, though they are not from a non-ordinand population, are for a large sample (1775) of male theological students in 53 American colleges in 1963, from Dittes 1964, Appendix II, Table 1.
3. Means for variables 11 and 12 are for a sample of 2000 male and female respondents from Eysenck and Eysenck 1964, pp. 16–17.

TABLE 14   Means and standard deviations of scores on 12 variables for total sample (N = 76) and for normal and late groups (N = 49 and 27, respectively) within it

	Variables											
	1	2	3	4	5	6	7	8	9	10	11	12
Total												
Mean	24·9	24·7	24·3	40·4	22·9	42·9	46·3	55·1	56·2	50·7	10·4	14·2
SD	5·4	6·3	8·1	5·0	5·6	9·6	7·4	9·1	8·2	8·4	4·1	3·7
Normal												
Mean	25·2	24·4	25·6	40·4	23·3	41·1	45·8	54·4	54·7	53·0	11·0	14·0
SD	6·3	6·5	8·5	4·7	5·6	9·6	8·1	9·0	7·1	7·2	4·2	3·9
Late												
Mean	24·9	25·0	22·0	39·6	21·9	46·7	47·2	56·9	59·6	47·0	9·3	13·9
SD	4·6	5·9	6·8	5·5	5·5	7·7	5·9	8·2	8·2	9·7	3·8	3·1

Notes. Variables as in Table 13; SD = standard deviation.

TABLE 15   Means of scores on 12 variables for total sample and for college groups within it, and ranges of means for each variable

Variable	Total	St Chad's	Oak Hill	Mirfield	Westcott	Range
1	24·9	29·6	22·7	24·9	23·6	6·9
2	24·7	25·0	24·8	24·7	25·0	0·3
3	24·3	30·1	18·4	23·2	28·3	11·7
4	40·4	40·2	40·0	41·3	40·0	1·3
5	22·9	22·0	23·2	22·9	22·8	1·2
6	42·9	33·3	50·9	43·1	40·0	17·6
7	46·3	44·4	47·7	44·7	46·9	3·3
8	55·1	51·0	60·7	56·8	50·2	10·5
9	56·2	51·9	63·6	54·7	51·5	12·1
10	50·7	55·8	43·4	53·7	53·8	12·4
11	10·4	12·9	9·9	10·6	9·5	3·4
12	14·0	13·7	13·8	14·4	14·6	0·9
N	76	14	22	15	21	

Note. Variables as in Table 13.

TABLE 16   Loadings on 6 rotated factors of 12 variables

Variables	Factors					
	I	II	III	IV	V	VI
1. Theoretical interest	+28	−39	+07	−08	+78	+11
2. Economic interest	+10	−02	−01	+95	+02	−13
3. Aesthetic interest	+73	+06	+12	−51	+06	−11
4. Social interest	−13	−32	+65	−09	−44	−21
5. Political interest	−06	−21	−87	+01	−17	+10
6. Religious interest	−74	+47	+03	−10	−18	+17
7. Natural vocation	0	+20	−15	−09	−01	+88
8. Supernatural vocation	−75	+09	−20	−15	−06	−34
9. Concept of the call	−86	−10	+05	−10	0	−14
10. Flexibility	+71	−07	−43	−14	−18	−18
11. Neuroticism	+02	−83	−07	+01	+06	−10
12. Extroversion	+28	−23	−08	−11	−58	+42
Latent root	3·08	1·32	1·45	1·27	1·24	1·24
Percentage of total variance	25·7	11·0	12·1	10·6	10·3	10·3 (80·0)

TABLE 17   Churchmanship and vocation type

Churchmanship	Total	Vocation type		
		Puritan	Antipuritan	Neither
Catholic	30	4	11	15
Modernist	13	1	10	2
Evangelical	25	20	1	4
Totals	68	25	22	21

TABLE 18   Eysenck Personality Inventory lie-scale scores and views on sexual morality (N = 76)

Lie-scale score	Do you think that sexual relations outside marriage are always wrong?	
	Yes	No
0–1	24	27
2–4	20	5
Totals	44	32

On the chi-square test: $0.01 > p > 0.001$.

TABLE 19 Puritan and antipuritan sub-groups divided by normal and late; and for evangelicals and others

1. For all those who are either puritan or antipuritan there appears to be a relationship:

	Puritan	Antipuritan
Normal	14	18
Late	11	4

On the chi-square test: $0·05 < p < 0·1$

2. It disappears, however, when we consider evangelicals and non-evangelicals separately:

	Puritan	Antipuritan
Evangelicals		
Normal	10	0
Late	10	1
Non-Evangelicals		
Normal	4	18
Late	1	3

TABLE 20 Degree of satisfaction with training, mean values on a scale 0–100

	N	1966	1967	1968
Total	67	75	41	32
St Chad's	11	54	13	9
Oak Hill	21	88	66	45
Mirfield	15	76	60	43
Westcott	20	72	15	25
Puritans	23	85	71	45
Antipuritans	19	68	25	18

Notes
1. Queen's College, Birmingham, is omitted because it contributed too few cases.
2. Figures were computed by scoring 'dissatisfied', 'fairly satisfied', and 'completely satisfied' as 0, 1 and 2 respectively, and rescaling.

TABLE 21   Clergymen in three categories in the Church of England, 1959–68

As at 31 Dec (except 1977 and 1978) in the years	Incumbents	Assistant curates	Non-parochial clergy
1959	9386	2700	2583
1960	9372	2781	2825
1961	9386	3039	2939
1962	9355	2988	3441
1963	9385	3047	4122
1964	9374	3146	4207
1965	9321	3210	4420
1966	9232	3262	4474
1967	9213	3317	4652
1968	9110	3317	4652
Mid-1977	9197	1979	
Mid-1978	8905	1823	

Notes

1. Systems of classification have changed from time to time, making comparisons difficult; one change occurred between 1962 and 1963.
2. Non-parochial clergy for 1959 to 1968 included the semi-retired parochial clergy as well as non-parochial clergy-men, but the rate of retirement by no means accounts for the increase in this column over the period.
3. The Church Commissioners, from whom the figures have been obtained, are unable to provide comparable figures for *all* clergymen up to the present time, but only for full-time clergy.
4. Data for 1977 and 1978 are reported as available under comparable headings.

TABLE 22 Theological radicalism: replies to the question, 'What do you think of the "new theology"?'

| | Percentages | | |
	1966	*1967*	*1968*
Total			
Strongly agree	35	48	58
Agree	17	13	17
Disagree	48	39	25
St Chad's			
Strongly agree	55	64	64
Agree	27	9	27
Disagree	18	27	9
Oak Hill			
Strongly agree	10	10	14
Agree	10	4	24
Disagree	80	86	62
Mirfield			
Strongly agree	40	60	80
Agree	27	13	7
Disagree	33	27	13
Westcott			
Strongly agree	47	74	84
Agree	11	21	11
Disagree	42	5	5

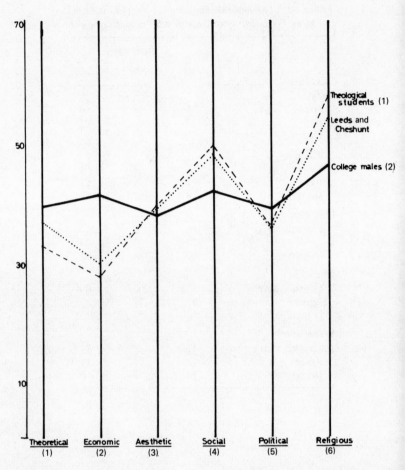

FIGURE A1 Study of values: comparative profiles for (1) British and American ordinands, and for (2) American college males

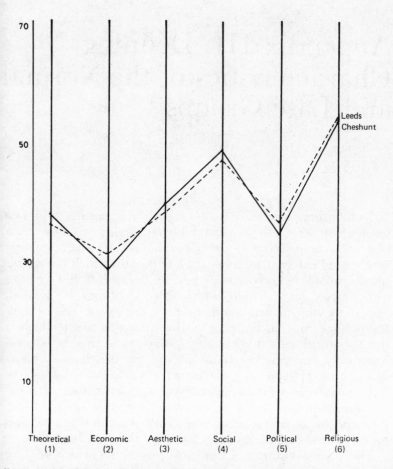

FIGURE A2   Study of values: comparative profiles for Hostel of the Resurrection, Leeds, and Bishops' College, Cheshunt

Appendix III: Defining Characteristics of the Normal and Late Groups

In establishing the difference between the normal and late groups, attention has been focused upon single attributes, taken one at a time. Normal-group ordinands are predominantly single, tend to have left school at a later age than their late-group fellows, are more likely to have a degree, and so on. But we have glossed over the extent to which these attributes are related, except for the association between school type and school-leaving age. But, again, people who leave school later have a much high chance of becoming graduates – that is, school-leaving age and graduate status are strongly associated. If many of the characteristics are correlated, then a good deal of the information given for single characteristics is redundant; what we should prefer would be to know both how well a given attribute discriminates between the normal and late groups, and also what combinations of attributes are the most important.

There are a number of statistical procedures which offer an answer to this question of determining the best predictor or predictors of a given dependent variable, but until recently few models were available for coping with a situation where the predictors concerned are of differing measurement type (for example, marital status, churchmanship and number of clerical relations), and which could be used on a sample of relatively few cases. One model which is well adapted to these data is the variant of stepwise regression known as AID II (Automatic Interaction Detection, version II; see Sonquist and Morgan 1964). Even though subsequently it has been found to have some undesirable properties (Fielding 1975), its careful use can reveal useful information of the sort we seek.

THE MODEL

Given a dependent variable (which in this instance might be number of years in a full-time occupation other than the ministry), and a set of independent variables (marital status, rank in family, and so on), the purpose of the procedure is to find out what *combination* of independent variables best explains the variation in the dependent variable. In the present case, the aim is to find out what combination of social variables best discriminates between the normal and late groups.

The program begins by finding the variable which explains the most variation in the dependent variable, and then it splits the subjects into two groups. For each of these two groups in turn (i.e. taken separately) the process is repeated, until the resulting groups are too small to allow further splitting, or there is not sufficient variation in a group to justify its being split. The technical criteria are given below.

The variables chosen for analysis are:

Dependent variable: normal vs late

This takes the forms:

(a) the length of time in full-time occupations (FTO) (the variable defining the normal/late groups); and
(b) the normal/late dichotomy itself (NL).

Independent variables

(a) *Background variables*

1. Marital status	(single, engaged, married)
2. Number of children in family of origin	(1, 2, 3, 4, or more)
3. Rank position of subject in family	(1st, 2nd, 3rd, or later)
4. School-leaving age	(15 or less, 16, 17, 18 or more)
5. School type	(public/independent, grammar, other)
6. Highest educational certificates	(degree, 'A'-level, 'O'-level, none)
7. Socio-economic group of parent's occupation	(employer/manager, professional, non-manual, skilled manual, other)

	8. Father's 'social class'	(I, II, III, IV and V, not easily classified)
	9. Clerical relations	(yes, no)

(b) *Attitudinal variables*

	10. Churchmanship	(catholic, central church-man/modernist, evangelical, other)
	11. Interest in politics	(very indeed, quite, not very, not at all)
	12. Political allegiance	(left, liberal, right, no allegiance)
	13. Class identification	(upper/upper-middle, middle, lower-middle, working, not early classified)

(c) *Age*

	14. Age in years	(19–21, 22–24, 25–27, 28–30, 31–40, over 40)

ANALYSIS

In the first analysis, *age* (14) was such a strong predictor of FTO that it 'drowned out' the effect of the other independent variables, with the exception of *school-leaving age* (4). Since *age* is so strongly correlated with the dependent variable, it was left out of subsequent analysis.

In the second analysis, *school-leaving age* at 18 turns out to be most important in predicting the number of years in a full-time occupation, followed by *marital status* (1). The range of variation accounted for by these two predictors is very considerable, ranging from an average of 8·74 years in a full-time job in the case of the 94 ordinands who are married and who left school before 18, to an average of 1·15 years for the 220 single ordinands who left school at 18 or later. Beyond this point, no variable has a systematic (additive) effect. The overall impression is of the profound and cumulative effect of eductional variables in predicting the number of years in a full-time occupation. The only other variables which have any noticeable effect are *parental occupation* (7), *political allegiance* (12) and *churchmanship* (10), and then only in the case of the late group.

TECHNICAL NOTE: AID II parameter settings used for determining the stopping point for splitting groups were:

p_1	proportion of total sum of squares in the dependent variable that a group must contain before it is to become a candidate for splitting	0·005
p_2	the 'best' split must reduce the unexplained sum of squares by this proportion before it may be split	0·005
MAXGP	maximum allowable number final groups	16
NMIN	smallest allowable group	30
TLEV	test of significant difference between the means of two groups before a split is made	2·50

In the third analysis, the dependent variable is simply whether or not a subject is classified as normal or late group and the 'average' is simply the proportion who are late-group subjects. Once again, *age* is excluded as a predictor. (In this analysis, the splitting criteria are relaxed slightly: $p_1 = p_2 = ·001$; $TLEV = 0$, $MAXGP = 30$; $NMIN = 5$. The effect is that a much finer typology, or combination of variables, is produced; the more relaxed criteria also allow more of the variables to enter as predictors.)

Up to the second level, the same variables affect both groups, and in the earlier stages, the strong cumulative effects of educational factors are again very obvious.

But in the later branching levels, a number of other variables enter: *clerical relations* (9) enters fairly early in the predominantly normal-group (lower) branches, and *churchmanship* (10), which occurs as a fairly important predictor in the late-group branches, is a rather unimportant one in the normal-group branches. Other variables – *number of children* (2), *class identification* (13), *political affiliation* (12) – occur only in relatively unimportant branches, and several variables, such as *rank in family* (3), *father's class* (8) and *political interest* (11), do not appear at all.

CONCLUSIONS

Educational variables very predominantly explain the normal-/late-group differentation, followed by marital status.

The most significant fact about the normal group is that its members left school already prepared for university entrance, and are not married. They are also much more homogeneous than the late group.

When the educational and marital differences have done their share of explanation, other predominantly class and political variables come into play. Parental, or self-identified, middle-class status tends to increase the likelihood that an ordinand is in the normal group, as does a leftward political orientation (the extent to which this is an effect rather than a cause is, of course, moot). Perhaps the most interesting factors are those which do not seem to be systematic in their effect, especially the fact of having clerical relations, and churchmanship.

Having clerical relations does have an important effect, but only, apparently, when the ordinand is educationally qualified and already married. The effect of churchmanship is relatively minor, yet quite widespread, but the type of its effect differs: by and large, catholic churchmanship predisposes towards normal-group membership, except for single, upper and middle-class graduates who attended public school, in which cases it seems to have the contrary effect; but this is based on branching at the least reliable end of the procedure.

The 'negative information' also is interesting: none of the demographic variables has a significant effect upon differences between the two groups.

Appendix IV: A Note on the More Recent Literature on Professions with Special Reference to the Clergy

We have avoided using the word 'professionalisation' to refer to professional socialisation, but the usage is common. It may help if we distinguish some of the principal areas of research represented in the literature which are relevant to the general subject of the present volume, simply noting main references.

1. Professionalisation as the taking-on of a professional self-image while undergoing training, or professional socialisation as discussed here in Chapter 7: Kunitz 1974; Liebhart 1970; Luecke 1970, 1971; Mauer 1959; Ondrack 1975; Pavalko and Holley 1974.
2. Defence of professional status and problems with achieving professional status experienced by occupations: Hammond 1966; Klegon 1975; Mendenhall 1975; Portnory 1975; Visentini 1975.
3. Professionalisation as the taking on by an occupation of the characteristic traits of a profession: Amano 1969; Atal 1971; Banaitis 1975; Fichter 1970; Hickson and Thomas 1969; Hill 1973; Luecke 1970; Wisneski 1974.
4. Professionalisation as the changes to occupational organisation and practice which are analysed in a Weberian manner as rationalisation and bureaucratisation: Bell 1968; Charlott 1973; Durand 1974; Ference et al. 1973; Johnson 1961; Johnson 1972; Leat 1973; Ritzer 1975; Steudler 1973; Vickers 1974.
5. Professionals at odds with bureaucracy: Blackie 1974; Epstein 1970; Forney 1975; Lawer 1973; Perrucci 1973; Struzzo 1969.
6. Professionals at odds with their clients: Braude 1961; Demsey 1973; Emmis 1975; Garrett 1973; Maddock et al. 1973.

7. Deprofessionalisation, or the lowering of occupational status: Brawley 1974; Chapman 1944; Goldner *et al*. 1973; Haug 1973, 1975; Hagstrom 1957; Illich 1973; Jarvis 1975; Peters 1970; Stinson 1971.
8. Questions about the concept of profession: Gannon 1971.

We might have made reference to almost every one of these works in the course of the discussion, but it would have made the treatment unbearably long. As it is we have contented ourselves with noting their various arguments and findings in developing our own discussion.

Notes

1. The correlations between prestige rating, income, and educational achievement are high. American evidence shows that the rank-order correlation of median income level with National Opinions Research Center prestige scores is +0·85, and +0·83 for median level of educational achievement: thus '72% of the variance in prestige scores is therefore accounted for by income, and 69% of this variance is accounted for by educational attainment. Hence either income level or educational attainment is a surprisingly good predictor of judgements of the 'general standing' of an occupation' (Reiss 1961, p. 84). An extended discussion of the validity of such scales is contained in Coxon and Jones (1978, p. 15).

2. The relationship between values as they are referred to in psychology and in sociology is not easy to clarify, but scores on the Study of Values variables have a definite significance for sociology. Kluckhohn (1951) defines a value as 'a conception, explicit or implicit, distinctive of an individual or characteristic of a group, of the desirable which influences the selection from available modes, means, and ends of action' (p. 395), and gives an alternative definition for use in psychological contexts whereby it is 'that aspect of motivation which is referable to standards, personal or cultural, that do not arise solely out of immediate tensions or immediate situation' (p. 425). Most psychological tests attempt to assess attitudes, which differ from values by being referable exclusively to the individual and by not containing the evaluative element, but the Study of Values, its own shortcomings notwithstanding, is an exception to this and is concerned with values (ibid., p. 423).

3. The most obvious drawback to the Study of Values as a test is that the scores a person obtains on its six variables are not independent. Each question in the text asks the person doing it to evaluate a number of alternatives, each of which relates to one of the values being assessed. The result, therefore, is an order of priorities, because a higher score on one variable necessarily means a lower score on some other.

4. The rotated factors were produced using the Varimax solution, which aims to simplify each column rather than each row of the factor matrix and thus to preclude the generation of a general factor (Cooley and Lohnes 1962, p. 162; Harman 1967, p. 304), and so the first factor was notable not only for the proportion of variance for which it accounted, but also for having five high loadings, compared with the one or two on succeeding factors.

5. The flexibility measured by variable 10 bears a certain similarity to the well known California F scale (Adorno *et al* 1950), though without the same

231

bias towards right-wing authoritarianism; nor is it unlike the Gough–Stanford rigidity scale; but it most closely resembles Rokeach's dogmatism scale – only in reverse, of course (Rokeach 1960).

6. A man is identified as a puritan if at least four of his scores on the five relevant variables (3, 6, 8, 9 and 10) deviate from the means for the total group in the sequence +, −, −, −, +, and when the score on a fifth variable falls less than one standard deviation on the 'wrong' side of the mean; and *vice versa* for an antipuritan. We found that 36·8 per cent of the men fitted the pattern perfectly, and are thus 'pure' puritans or antipuritans, although the factor accounted for only 25·6 per cent of the variance; a further 25 per cent satisfy our more relaxed condition, and thus 61·8 per cent of the group were counted as being either puritans or antipuritans.

7. Scale values were produced from the 1962 data by using a rank equivalent of the paired-comparison method and Thurstone's Law of Comparative Judgement (Torgerson 1959; Edwards 1957); responses to the question in the 1966 study were scored 2, 1 and 0 for each role component, to produce a crude measure.

8. Crown appointments are made on the advice of the Prime Minister or some other government minister, though it is assumed that the archbishops and bishops are consulted as may be appropriate. Crown appointment to diocesan sees has been a sensitive area for a very long time, and the procedure by which a name, or a list of names, to be presented to the Sovereign by the Prime Minister used to be agreed upon is shrouded in mystery, though it is thought that the Prime Minister's Appointments Secretary 'consulted widely'. From 1977, a list of at least two names, which may be in order of preference, is forwarded to the Prime Minister by the Crown Appointments Commission, though this body acts only in the appointment of diocesan bishops; the Commission is composed of the two archbishops, three clergy and three laymen elected by the General Synod of the Church of England, four representatives of the diocese (who may be clerical or lay) elected by the vacancy in see committee, the Prime Minister's Appointments Secretary, and the Archbishop's Patronage Secretary.

9. A follow-up of our 1966 group, ordained in 1968 and 1969, provides further evidence to support the impression that the patterns described here remain applicable. The adjustment for war service referred to above amounted to removing 3 per cent from group 4 and including them under group 2 (men who would have had a period as chaplains to the forces in another period), and reducing group 2 by 7 per cent and increasing group 1 by the same proportion (for the same reason), on the assumption that men who, effectively, are obliged to become military chaplains are not thereby influenced to remain in the Forces.

10. Our sample was drawn from the published lists of men ordained which used to appear in the pages of *The Times*, but since the lists are no longer

published it is impossible to draw comparable samples. Had it been possible, we should, in view of the importance of what has happened to recent cohorts, have presented data for all men ordained in 1970, at least, as we have done for the bishops.

Bibliography

Adorno, T. W. *et al.*, 1950, *The Authoritarian Personality* (New York: Harper).

Amano, Masako, 1969, 'The structure of teachers' consciousness on professionalization of teaching careers', *Journal of Educational Sociology* (Japan) 24, 158–76.

Anon., 1959, *Bishops' College, Cheshunt: A Jubilee Portrait* (Ossett, Yorks: Shaw Pearce).

Anson, P., 1956, *The Call of the Cloister* (London: SPCK).

Atal, Yogesh, 1971, 'Professionalization of sociologists', *Indian Journal of Social Research*, 12, 2, 137–42.

Banaitis, D. A., 1975, 'Professionalization of physical therapy and the preparation of physical therapists for professional autonomy', (unpublished PhD thesis, Southern Illinois University).

Barry, F. R., 1958, *Vocation and Ministry* (London: Brisbet).

Becker, H. S., and Geer, B., 1958, 'The fate of idealism in medical school', *American Sociological Review*, 23, 1, 50–6.

Bell, D., 1968, 'The measurement of knowledge and technology', in Shaldon and Moore 1968.

Bennett, T. R., 1959, 'Some sociological considerations on motivation for the ministry', in Southard 1959.

Berger, P. L., 1966, 'Identity as a problem in the sociology of knowledge', *European Journal of Sociology*, 7, 1, 105–15.

Blackie, N. W. H., 1974, 'Altruism in the professions: the case of the clergy', *Australian and New Zealand Journal of Sociology*, 10, 2, 84–9.

Blau, P. M., 1956, 'Occupational choice: a conceptual framework', *Industrial and Labor Relations Review*, 9, 4, 531–43

Blizzard, S. W., 1956, 'The minister's dilemma', *Christian Century*, 25 Apr.

Bowers, M. K., 1963, *Conflicts of the Clergy* (New York: Nelson).

——, 1966, 'Address to the Ministry Studies Board Conference', in De Wire 1966.

234

Braude, L., 1961, 'Professional autonomy and the role of the layman', *Social Forces*, 39, 4, 297–301.

Brawley, E. A., 1974, 'The non-professional and the professional culture: a dilemma for social workers', *Journal of Sociology and Social Work*, 2, 2, 182–97.

Brothers, J., 1963, 'Social change and the role of the priest', *Social Compass*, 10, 6, 477–90.

Brown, L. B., 1966, 'The structure of religious belief', *Journal for the Scientific Study of Religion*, 5, 2, 259–72.

CA: Reports to Church Assembly, London.

Campbell, E. Q., and Pettigrew, T. F., 1959, 'Racial and moral crisis: the role of the Little Rock ministers', *American Journal of Sociology*, 64, 5, 509–16.

Caplow, T., 1954, *The Sociology of Work* (Minneapolis: University of Minnesota Press).

Carr-Saunders, Sir A. M., and Wilson, P. A., 1933, *The Professions* (Oxford: Oxford University Press).

CC: *My Call to the Sacred Ministry of Christ's Holy Catholic Church*, Commission Report, on Recruitment of the Anglican Church of Canada (Ottawa, 1959).

Chadwick, W. O., 1971 and 1972, *The Victorian Church*, 2 vols (London: A. & C. Black) (first edition 1966 and 1970).

Chapman, S. H., 1944, 'The minister: professional man of the church', *Social Forces*, 23, 202–6.

Charlott, J., 1973, 'Les élites politiques en France de la IIIe à la Ve République', *European Journal of Sociology*, 14, 78–92.

Church Congress, 1872, *Authorised Report of the Church Congress, 1872* (London: John Hodges, 1873).

Cooley, W. W., and Lohnes, P. R., 1962, *Multivariate Procedures for the Behavioral Sciences* (New York: Wiley).

Coxon, A. P. M., 1964, 'An élite in the making', *New Society*, 26 Nov.

——, 1965, 'A sociological study of the social recruitment, selection and professional socialization of Anglican ordinands' (unpublished PhD thesis, University of Leeds).

——, 1967, 'Patterns of occupational recruitment', *Sociology*, 1, 73–9.

——, and Jones, C., 1978, *The Images of Occupational Prestige: A Study in Social Cognition* (London: Macmillan).

Cupitt, D., 1977, 'The Christ of Christendom', in Hick 1977.

Delumeau, J., 1977, *Catholicism between Luther and Voltaire* (London: Burns & Oates) (original French ed. 1971).

Demsey, K., 1973, 'Secularization and the protestant parish

minister', *Australian and New Zealand Journal of Sociology*, 9, 46–50.

De Wire, H., 1959, *Motivation for the Ministry* (Dayton, Ohio: Ministry Studies Board, mimeo).

——, (ed.) 1966, *The Guidance of Ministerial Candidates* (Washington, DC: Ministry Studies Board).

Dittes, J. E., 1964, *Vocational Guidance of Theological Students* (Dayton, Ohio: Ministry Studies Board).

Dunstan, G. R., 1967, 'The sacred ministry as a learned profession', *Theology*, 70, 433–42.

Durand, M., 1974, 'Professionalizzazione e lealtà verso l'organizzazione' ('Professionalisation and organisational loyalty'), *Rassegna Italiana di Sociologia*, 15, 51–81.

Durkheim, E., 1915, *The Elementary Forms of the Religious Life*, trans. J. W. Swain (London: Allen & Unwin, 1976) (Original French ed. 1912).

Edwards, A. L., 1957, *Techniques of Attitude Scale Construction* (New York: Appleton-Century-Crofts).

Ellison, G., 1968, *Progress in Ministry* (London: Faith Press).

Emmis, J. G., 1973, 'The role expectations of Roman Catholic campus chaplains and Roman Catholic undergraduates for the Roman chaplain' (unpublished PhD thesis, St John's University).

Epstein, I., 1970, 'Professionalization, professionalism, and social worker radicalism', *Journal of Health and Social Behavior*, 11, 67–77.

Etzioni, A., 1961a, *Comparative Analysis of Complex Organizations* (Glencoe, Ill.: Free Press).

—— (ed.), 1961b, *Complex Organizations* (New York: Holt, Rinehart & Winston).

—— (ed.) 1969, *The Semi-professions and their Organization* (New York: Free Press).

Eysenck, H. J., 1954, *The Psychology of Politics* (London: Routledge).

——, and Eysenck, S. B. G., 1964, *Manual of the Eysenck Personality Inventory* (London: London University Press).

Eysenck, S. B. G., and Eysenck, H. J., 1963, 'An experimental investigation of "desirability" response set in a personality questionnaire', *Life Sciences*, 2, 5, 343–55.

Ference, T. P., Goldner, F. H., and Ritti, R. R., 1973, 'Priests and church: the professionalization of an organization', in Friedson 1973.

Festinger, L., Schachter, S., and Back, K., 1955, 'Matrix analysis of group structures', in Lazarsfeld and Rosenberg 1955.

F.F.C.E.: *Facts and Figures about the Church of England*, ed. R. F. Neuss (London: Church Information Office, 1959–65).

Fichter, J. H., 1961, *Religion as an Occupation* (Notre Dame, Ind.: University of Notre Dame Press).

——, 1970, 'Catholic church professionals', *Annals of the American Academy of Political and Social Science*, 12, 137–42.

Fielding, A., 1975, 'A study of statistical stability of binary branching algorithms', London, LSE, mimeo.

Floud, J., 1961, 'Social class, intelligence tests and selection for secondary schools', in Halsey, Floud and Anderson 1961.

——, and Halsey, A. H., 1961, 'English secondary schools and the supply of labour', in Halsey, Floud and Anderson 1961.

Forney, J. G., 1975, 'Transition: a study of the United Methodist clergy of the Southern California–Arizona Conference who have left the parish ministry' (unpublished PhD thesis, School of Theology at Claremont, Cal.).

Friedson, E. (ed.), 1973, *The Professions and Their Prospects* (Beverly Hills, Cal.: Sage Publications).

Furlong, M., 1966, 'Address to a conference of clergy in the Diocese of Wakefield', mimeo.

Gannon, T. M., 1971, 'Priest/minister: profession or non-profession?' *Review of Religious Research*, 12, 66–79.

Garrett, W. R., 1973, 'Politicized clergy: a sociological interpretation of the "new breed" ', *Journal for the Scientific Study of Religion*, 12, 383–99.

Gellner, E., 1974, *Legitimation of Belief* (London: Cambridge University Press).

Ginzberg, E., *et al.*, 1951, *Occupational Choice: An Approach to a General Theory* (New York: Columbia University Press).

Glass, D. V. (ed.), 1953, *Social Mobility in Britain* (London: Routledge).

Glock, C. Y., and Ringer, B. B., 1956, 'Church policy and attitudes of ministers on social issues', *American Sociological Review*, 21, 2, 148–56.

Goffman, E., 1961, 'The character of total institutions', in Etzioni 1961b.

Goldner, F. H., Ference, T., and Ritti, R. R., 1973, 'Priests and laity: a profession in transition', *Sociological Review Monographs*, 20, 119–37.

Goode, W., 1969, 'The theoretical limits of professionalization', in Etzioni 1969.

Gould, J. (ed.), 1965, *Penguin Survey of the Social Sciences 1965* (Harmondsworth: Penguin).

Greenwood, E., 1957, 'The attributes of a profession', *Social Work*, 2, 44–55; repr. in Vollmer and Mills 1966.

Hadden, J. K., 1969, *The Gathering Storm in the Churches* (New York: Doubleday).

Hagstrom, W., 1957, 'The protestant clergy as a profession: status and prospects', *Berkeley Publications in Society and Institutions*, 3, 54–68.

Hall, O., 1948, 'The stages of a medical career', *American Journal of Sociology*, 53, 5, 327–36.

Halsey, A. H., Floud, J., and Anderson, C. A. (eds.), 1961, *Education, Economy and Society* (Glencoe, Ill.: Free Press).

Hammond, P. E., 1966, *The Campus Clergyman* (New York: Basic Books).

Harman, H. H., 1967, *Modern Factor Analysis*, 2nd ed. (Chicago: University of Chicago Press).

Haug, M. R., 1973, 'Deprofessionalization: an alternative hypothesis for the future', *Sociological Review Monographs*, 20, 195–211.

——, 1975, 'The deprofessionalization of everyone?', *Social Forces*, 8, 197–213.

Hick, J. (ed.), 1977, *The Myth of God Incarnate* (London: SPCK).

Hickson, D. J., and Thomas, M. W., 1969, 'Professionalization in Britain: a preliminary measure', *Sociology*, 3, 1, 37–53.

Hill, S. C., 1973,'Professions: mechanical solidarity and process or: "How I learnt to live with a primitive society" ', *Australian and New Zealand Journal of Sociology*, 9, 30–7.

Hunt, R. A., 1968, 'The interpretation of the Religious scale of the Allport–Vernon–Lindzey Study of Values', *Journal for the Scientific Study of Religion*, 7, 65–77.

Illich, I., 1973, 'The professions as a form of imperialism', *New Society*, 13 Sep, 633–5.

Inglis, K. S., 1963, *Churches and the Working Classes in Victorian England* (London: Routledge).

Interim Report of the Archbishops' Commission on Training for the Ministry, 1942 (London: Church Assembly).

Jarvis, P., 1975, 'The parish ministry as a semi-profession', *Sociological Review*, 24, 911–22.

Johnson, C. D., 1961, 'Priest, prophet, and professional man: a study of religious leadership in a small community' (unpublished PhD thesis, University of Minnesota).

Johnson, T. J., 1972 *Professions and Power* (London: Macmillan).

Kandell, D. B., 1960, 'The career decisions of medical students' (unpublished PhD thesis, Columbia University).

Kelsall, R. K., 1953, 'Self-recruitment in four professions', in Glass 1953.

Klegon, D. A., 1975, 'Lawyers and the social structure: an historical analysis of the role of professionalization among lawyers in the United States' (unpublished PhD thesis, University of Wisconsin).

Kluckhohn, C., 1951, 'Values and value-orientations', in Parsons and Shils 1951.

Kunitz, S. J., 1974, 'Professionalism and social control in the progressive era: the case of the Flexner Report', *Social Problems*, 22, 16–27.

Lawer, E., and Hage, F., 1973, 'Professional–bureaucratic conflict and interorganizational powerlessness among social workers', *Journal of Sociology and Social Work*, I, 92–102.

Lazarsfeld, P. F., 1931, *Jugend und Beruf* (Jena: Gustaf Fischer).

——, and Rosenberg, M. (eds), 1955, *The Language of Social Research* (Glencoe, Ill.: Free Press).

Leat, D., 1973, 'Putting God over: the faithful counsellors', *Sociological Review*, 21, 561–72.

Leiffer, M. H., 1959, 'The influence of denominational appeals upon motivation for the ministry', in Southard 1959.

Liebhart, E. H., 1970, 'Sozialisation im Berufergebnisse: Panelbefragung von Studienreferendaren' ('Occupational socialization: results of a panel study among students training to become high school teachers'), *Kölner Zeitschrift für Soziologie und Sozialpsychologie*, 2, 715–36.

Lindzey, G. (ed.), 1954, *Handbook of Social Psychology*, 2 vols (London: Addison-Wesley).

Lindzey, G., and Borgatta, E. F., 1954, 'Sociometric measurement', in Lindzey 1954, vol. I.

Ling, T. O., 1967, 'Religion, society and the teacher', *Modern Churchman*, 10, 142–51.

Luecke, D. S., 1971, 'The professional as organizational leader: an organizational behavior study of parish ministers' (unpublished PhD thesis, Washington University).

Luecke, R. H., 1970, 'Protestant clergy: new forms of ministry, new forms of training', *Annals of the American Academy of Political and Social Science*, 387, 86–95.

MacDonnell, J. C., 1896, *The Life and Correspondence of William Connor Magee* (London: Isbister).

Maddock, R., Kenny, C. T., and Middleton, M. M., 1973, 'Preference for personality versus role-activity variables in the choice of a pastor', *Journal for the Scientific Study of Religion*, 12, 449–52.

Major, H. D. A., 1925, *The Life and Letters of William Boyd Carpenter* (London: John Murray).

Martin, D. A., 1965, 'Towards eliminating the concept of secularisation', in Gould 1965.

——, 1966, *A Sociological Yearbook of Religion in Britain*, 2 (London: SCM Press).

Mauer, B. B., 1959, 'A study of selected factors associated with the professional behavior-image of protestant parish ministers' (unpublished PhD thesis, Pennsylvania State University).

Mayne, W. C., 1959, 'A continuing tradition', in Anon. 1959.

Mead, G. H., 1934, *Mind, Self, and Society* (Chicago: University of Chicago Press).

Mendenhall, W. R., 1975, 'A case study of the American College Personnel Association: its contribution to the professionalization process of student personnel work (unpublished PhD thesis, Florida State University).

Menninger, K., 1942, *Love against Hate* (London: Allen & Unwin).

Merton, R. K., 1957, *Social Theory and Social Structure*, rev. ed. (New York: Free Press).

——, Reader, G. R., and Kandell, P. (eds), 1957, *The Student Physician: Introductory Studies in the Sociology of Medical Education* (Cambridge, Mass.: Harvard University Press).

Miller, D. C., and Form, W. H., 1964, *Industrial Sociology*, 2nd ed. (New York: Harper and Row).

Moberg, D. O., 1962, *The Church as a Social Institution* (Englewood Cliffs, NJ: Prentice-Hall).

Morris, W., 1949, *The Christian Origins of Social Revolt* (London: Allen & Unwin).

Niebuhr, H. R., 1956, *The Purpose of the Church and its Ministry* (New York: Harper).

O.D.C.C.: *Oxford Dictionary of the Christian Church*, 2nd ed., ed. F. L.

Cross and E. A. Livingstone (London: Oxford University Press, 1974).

Ondrack, A., 1975, 'Socialization in professional schools: a comparative study', *Administrative Science Quarterly* 20, 97–103.

Parsons, T., 1954, *Essays in Sociological Theory*, rev. ed. (London: Collier-Macmillan) (1st ed. 1949).

——, and Shils, E. A. (eds), 1951, *Toward a General Theory of Action* (Cambridge, Mass.: Harvard University Press).

Paul, L., 1964, *The Payment and Deployment of the Clergy* (London: Church Information Office).

Pavalko, R. M., and Holley, J. W., 1974, 'Determinants of a professional self-concept among graduate students', *Social Science Quarterly*, 52, 462–77.

Perrucci, R., 1973, 'In the service of man: radical movements in the professions', *Sociological Review Monographs*, 20, 179–94.

Peters, H., 1970, 'Die misslungene Professionalisierung der Sozialarbeit. Das Verhältnis von Rolle, Handlungsfeld und Methodik in der Fürsorge' ('The failed professionalisation of social work. The relationship of role, field of action, and methods in social work'), *Körner Zeitschrift für Soziologie und Sozialpsychologie*, 22, 335–55.

Petre, M. D., 1912, *Autobiography and Life of George Tyrrell*, 2 vols (London: Edward Arnold).

Phillips, E., 1863, *The Church and the Ecclesiastical Commissioners* (London: Bell and Daldy).

Portnoy, F. L., 1975, 'What keeps an occupation in its place? A case study of blocked mobility in the occupation of nursing' (unpublished PhD thesis, Florida State University).

Reiss, A. J., Jr, 1961, *Occupations and Social Status* (Glencoe, Ill.: Free Press).

Report [1908] *on the supply and Training of Candidates for Holy Orders* (Poole: Hunt).

Richards, N. D., 1962, 'An empirical study of the prestige of selected occupations' (unpublished MA thesis, University of Nottingham).

Richardson, S., 1965, *Manual* for the British version of the Study of Values test (Slough: National Foundation for Educational Research).

Ritzer, G., 1975, 'Professionalization, bureaucratization and rationalization: the views of Max Weber', *Social Forces*, 53, 627–34.

Roe, A., 1953, 'A psychological study of eminent psychologists and anthropologists, and a comparison with biological and physical scientists', *Psychological Monographs*, 67, 2, 1–55.

——, and Siegelman, M., 1964, *Origin of Interests* (Washington, DC: American Personnel and Guidance Association).

Rogoff, N., 1957, 'The decision to study medicine', in Merton *et at*. 1957.

Rokeach, M., 1960, *The Open and Closed Mind* (New York: Basic Books).

Rosenberg, M., 1957, *Occupations and Values* (Glencoe, Ill.: Free Press).

Russell, A. J., 1976, *Two Surveys of Ordinands in the Church of England: A Comparative Analysis* (London: Advisory Council for the Church's Ministry [Church of England] Occasional Papers, no. 4).

Sanderson, A., 1963, 'Parental influences and the sense of vocation in emotionally disturbed theological students' (unpublished DPM dissertation, London University).

Sanford, R. N., 1950, 'Ethnocentrism in relation to some religious attitudes and practices', in Adorno *et al*. 1950.

Schreuder, O., 1965, 'Le caractère professionel du sacerdoce', *Social Compass*, 12, 1–2, 5–20.

Shaldon, E. B., and Moore, W. E. (eds), 1968, *Indicators of Social Change* (New York: Russell Sage Foundation).

Sklare, M., 1955, *Conservative Judaism* (Glencoe, Ill.: Free Press).

Smith, H. T., 1959, *Theological Education* (Kelham: SSM Press).

Sonquist, J. A., and Morgan, J. N., 1964, *The Detection of Interaction Effects* (Ann Arbor, Mich.: Institute of Social Research).

Southard, S. (ed.), 1959, *Conference on Motivation for the Ministry* (Louisville, Ky: Southern Baptist Seminary, mimeo).

Spranger, E., 1928, *Types of Men: The Psychology and Ethics of Personality*, trans. P. J. W. Pigors (New York: Johnson Reprints) (Original German ed. 1922).

Stark, R., and Glock, C. Y., 1968, *American Piety: The Nature of Religious Commitment* (Berkeley and Los Angeles: University of California Press).

Steudler, F., 1973, 'L'Évolution de la profession médicale: essai d'analyse sociologique', *Cahiers de sociologie et de demographie médicales*, 13, 61–7.

Stinson, S. M., 1971, 'Deprofessionalization in nursing?', Canadian Anthropology and Sociological Association, 1971 Annual Meeting, Sociological Abstracts no. E9323/CSAA 1971.0045.

Strong, E. K., 1942, *Vocational Interests of Men and Women* (Stanford, Cal.: Stanford University Press).

Struzzo, J. A., 1970, 'Professionalism and the resolution of authority conflicts among the Catholic clergy', *Sociological Analysis*, 31, 92–106.

Super, D. E., 1949, *Appraising Vocational Fitness* (New York: Harper).

——, 1957, *The Psychology of Careers* (New York: Harper).

—— *et al.*, 1963, *Career Development: Self Concept Theory* (New York: College Entrance Examination Board).

——, 1966, 'Current trends in career development', in De Wire 1966.

Thielens, W., Jr, 1957, 'Some comparisons of entrants to medical and law schools', in Merton *et al*. 1957.

Torgerson, W. S., 1959, *Theory and Methods of Scaling* (New York: Wiley).

Towler, R. C., 1969, 'Puritan and antipuritan: types of vocation to the ordained ministry', in Martin 1966.

——, 1970, 'A sociological analysis of the professional socialization of Anglican ordinands' (unpublished PhD thesis, University of Leeds).

Vickers, G., 1974, 'The changing nature of the professions', *American Behavioral Scientist*, 18, 164–89.

Visentini, L., 1974, 'Alla ricerca della sociologia delle professioni: note per una ressegna critica' ('Search for a sociology of professions: note for a critical survey'), *Rassegna Italiana di Sociologia*, 15, 11–32.

Vollmer, H. M., and Mills, D. L. (eds), 1966, *Professionalization* (Englewood Cliffs, NJ: Prentice-Hall).

Watts, A. G., 1973, reported in *Sunday Times*, 7 Oct.

Weber, M., 1930, *The Protestant Ethic and the Spirit of Capitalism*, trans. T. Parsons, (London: Allen & Unwin) (First German ed. 1904–5).

Whitesel, J. A., 1952, 'Parental relationships of theological students in reference to dominance–submission' (unpublished PhD thesis, Boston University).

Wilensky, H. L., 1964, 'The professionalization of everyone?' *American Journal of Sociology*, 70, 2, 137–58.

Wilson, B. R., 1959, 'An analysis of sect development', *American Sociological Review*, 24, 1, 3–15.

——, 1966, *Religion in Secular Society* (London: C. A. Watts).

Wise, C. A., 1958, 'The call to the ministry', *Pastoral Psychology*, 9, 9–17.

Wisneski, C. A., 1974, 'A contribution to the media field through the development of a media doctoral program model' (unpublished PhD thesis, Temple University, Philadelphia). (Survey of existing PhD programs in the field.)

Wrong, D., 1961, 'The oversocialized concept of man', *American Sociological Review*, 26, 2, 183–93.

Index

Adorno, T. W., 102–4, 231
Advisory Council for the Church's Ministry (ACCM), formerly CACTM, 25, 69, 71, 82–5, 140
Allport, G. W., 91
Anglican–Methodist reunion, 201
Arnold, Dr Thomas, 16, 106
Articles, Thirty-Nine, 12, 44–5
The Authoritarian Personality, see authoritarianism
authoritarianism, 102–5, 231–2
Auxiliary Pastoral Ministry (APM), 53, 87–8, 134, 142, 188, 190

Barry, F. R. (Bishop of Southwell 1941–63), 57
Bennett, T. R., 59
Berger, P. L., 47
bishops: in mediaeval England, 5; in 19th-century England, 15–16; careers of, 182–6
Blau, P. M., 61
Bowers, M. K., 60
Blizzard, S. W., 35, 109, 110, 151–2
Brothers, J., 37
Brown, L. B., 94

'Call to the Nation', the archbishops', 201
Cambridge University: Theological Colleges' Union, 163; Divinity School, 163
Campbell, E. Q., 104
Caplow, T., 42
careers, clerical, 170–86; of bishops, 182–6; curacies, 175–6; and educational background, 176–8; highest points of, 178; patterns of, 179–82; 'post-curacy' jobs, 178–9
Carpenter, W. B. (Bishop of Ripon 1884–1911), 20

Carr-Saunders, Sir A. M., 48, 49
Central Advisory Council for Training for the Ministry (CACTM), *see* ACCM
Chadwick, W. O., 4, 17, 33
Charismatic movement, 3, 198–9
churchmanship, 19–20, 89, 98, 106–15, 164–5; Catholic and Protestant concepts of vocation, 59; Catholic and Protestant traditions of ordination training, 129–30; greater efficiency of evangelical training, 75, 165–9, 203
Community of the Resurrection, 26, 134–43
conservative *vs* radical split, 3, 165, 196–205
conversion, 165–6
Coxon, A. P. M., 77
Crockford's Clerical Directory, 36

Delumeau, J., 3
De Wire, H., 73
Dittes, J. E., 93, 148
Dunstan, G. R., 40
Durham University, 16–17

education, the clergy and, 6, 10–15
Elizabeth I, 12
Elizabethan Settlement, 12
Ellison, G., 150
Etzioni, A., 42, 127–9
Eysenck, H. J., 94, 102, 114
Eysenck, S. B. G., 94, 114
Eysenck Personality Inventory, 94–5; lie scale, 113–14

factor analysis, 98–9
Fayers-Heawood data, 84, 87
Festival of Light, 201
Fichter, J. H., 59, 71, 118

Floud, J., 81
Froude, Hurrell, 22
Furlong, M., 41

Gellner, E., 31
General Ordination Examination,
    139, 144, 145, 160
Ginzberg, E., 62, 68
Glock, C. Y., 104, 165
Goffman, E., 122–6
Goode, W., 42
Gore, Charles, founder of the Com-
    munity of the Resurrection, 26, 135
Greenwood, E., 42
group dynamics, 168

Hadden, J. K., 104, 145, 165
Hall, O., 66
Halsey, A. H., 81
Hickson, D. J., 42
Howson, J. S. (Dean of Chester
    1867–85), 22
Hunt, R. A., 92, 93

incomes, clerical, 7, 22–3

Kandell, D. B., 62, 68
Keble, John, 15
Keble College, Oxford, 19
Kelsall, R. K., 80

Lampeter, St David's College, 14
late vocations, 63–6
Law, G. H. (Bishop of Chester
    1812–24), 14
law students, 80
Lazarsfeld, P. F., 61
Leeds University, 26, 35, 136–7,
    139–40, 142
Liddon, H. P., 20
Lindzey, G., 91
Ling, T. O., 35
London, University College, 18

MacDonnell, J. C., 20
Magee, W. C. (Bishop of
    Peterborough 1868–91), 20
Major, H. D. A., 20

Malmesbury, Lord, 22
Mead, G. H., 145
medical students, 66, 68, 71, 81,
    117–18, 120, 168
Menninger, K., 60
Melvin-Eysenck test, 102–4
Merton, R. K., 62, 116–17, 144
Moberg, D. O., 72
Mormons, 39

Newman, John Henry, 15
Niebuhr, H. R., 58, 59
normal *vs* late groups of ordinands,
    63–6, 70, 75–83, 96–7, 193–7
occupation, the clergy as an, 47–9, 51–5
occupational choice of ordinands,
    56–87; age of first thoughts, 62–7;
    age of definite decision, 68–71;
    compared with Roman Catholic
    ordinands, 63, 71; compared with
    other professions, 66, 68, 71; influ-
    ences on, 66–7, 71–4; psychological
    approach to, 59–60; sociological
    approach to, 60–2, 68; theological
    approach to, 57–9; two patterns of,
    63–6, 70
open *vs* closed models of ordination
    training, 118–22, 126–7, 128, 130,
    143
*Oxford Dictionary of the Christian Church,
    The*, 12, 171

parochial structure, changes in, 190–1
Parsons, T., 42
Paul, L., 78, 84
'People Next Door', 38
Petre, M. D., 132
Pettigrew, T. F., 104
Phillips, E., 23
profession, medicine as, 50–1; profes-
    sional status of clergy, 40–7, 49–51;
    sociological characteristics of, 41–2;
    theology and clerical professional-
    ism, *see* theology
puritan *vs* antipuritan ordinands,
    100–15, 162, 196–200, 202–4; and
    churchmanship, 106–13; at different
    colleges, 105; and scores on EPI lie
    scale, 113–14; and sexual morality,
    113, 164

Queen Anne's Bounty, 7

Richards, N. D., 32
Richardson, S., 91, 92
Ringer, B. B., 104
Robinson, J. A. T. (Bishop of Woolwich 1959–69), 161, 163
Roe, A., 60
Rogoff, N., 66, 80
role of the clergy, uncertainty about,
34, 39–40; components of the clergyman's role, 34–40, 108–13, 151–4;
role as prophet, 55
Roman Catholic Church, 2–3, 37, 121,
175; conservatism in, 203; ordinands
in, 63, 71; priests in, 46; seminaries
in, 118–19, 147; and the universities,
13, 19
Rosenberg, M., 67
Russell, A. J., 77

Sanford, R. N., 103
Schreuder, O., 49
Second Vatican Council, 2, 37
secularisation, 3, 26–7, 31–2, 191–3; in
the Tudor period, 5–6, 191–2; of the
universities, 11–13, 18–19; and
urbanisation, 23–4; in the Victorian
period, 8–9, 192–3
selection of ordinands, 83–5; biases in,
84–5
'self concepts', 60
self-recruitment to the ministry, 80–81
Selwyn College, Cambridge, 19
Siegelman, M., 60
Simeon, Charles, 14
Sklare, M., 109, 152
social characteristics of ordinands: age,
75–6; educational background,
81–3; marital status, 76–8; normal *vs*
late groups, 75–83, 193–4; social
class, 79–81
social class, the clergy and, 6–9, 21–4,
26, 79–81, 88, 159
socialisation, defined, 116–17
socialisation of ordinands, 116–34,
144–69; compared with socialisation
of medical students, 117–18; and
experience of conversion, 165–6;
patterns of, 165–6, 194–6; as professional socialisation, 144–5, 159–60,
166–9, 194–5; role of clergy in, 145,
158; role of fellow students in, 145–46
socialisation of ordinands, changing
attitudes during: to churchmanship
self-definitions, 164–5; to clergymen's roles, 151–4; to the ministry,
150–1; to moral questions, 163–4; to
social class, 159; to social and political concerns, 155–9; to specialist
ministries, 154; to theological questions, 160–3; to training, 147–50
Society of Jesus, 132
Society of the Sacred Mission, 26, 123,
125
Spranger, E., 92
Stacey, Nicolas (Rector of Woolwich
1959–68), 201
Stark, R., 165
status of the clergy, 6–9, 31–4
'street wardens', 38
Strong, E. K., 60
Stubbs, William, 21, 22
Study of Values test, 91, 95–115
Super, D. E., 60, 92

team ministries, 188–9
theological colleges, 14, 17–20, 116–43,
187; and churchmanship, 19–20,
107–8, 129–30; forms of authority in,
127–9, 130–4; open and closed types
of, 118, 126–7, 128, 130, 143; theology in, 121–2, 160, 169; as total
institutions, 122–7
theological colleges: Bernard Gilpin
Society, 141; Bishop Wilson, I. O.
M., 14; Bishops' College, Cheshunt,
96, 102–4, 187; Brasted Place, 141;
Chichester, 17; Cuddesdon, 19, 77,
122; Ely, 19, 122, 187; Exeter, 19;
Gloucester, 19; Kelham, 26, 123–6,
187; Leeds, Hostel of the Resurrection, 96, 102–4, 136–42; Lichfield 19,
122, 187; Lincoln, 19; Mirfield, College of the Resurrection, 26, 90,
97–114, 134–43, 156–8, 161, 164–5;
Oak Hill, 90, 97–114, 133–4, 158–9,
161, 164–6, 195, 198–9, 203; The
Queen's College, Birmingham, 90,
96, 156; Ridley Hall, 19; Ripon Hall,

122; Rochester, 187; St Aidan's, Birkenhead, 187; St Bee's, 14; St Chad's, Durham, 90, 97–114; St Stephen's House, 19, 109; Salisbury, 19, 122; Southwark Ordination Scheme, 142; Wells, 17, 122; Westcott House (formerly Clergy Training School), 19, 90, 97–114, 161, 164–5; Worcester Ordination College, 187; Wycliffe Hall, 19; missionary colleges, 14

Theological School Inventory, 93–4, 95–115

theology: Cambridge theological tripos in, 19; degrees in, for ordinands, 82–3; Oxford honours school of, 19; ordinands' attitudes to the 'new theology', 161–3; as professional knowledge, 17–19, 46–7; teaching of, at Oak Hill, 168–9; in theological colleges, 121–2, 160, 169

Thielens, W., 80

Thomas, M. W., 42

total institutions, theological colleges as, 122–7

Towler, R. C., 100

Tyrrell, George, 132

van Mildert, William (Bishop of Durham 1826–36), 17

Vernon, P. E., 91

vocation, the ministry as a, 57–60

Watts, A. G., 82

Weber, M., 57–8

Wellington, 1st Duke of, 11

Wilberforce, Samuel (Bishop of Oxford 1845–69), 20, 22

Wilensky, H. L., 42

Wilson, B. R., 31, 74, 100, 200

Wilson, P. A., 48, 49

Wilson, Thomas (Bishop of Sodor & Man 1698–1755), 14

Windross, Andrew, 77, 89, 109

Wise, C. A., 59

Wrong, D., 117